IS MAN A
ROBOT ?

IS MAN A ROBOT?

GEOFF SIMONS
Chief Editor, The National Computing Centre, UK

John Wiley & Sons
Chichester • New York • Brisbane • Toronto • Singapore

Library of Congress Cataloging in Publication Data:
Simons, G.L.
 Is man a robot?

 Includes index.
 1. Robotics.   I. Title
TJ211.S56 1986   629,8'2   86-9241

ISBN 0 471 91106 2

British Library Cataloguing in Publication Data:

Simons, Geoff
 Is man a robot?
 1. Human behavior
 I. Title
 150'.1   BF121
 ISBN 0 471 91106 2

Print and Bound in Great Britain

'Joe himself became less docile and more rebellious. For the most part he would still be the Kallingers' *obedient robot*.* But there would also be lapses.'
(Flora Rheta Schreiber, *The Shoemaker: Anatomy of a Psychotic*, Penguin, 1984, p. 49)

'Now they swarm in huge colonies, safe inside *gigantic lumbering robots*, sealed off from the outside world, communicating with it by tortuous indirect routes, manipulating it by remote control.... They have come a long way, those replicators. Now they go by the name of genes, and we are their survival machines.'
(Richard Dawkins, *The Selfish Gene*, Paladin, 1982, p. 21)

'But we must now raise the question in an ultimate form: among contemporary men will there come to prevail, or even to flourish, what may be called *The Cheerful Robot?*'
(C. Wright Mills, *The Sociological Imagination*, Pelican, 1970, p. 189)

'Japan's industrial eminence was still down to its *human robots*.'
(*The Sunday Times*, 17 April 1983)

'For the many there is hardly concealed discontent.... "I'm a machine," says the spot welder. "I'm caged," says the bank teller, and echoes the hotel clerk. "I'm a mule," says the steel worker. "A monkey can do what I do," says the receptionist. "I'm less than a farm implement," says the migrant worker. "I'm an object," says the high fashion model. Blue collar and white call upon the identical phrase: "*I'm a robot.*"'
(S. Terkel, *Working*, Pantheon, New York, 1974, p. xi)

'*I'm not a robot.*'
(John McEnroe, *The Sunday Times Magazine*, 3 November 1985, p. 81)

*My italicized quotations throughout.

Notes to:

Feminists

Yes, 'man' and 'he' are much in evidence in this tract. This is simple linguistic convenience, nothing more. *Is Person a Robot?* seems to lack something. But remember, there is plenty of talk also of 'human beings'. Women are not left out. Be assured that they too are robots.

Human robots (male and female)

Don't worry about it. You are still remarkably complex, the most sophisticated systems — we yet know about — in the universe. The doctrine of robotic man will still let you enjoy the sunshine, write sonnets, choose a course in life, learn judo, eat to excess, and be unfaithful.

Artificial robots

OK, so you're learning to think, decide, create, move. . . .

OK, so human beings are robots, of a sort, too. . . .

Just don't get too cocky about it. You've a long way to go. We managed it in a couple of million years. You'll need less, but you've scarcely got started.

Reviewers

Try reading it first.

Contents

Thesis

This book argues that there is an important sense in which man is a robot, i.e. that every human being is a deterministic system subject to the constraints of natural law. The argument rests on three central propositions:

1. that man is an anatomy, a physical structure engineered by biological evolution (Chapter 3),
2. that man is a cybernetic system, regulated by a complex of definable processes of a certain sort (Chapter 4),
3. that man is programmed for performance, in all he thinks and does (Chapter 5).

These three propositions are held to provide a framework within which man can be defined *in toto*. Freedom, creativity, ethical sensitivity, human attachment, etc., can all be accommodated within the doctrine of robotic man. This is because physical events — at one level or another (physics, chemistry, cognitive and conative information processing, etc.) — are the only phenomena that are relevant to human existence and to an understanding of human activity.

This doctrine, superficially dehumanizing, is in fact a humanistic tribute to human potential. *True* dehumanization occurs when man can only be celebrated by packaging him in false categories, where superstition, mystery, and obscurity are the perennial points of faith, i.e. when man — *as he is* — is too depressing to contemplate. To face man's real nature — and still be optimistic — is the only humanism worth supporting.

Introduction

Today we are about forty years into the age of the electronic computer, and already computer-based systems have revolutionized human activities in every area, in every conceptual and practical field. We cannot think of an area of interest to human beings that has not felt the impact of logic encapsulated in electronic circuits. Already we have witnessed the dramatic procession of computer generations, from thermionic valve to transistor to integrated circuit to large-scale integration of electronic components; already we have seen computer power leap forward in performance and computer size shrink to microscopic proportions. Today a rapidly evolving computer intelligence can be embedded in artefacts of every type and size: in cars, medical equipment, radios, machine tools, weapons, teaching aids, heart implants, video games, artificial satellites, automatic submarines, watches, aeroplanes, sewing machines, power stations, chemical plant, knitting machines — and *robots*.

The modern robot — found mainly in industry — is rapidly acquiring computer-based intelligence, sensory faculties, and a degree of mobility in its physical environment. We have already moved through one or two robot generations, from the early 'pick and place' devices to the highly sophisticated modern systems run by mainframe computers, minicomputers, or embedded microprocessor-controlled intelligence. Today artificial robots are developing immense functional versatility and, many would say, powers of judgement, reason, and the ability to discriminate between behavioural options (the rudiments of 'free will').

Many of the most intriguing robot systems have been designed for experimental or entertainment purposes. For example, the Japanese firm, Sumitomo Electric, has built a robot that can read music and play the tune on an organ — using the fingers of two hands to play notes on the keyboard at the rate of fifteen a second, and treading the pedals as required! Toshiba's Amooty robot employs three-pronged legs to climb up and down stairs, using an artificial eye to see where it is going. In the same way, a mobile robot from Hitachi can watch what it is doing, travelling on level terrain or adapting its versatile crawlers to mount steps or ladders, and it can remember the environments that it encounters in order to aid future navigational activity. Such skilled robots are becoming increasingly common in the laboratories of the world. (More examples are given in Chapter 1.)

In December 1985, a robot 'danced' the central role in a 45-minute modern ballet at Stanford University in California. Here the robot is simply a mechanical arm with joints that can be programmed in various ways: the result is a smoothly bending and twisting artefact. The robot performed a dance in a work, *Invisible Cities*, written by Michael McNabb from the Stanford Centre for Computer Research in Music and Acoustics. The sound of the arm's motors, like a cello when amplified, have been incorporated into the score. The ultimate aim is to make the robot mobile to serve as an aid for the disabled.

Another robot — Ole (pronounced 'Oh-lee') — is said to be able to perform brain surgery faster, and with greater precision, than can a human being! Based on a Unimation Puma robot arm, this device is helping neurosurgeons at the Memorial Centre in Long Beach, California. After the patient's head is bolted into a restraint, a computer-aided tomography scanner is used to take images of skull cross-sections, after which the patient is slid out of the scanner into Ole's work area. The human surgeon, Dr Yik San Kwoh, director of tomography research, guides the robot to a suitable entrance point to enable it to assist in drilling a burr hole through the skull. Ole ensures that probes stay on course and prevents them from penetrating too deeply. It is said that the robot can reduce operating times from three hours to 45 minutes, and also remove human error by calculating probe trajectories from scan information. It is expected that before long Ole will be allowed to drill holes and take tissue samples automatically, and to build up an extended repertoire of surgical operations.

Every month new technical robot advances are reported in the literature — in artificial eye technology, in sensor electronics, in actuator engineering, in artificial intelligence. A recent robot article in *Personal Computer World* (January 1986) saw robots being given 'a sense of awareness', though at the same time we should remember that not all robot applications are intended to be benevolent (a military robot, a 'mechanical Rambo', reported in *The Sunday Times*, 29 December 1985, has been designed to 'fight tanks, shoot down aircraft, interrogate prisoners, and rescue the wounded'). In this context it is worth quoting the cliché that (robot) tools take on the morality of their users.

This then is one side of the story — to be expanded (to some extent) in what follows. It consists in the idea that computer-based systems, in particular those that are intended to simulate or mimic human activities, are increasingly coming to acquire human characteristics. Of course to an extent this is entirely deliberate: after all, a robot is generally reckoned to be a machine 'made in man's image'. However, progress in this area — staggering, when we remember that it has been underway for only two decades or so — is pregnant with other possibilities. For example, we can ask the all-embracing question: are there *any* human functions that robots, one day, will not be able to mimic or duplicate? This immediately suggests the complementary question: can human activities — mental and physical — be interpreted *in toto* in robotic terms? How far will such an approach to *Homo sapiens* take us? Is man a robot?

We have already presented the thesis of the present book: that there is in fact a sense in which man can be interpreted as a robot. We aim to present the robot background to the argument, to establish the thesis, and to explore its implications in particular areas.

Chapters 1 and 2 profile the extent to which robot concepts have prevailed in different historical cultures, indicating both mythological notions and the birth of practical automata; they also consider different ways in which man has been viewed at different times and by different thinkers. It is inevitable that such 'models of man' are conditioned by historical circumstance, by the level of technology and economics, by prevailing prejudice and taboo, by the status of science and rational enquiry. It is clear that the model of 'man as robot' is similarly conditioned by historical contingency: a future age may well have a different bias.

It is then necessary to propound the central thesis — in Chapters 3 to 5. Here we argue that every human being is an engineered anatomy — a cybernetic system programmed to perform in various ways. Such a view has inevitable implications for such matters as human freedom, ethical response, political commitment, and human relationships (explored in Chapters 6 to 9). I believe that the arguments on free will and decision making are very strong, not least because the opponents of such arguments rarely realize that an *uncaused* scenario does nothing for human moral responsibility: if events — including mental events — can occur *for no reason*, then that is no help to anyone who is worried about preserving conventional attitudes to ethical responsibility.

At the same time, some of the ideas on the consequences for morality, politics, and human attachment are only sketched — if only to keep this volume within manageable proportions. There is much to be said in all these areas — perhaps in another book!

The doctrine of robotic man belongs in a certain philosophic tradition — the one that is characterized by materialism, biological determinism, rationalism, and the empirical approach to what may optimistically be deemed 'objective truth' (I cannot sympathize with those pessimistic souls who, full of trepidation, assert that the quest for objectivity is a foolish endeavour — at the same time declaring with conviction that such and such is certainly the case). In this approach, man is most realistically viewed as a machine, a system, an animal, etc. (I well remember being impressed to learn that a human being differs from a chimpanzee in only 1.1 per cent of his genetic material: *Homo sapiens* and *Homo troglodytes* are almost siblings). The realistic model that we select depends in part upon our immediate purposes: which particular language, necessarily congenial to the doctrine of robotic man, best helps us in the task in hand? Are we trying to educate, analyse, or celebrate? Are we trying to remove imperfection or celebrate mental complexity? Are we in a polemical or philosophic mood? In any event, I suggest, there will be a way of interpreting the selected model, the selected language, in robotic terms.

We have not explored in any detail the possible consequences of such a doctrine for the matters of most *human* concern — such topics as guilt, love, fulfilment, and happiness. A few pointers are offered in Chapters 8 and 9 but these are pregnant with unanswered questions, unexplored terrains. For instance, the 'scenarios' given in Chapter 9 invite considerable comment (the first can be given *many other* interpretations, the second is subject to *unstated insecurities,* the third takes too little account of *need* — but more of this in a sequel?).

We emphasize that the doctrine of robotic man is a bracing notion, powerful in its directness, and in its way more humanistic than the bogus celebrations that rest upon intellectual confusion and moral hypocrisy. There is nothing *diminishing* in the doctrine of robotic man — our sensitivities and potential are unchanged and we are encouraged to be robust.

1 Background

Preamble

The idea that man is *akin* to a robot is not new, though in earlier times the notion was inevitably cast in terms that were not obviously robotic. A truly robotic view of man may be regarded as essentially a modern concept. Many, perhaps all, ancient cultures developed the idea of intelligent machines, mythical artefacts that could act with wisdom and purpose: the clever robot has a long tradition in human imagination. However, man has usually been seen as something *more* than a mechanistic artefact, as a creature embracing spiritual or metaphysical elements in addition to the indubitably physical frame. At the same time there are many historical philosophic threads that are sympathetic to the idea of robotic man.

The atomic theories of Democritus in ancient Greece, the irreverent scepticism of Lucretius and Lucian, the hedonistic materialism of the Charvaka of ancient India, the mechanistic philosophy of the eighteenth century La Mettrie and his followers, the modern neurophysiological theories of mind — all contribute, often unwittingly, to a robotic interpretation of the human species. Modern science and technology — particularly the allied disciplines of information science and computer technology — have encouraged, albeit often obliquely and in unexpected ways, the notion that man is a robot. What are the essential elements in such an idea? First we should indicate the obvious sense in which man is *not* a robot.

Human beings are not generated in some workshop or factory: they are not assembled, by people or automated machines, out of pieces of metal and electrical circuits. They are not the mechanical output of some industrial production line. Nor were they planted on earth by some cosmic master of the mechanical arts. People are soft and warm, endearingly prone to error and confusion. They have little about them of the stereotypical robot. People, it seems, are one type of phenomenon; robots are quite another. Yet we will see that there is a sense in which man *is* a robot, relying totally upon an anatomy that functions according the mechanical, electrical, and other physical principles, and completely dependent upon a sophisticated complex of *programs*, laid-down routines that define all human behaviour, all

1

modes of intercourse, all flights of fancy, all movement, decision making, and creative endeavour. We will also see that such a view of man, compelling in the light of modern knowledge, has profound implications for human self-image and human attitudes to ethics, politics, and human relationships. It can be argued that man is a robot — a special kind of robot, but a robot nonetheless.

Man as Robot

We often see suggestions in books, newspapers, and elsewhere to the effect that man is a robot. Thus Richard Dawkins (1976), discussing the survival strategy of the selfish gene, observes: 'Now they swarm in huge colonies, safe inside gigantic lumbering *robots*, sealed off from the outside world, communicating with it by tortuous indirect routes, manipulating it by remote control. 'In a completely different context, Flora Rheta Schreiber (1983) writes about the early life of the rapist and murderer Joseph Kallinger: 'Joe himself became less docile and more rebellious. For the most part he would still be the Kallingers' obedient *robot*. But there would also be lapses.' And again: 'He was not treated as a child, but as a shoemaker's *robot* that, duly programmed, would become a shoemaker.' A report in *The Guardian* (8 October 1985) describes the behaviour of a drug-taking business studies student who became 'an axe-wielding "*robot*" and nearly bludgeoned his father to death'. Three psychiatrists were quoted as being completely satisfied that the youth 'was acting as an *automaton*'. (My italics in each case.)

In these instances people are compared with robots so that particular conceptual or psychiatric points can be made. There is no suggestion that people are *really* robots. The term 'robot' is used as a metaphor or to denote a singular aspect of a person's behaviour. It is inevitable that in such a context the idea of man is *contrasted* with the idea of a robot. Dawkins suggests that individuals are exploited by their genes, serving only to ensure their security: man, in the survival stakes, is somehow less than the gene. Where, in a psychiatric context, a person is likened to a robot the aim is similarly to portray the individual as diminished, as less than fully human. This is an objective that can also be served by portraying man as a robot in a political or industrial context.

People, we are told, can be brainwashed into being robots, unthinking agents of malevolent programming (it is always the other side that does the brainwashing). The same robot metaphor can be used where people are exploited in employment. Thus *The Sunday Times* (17 April 1983) ran extracts from a book by the Japanese journalist Satoshi Kamata under the heading 'Diary of a human robot'. The man had worked on an automobile assembly line for the Toyota company as a temporary worker, and found mindless toil and gross exploitation. The blurb introducing the extracts observes that 'Japan's industrial eminence was still down to its *human robots*' (my italics). Here again there is the attempt to contrast people properly viewed with their treatment as things, as unfeeling elements in an industrial process, as robots. In such a context we may assume that the phrase 'human robot' is intended to cause indignation or revulsion in the reader. We are expected to feel that people should not be treated like that. Again people, rightly viewed, are more than robots.

Sometimes the idea of 'man as robot' has been introduced to serve pieces of sociological commentary. For example, C. Wright Mills (1959) highlights the awareness in a number of writers of how man may be turned into a robot by political and other pressures. Fromm had a concept of the social 'automaton' and Orwell's *1984* conveyed a pessimistic image of robotic man, a depressing picture of people programmed for labour, obedience, and little else. Mill's robot metaphor has a more optimistic flavour: 'Among contemporary men will there come to prevail, or even to flourish, what may be called The Cheerful Robot?' Here it is assumed that a striving after reason and freedom is at odds with a robot role for people in society: the question 'can men be made to want to become *cheerful* robots?' (original italics) is seen as lying on the negative side of the dilemma. If people are content but unthinking, are they betraying their humanity? We are encouraged to think so. To be a robot, cheerful or not, is to be less than fully human. So the argument runs.

The idea that emerges is that 'man as robot' is a depressing image. The notion is inevitably associated with human exploitation, unthinking responses, abject slavery, mindless obedience, and diminished human status. Even if a person is a *cheerful* robot we are faced with a betrayal of human significance, a neglect of the essential areas of humanity that should rightly be fostered and encouraged. But this image of 'man as robot' is necessarily rooted in prescientific attitudes. It is the supposed contrast between mechanisms and men that has allowed the robot metaphor to be used in a particular way. If it is once understood that the contrast cannot be sustained on a rational basis then the metaphor at once loses its potency as a dramatic device, as a means of highlighting particular aspects of man's condition.

If man *is* a mechanism then this fact obtains for every individual — exploited or exploiter, lover or murderer, genius or buffoon, young or old, materialist or mystic. If man is truly a robot then many people will perceive a threat to human status, but only because they have been led to false expectations. Man may or may not be a robot. We will not settle the question by a simple reiteration of metaphor. It will be settled, if at all, by rational enquiry using what knowledge we have. We may even find, following such an investigation, that human status is enhanced, rather than diminished, by an updated robot metaphor.

In calling people robots, Dawkins was saying something interesting about genes; we will find that genes are highly relevant to the man/robot question. In another context, J.J.C. Smart (1959) has suggested that if the story of Genesis is true then Adam and Eve may rightly be regarded as artefacts made by God, as *robots* given their programs in the form of genes. In this spirit, Ninian Smart (1959) has suggested that whereas a robot can be given a number of different programs, every individual is condemned to one set of programs for life. Thus we may imagine that in the long term man-made robots have more potential than human beings. In fact human programs are far more complex than the programs of any artefact, but this is not the important point when starting to think of 'man as robot'. What is significant is how human beings can be discussed in programming terms. To concede that human beings are programmed systems is largely to acknowledge the reality of robotic man.

What is a Robot?

Throughout history — in myth, fiction, and reality — there have been many devices and concepts which today we might dub *robots*. These range from the mobile tripods of Homer's *Iliad* to the mechanical moving elephants of Indian legend, from the clockwork figures designed to amuse the wealthy to the computer-controlled industrial robots of the modern age. In the twentieth century, fictional robots have proliferated in books, films, and magazines, and the robotic concept has even influenced theatre, dance, sculpture, and painting.

It is easy to see that the robot is not a single species in imagination or the real world. It may be mobile or not, friendly or malevolent, blind or sighted, capable of flexible response, or alarmingly dull witted. There is not *one* creature in the pantheon of robots but a myriad of species, a rich diversity stimulated by the many purposes — in entertainment, industry, the home, etc. — that the robot is expected to serve. Even in modern technology, one relevant field among many, *robot* is a loose term. It may denote a machine that somewhat resembles a human being in having a torso, limbs, senses, and a (computer) brain. Or it may signify little more than a box of electronic circuits, as with the 'robot pilots' used in some modern aircraft.

Industrial robots, a growing family of robot species, are perhaps the most prolific real robots in the world today (we may find *toy* robots too simple to qualify as *real* robots). There are many different types of robots used for industrial purposes: most are fixed (few are able to leave the factory when bored or angry); most have no sensory capabilities (though some are sprouting 'eyes' and 'ears'); and many — an increasing number — are programmable, though with very limited scope for flexible response.

The typical industrial robot comprises such elements as a central pedestal (the torso), an articulated arm which may terminate in a wrist, grippers (effective hands), a control system (the brain), and a power source. It is easy to view such a device in anthropomorphic terms. The control system that governs robot behaviour can be simple or complex. The simplest controllers are electronic matrix boards or pneumatic logic systems, allowing little scope for versatile behaviour. Computers — micros, minis, or mainframes — can serve as sophisticated controllers, enabling the robot to adapt to new circumstances, to cope with unexpected contingencies, and to 'think about' the options. The modern robot with a computer brain can adapt in a changing environment, often able to use sensory inputs to achieve objectives. It is important to realize that *purpose*, a seemingly human abstraction, can be incorporated into robot software. The modern working robot, finding one functional route blocked, can search elsewhere in the persistent attempt to achieve a defined goal.

The similarity between man and the robot has been pointed out by many modern writers — authors of fiction trade on the resemblance. Aleksander and Burnett (1983), in a factual and discursive exploration of the robot realm, see the robot as 'a machine made in the image of man'. There is ready acknowledgement that the robot occupies an uneasy ground between man and the machine. We may suggest that the robot is steadily traversing this ground towards man: as the robot becomes more human-like we also find it increasingly plausible to interpret man in machine terms. Man, we shall see, is a cybernetic system subject to the constraints of scientific law in a physical world. Definitions of the robot have variously focused on robot appearance, robot behaviour, or some amalgam of the two. It helps if a robot resembles a human being, though a computer-based system may be regarded as robotic where its actions can easily be interpreted in anthropomorphic terms. Various definitions have been attempted in the specific field of industrial robots and this has been important in studying aspects of robot demography. It is useless, for example, to attempt to compare national populations of robots unless common definitions are used. The Japanese Industrial Robot Association (JIRA) has defined 'robot' as denoting six separate categories (of ascending complexity): manual handling devices, pick-and-place devices, programmable variable-sequence manipulators, robots taught manually, robots controlled by a programming language, and robots that can react autonomously to their environments. It is clear that as one ascends the hierarchy of possible systems one is approaching, albeit slowly and at still great distance, the behavioural competence of the human being.

The first two classes of Japanese robot tend to be disregarded in Europe and the United States. For instance, the British Robot Association (BRA) has defined a robot as '*a reprogrammable device designed to both manipulate and transport parts, tools, or specialised manufacturing implements through variable programmed motions for the performance of specific manufacturing tasks*', which simply means that robots can use tools in various ways to make things. A definition from the Robot Institute of America (RIA) is very similar to the BRA version but talks of a *multifunctional manipulator*, so conveying the important idea that the modern industrial robot is not trapped in some rigid and repetitive procedure. Already it is becoming clear that the modern robot is far removed from the traditional stereotype. Today industrial robots are increasingly able to draw on computer developments in artificial intelligence (AI): e.g. in such areas as expert systems, problem-solving stategies, and visual perception. As robots become more intelligent and more adaptable it will become increasingly reasonable to view (intelligent and adaptable) man in robotic terms.

We can see that definitions of robots are becoming ever more ambitious. No self-respecting robot in the modern world would be satisfied with a single function, with a single programmed response. Increasingly we would expect the definition to include sensory skills (we will see that a sense of touch and visual capacities are commonplace in modern robots) and the ability to behave in an adaptive and versatile fashion. With the evolution of robots (and the accompanying definitions), the more reasonable it will seem to compare man and the machine in various ways. If we are to see man in truly robotic terms it is first necessary to abandon the early robot definitions, connotations, and stereotypes, the relatively primitive complex of impressions generated before robots had begun to develop delicate senses and to think for themselves. We need to remind ourselves of how robots have been viewed in mythology and imagination.

Robots in Myth and Fiction

Many of the early creation myths bear on the robot theme. Gods of various types would take earth or blood and use it to fashion human beings: people were nothing more than artefacts fashioned by divinities. For example, creation myths in the Assyro-Babylonian tradition, known from tablets held in the library of Ashurbanipal in Ninevah, tell how the great divinity Marduk moulded the body of the first man using the blood of a defeated god. In the Judeo-Christian myth, God is said to have breathed life into a man formed out of the dust of the earth. In a Talmudic variation on the idea, the dust was collected from all over the world to be kneaded into a shapeless mass (golem) prior to the forming of the limbs and the infusion of a soul. (In a similar fashion, Prometheus created the first man and woman from clay, and animated them with fire stolen from heaven.)

The golem of Jewish legend could acquire human features when the appropriate rituals were performed, and could be brought to life by inscribing the name of God on its newly shaped forehead. Rabbis were said to create golems to work in their households or to perform specific tasks in the community. In one version of the legend the Rabbi Loew (or Liva) of Prague is said to have created a golem to protect the Jewish community from pogrom (see, for example, the tale by Yudl Rosenberg). This golem, immensely powerful, was apt to run out of control and to threaten its creator (the Frankenstein tale has many versions). Eventually Loew manages to pluck the magic formula from the golem's brow, and the creature is again reduced to harmless clay. It is interesting to remember that the religious myth regards both man and golem as artefacts, effective robots depending for their existence upon divine whim: here God is reckoned to have created man and also to have cooperated with the rabbis in shaping and animating their golems.

Outside the Judeo-Christian tradition there are many myths that deal with the creation of human beings and with the generation of animate substitutes. In Sumerian mythology the gods decided to create deputies — perhaps the earliest industrial robots — who could work for them. In this tale, dating to 2500 BC, the goddess Nammu modelled clay into the shape of a creature and then breathed life into it. A similar legend can be found in the Babylonian Epic of Gilgamesh. In some versions of such tales the creatures are animated by blood. In ancient Egyptian mythology, dating to around 1400 BC, the god Khnum made the first man from clay, but relied upon the goddess Hather to animate it by means of a magic staff.

It is obvious that clay is a favoured substance for such purposes. Swahili tales relate how clay models can be animated by secret words spoken by a god: blood spreads throughout the body, whereupon the muscles ripple and the eyelids tremble. In Maori lore a human figure formed from sand can be animated by the breath of a god, and in Melanesia it was thought that the first men and women were made like wooden puppets and brought to life by the beating of a drum. North American Indians believed that the first people were created by a god mixing earth and water and infusing life into shaped models. The Hopi Indians, for example, reckoned that the Spider Woman made the first human beings by mixing earth with her own saliva.

In the Sanskrit epic, the *Mahabharata*, which contains the Sacred Song, the *Bhagavad Gita*, we learn of how Visvakarman, the god of crafts and the mechanical arts, is asked to generate an artificial woman. The result is the beautiful Tilottama who causes gods to fight over her charms. Of particular interest are the metal humanoids found in the epic Asian poem, the *Epic of Gesar of Ling*. Here a young smith presents the king with magical creatures fashioned out of gold, silver, copper, iron, and bronze. The gold yielded the life-sized Lama and a thousand monks; the bronze, 700 officials and courtiers, and a king; the silver, one hundred singing girls; and the copper, a general and 10,000 soldiers. In this tale the creations are depicted in naturalistic fashion. For once the creator is a skilled human being, a master of crafts but lacking divine powers. In one sense this represents an important departure from traditional religious legend. It is one thing for a divinity to create men and women by means of magic powers, quite another for a human being to fashion realistic figures and then to bring them to life. Here we see the first fumblings after a naturalistic robotics technology. In the *Epic of Gesar of Ling* the various creations are referred to as 'magic dolls' and 'metal dolls', the author clearly torn between an occult and a naturalistic depiction. In yet another Asiatic work, the eleventh century *Brihatkathasaritsagara*, there are descriptions of mechanical humanoids that can speak and dance. We may compare such artefacts with the golden maidens — who could speak and walk, and who were filled with wisdom — manufactured by the Greek god Hephaestus. This divinity also laboured to build twenty tripods which 'run by themselves to a meeting of the gods and amaze the company by running home again' (*Iliad*, Book XVIII); and the giant Talus, made of brass, who guarded Crete by crushing intruders to death against his heated body. In another myth, Hephaestus is said to have created the first woman, Pandora, out of clay.

A popular belief in ancient China was that certain men could bring statues to life, a skill termed *khwai shuh*. In this vein we have the Greek myth of Pygmalion, King of Cyprus, who produces a beautiful ivory statue of a woman whom he names Galatea. Aphrodite, heeding the prayers of Pygmalion, brings Galatea to life who then becomes Pygmalion's spouse. Similarly in Giambattista Basile's *Pentamerone* (1636), the heroine fashions a young lover out of precious stones, scented water, sugar, and other ingredients, whereupon the goddess of love animates the statue, allowing the heroine to consummate her passion.

What we find is a rich tradition in religion and mythology, a multilayered tapestry in which artefacts are fashioned out of earth or clay or blood, and then animated by men or gods possessing occult or divine powers. We see the first strivings after a robotic culture, the first halting steps towards a practical realization of machines made in man's image. The early tale-tellers and myth-spinners had little contemporary technology to stimulate their imaginations: their stories were often inspired by religious commitment rather than by devotion to mechanical arts. However, with the development of science and technology in the modern age, the picture changed. It became possible, not only to imagine artefacts viewed in anthropomorphic terms but to construct machines that truly mirrored human potential in the real world. The mythical humanoid had matured into the functional robot, practical devices that could serve man in the home or factory. In such circumstances it was inevitable that imaginary robots, the creatures of fiction and fancy, would rapidly evolve in scope and potential and that man's view of himself would change. The easier it became to view robots in anthropomorphic terms, the easier it became to embrace the daunting notion of robotic man.

With the rapid development of industrial technology in the nineteenth century there was a corresponding evolution of fiction dealing with science in an imaginative way. Many of these tales concerned humanoids, robotic inventions that mimicked human behaviour and perplexed or terrified the men and women who confronted them. *L'Eve Nouvelle* (1879), later known as *L'Eve Future*, depicts an attractive artificial woman animated by electricity and possessing a soul. The author, Villiers de l'Isle Adam, is supposed to have declared: 'My master, Edison, will soon teach you that electricity is as powerful as God.' In Hoffman's *Der Sandmann* (1817) we find another female automaton, called Olympia, who winds herself up by sneezing! Yet another female robot is found in *Helen O'Loy* (1938), sent as a housekeeper to two bachelors and eventually marrying one of them.

One of the most celebrated fictional treatments of the human automaton theme is Karel Capek's *R.U.R.* (*Rossum's Universal Robots*), one of five plays on a utopian theme (*robot* derives from the Czech word for 'worker'). When Rossum's robots eventually acquire feelings and emotions they can no longer tolerate being treated as slaves by human beings. The robots rebel and soon all human life is destroyed — a familiar idea in robot fiction. Capek saw clearly that robots might one day evolve to the point when they would have needs not formerly associated with machines — for survival, for laughter, and for love. For our purposes this is an important idea. If computer-based artefacts could in principle evolve a capacity for human-like emotions — and many writers and philosophers have toyed with this notion — then the corollary is that a being (e.g. a human) with an emotional disposition could in principle be viewed in robotic terms. It is partly the convergence between our images of *Homo sapiens* and our images of intelligent machines that makes it increasingly plausible to talk of robotic man.

The Capek robots evolved to the point when they could only realize their ambitions by violent action directed against human beings. By contrast, Isaac Asimov was keen to develop the idea of a benevolent robot, an artefact that could respond with sensitivity and intelligence in the developing symbiotic relationship with man. The legend has it that Asimov was depressed by always reading stories about robots that attacked human beings, and so he wrote tales in which robots and people could become emotionally attached to each other. In one of his most famous short stories, Gloria is distraught at having lost her pet robot: 'He was a *person* just like you and me and he was my *friend*. I want him back. Oh, Mamma, I want him back.'

The Asimov interest in the general benevolence of fictional robots is shown by his stipulation of the 'Three Laws of Robotics' (supposedly deriving from the *Handbook of Robotics*, 56th edition, AD 2058). The laws (quoted *ad nauseam* in robot literature) run into a number of moral and practical problems, and these need not detain us here (more is said about the laws in Chapter 8). What is of more interest in the context of the present book is the idea that such laws, intended to restrain robot behaviour, should be necessary. Even Asimov, well disposed to robots as he is, is well aware that robots may pose a threat to mankind. In fact he is quite prepared to suggest that robots, at least in their fictional form, may be seen as superior to human beings. Thus the automaton Cutie (in the short story *Reason*) observes, in 'no spirit of contempt', that human beings are soft and flabby and that they lack endurance and strength, 'depending for energy upon the inefficient oxidation of organic material...'. Periodically, people are apt to pass into a coma 'and the least variation in temperature, air pressure, a humidity, or radiation intensity impairs your efficiency'. Cutie is in no doubt that robots are superior to human beings: 'You are *makeshift*. I, on the other hand, am a finished product. I absorb electrical energy directly and utilise it with an almost one hundred per cent efficiency. I am composed of strong metal, am continuously conscious, and can stand extremes of environment easily.'

The fictional portrayal of robots inevitably led to their depiction in film. Sometimes a robot tale could form the basis of a screen production, or particular robots could feature in films without any fictional precursors. The film robot has a surprisingly lengthy history. Georges Méliès, for instance, made *Gugusse and the Automaton* in 1897, and *Homunkulus* (1916) and *Alrauna* (1918) also handled the idea of artificial life-forms. The robot Homunkulus is driven to tyranny when he realizes he does not possess a soul: the world is saved from disaster by a fortunate flash of lightning. In *Alrauna*, a scientist uses artificial insemination to generate the daughter of a hanged criminal and a prostitute. And the first of the many Frankenstein films was made as early as 1910.

Perhaps uniquely among the early robot films, *Metropolis* (1926) aimed in part to publicize the poor conditions of industrial workers. Here the scientist/magician Rotwang makes a replica of Maria, the mediator in the underground city where the workers toil in dreadful conditions to keep the metropolis above fully serviced and able to continue functioning. (Rotwang: 'I have created a machine in the image of man, that never tires or makes a mistake. . . . Now we have no further use for living workers'.) The main objective is to counter Maria's compassionate efforts on behalf of the exploited workers. The robot replica first looks like a female warrior in gleaming armour; later, when covered in artificial flesh, the machine is indistinguishable from Maria. The robot strives to provoke the workers to violence so that they will destroy the underground city and be obliterated in the ruins. In due course the robot double is burnt at the stake, whereupon the workers see what has happened. The real Maria escapes and redoubles her efforts to save the suffering workers.

Robots have assumed many roles in modern films: developments in industrial technology and computer science have dramatically enlarged the scope of intelligent machines. Like Robbie in the Asimov tale, robots can sometimes be endearing pets (R2D2 in *Star Wars* is the obvious example) or they may be prodigiously talented servants (like Robby in *Forbidden Planet* and *The Invisible Boy*), omnipotent warriors (Gort, able to use death rays to destroy the world, in *The Day the Earth Stood Still*), lovers (as in *Westworld* and *Blade Runner*), rapists (*Demon Seed*), and space-ship crew members (*Alien*). The development of sophisticated computer-based systems in the real world has necessarily enlarged the scope for clever multifunctional robots in films and other forms of fiction. One consequence of this evolution is that film-makers no longer have to rely upon special effects. It is convenient, to say the least, that the robots in *Alien* and *Blade Runner* can be played by human beings: there is no longer any need for the slightly absurd metallic androids — which, in any case, often resembled human beings dressed in tin foil. As robots increasingly come to look like people, so — at least in films and fiction — their emotions can approach those of human beings.

The computer-controlled bombs in *Dark Star* have an evident inclination for philosophic debate, seemingly intrigued by the logical ramifications of certain lines of enquiry. The robots in *Silent Running* evince clear signs of a caring disposition, at one time carrying out successful surgery on a damaged human being. In *Blade Runner* (based on Philip Dick's novel *Do Androids Dream of Electric Sheep?*), the immensely competent Nexus Six robots — inevitably played by human beings — are capable of sexual delight and romantic love. There is certainly no paradox, in the world of the fictional robot, about intelligent machines being capable of emotional response.

What we find in myth and fiction is the persistent notion that artefacts, imbued with intelligence and purpose, can involve themselves in the problems and predicaments of human beings. We frequently encounter the idea that robots are *less than* human beings — less sensitive, less conscious of moral obligation, less able to simulate (or embody) the complex pattern of feelings, anxieties, and joys that characterize human beings. However we also find robots that are *more than* human beings — clearly more intelligent and physically stronger, but also wiser and capable of subtle and powerful emotions. This latter theme mirrors a persistent idea in robot myth and fiction — that a robot race will evolve beyond man, outstripping *Homo sapiens* in the evolution stakes, consigning the biochemical human systems to subordinate roles in society. In such a scenario, it will be human beings, not Robbie or R2D2, who are the pets, the slaves, the disposable devices. The projected evolution of the computer-controlled robot suggests the possibility of a superior intelligence on earth. It suggests also a new sociology of robotic man: in popular culture, *slaves* and *robots* have often been regarded as siblings. To be a slave or a robot is, so the theme runs, to be diminished as a human being, and nothing would diminish *Homo sapiens* more than to be outstripped by an artefact.

The mythical and fictional robot is clearly independent of the current state of practical technology, but also in a fundamental sense mediated by it. It is only in the modern age that fictional robots have been generated in a naturalistic way: the robots of earlier times were necessarily dependent upon occult or religious forces. The primitive mechanical automata, to be found in every age, bore little resemblance to the highly competent humanoid artefacts that ran through contemporary literature. From the earliest times it has proved possible to envisage artificial intelligence enshrined in functional devices, but it was generally thought that such phenomena necessarily derived from magical powers of divine fiat. The possibility of the purely mechanical, but intelligent, robot has taken on a dramatic impetus in the secular age. Another consequence of increased secularization is the possibility of embracing the concept of robotic man, not as a miraculous artefact deriving from magic or divine intervention but as a highly complex naturalistic phenomenon.

The idea that man can be viewed as a robot gains support from the increasing flexibility of modern computer-based systems. Before highlighting some of the more unusual activities of the modern robot, it is worth glancing at the incidence of automata in history.

The Coming of Automata

Inventors of mechanical devices have often been intrigued by the possibility of creating artefacts to resemble living creatures. It is a simple matter to construct a sculpture that *looks like* a bird or a man, but much more difficult to design a machine that *moves like* an animate creature. To this end the early engineers — Greeks, Ethiopians, Chinese, Babylonians, etc. — exploited whatever motive power was available. At many times, in many different cultures, ingenious inventors exploited the properties of water, air, steam, and gravity to cause devices to act out a series of motions and so create the illusion of life.

More than two thousand years ago, Hero of Alexandria wrote his celebrated *Treatise on Pneumatics* in which he described a wealth of automata — such as moving figures and singing birds (what one writer — Scott, 1984 — has dubbed 'an Ancient Greek Disneyland'). In Pindar (*Olympic Ode*, c520 BC) we find descriptions of the animated figures that seemingly adorned every public street and which appeared 'to breathe in stone, or move their marble feet'. The Athenian Daedalus was said to have created a range of humanoid automata: e.g. a bronze warrior and a wooden device animated by a flow of mercury through concealed channels. (Daedalus is also credited with the invention of the wedge, the axe, the level, and many mechanical devices.) Wooden statues called Daedala were carried in processions in Ancient Greece.

A statue of the king of Ethiopia, Memnon, dating to the fifteenth century BC, was supposed to emit melodious sounds when struck by the rays of the sun. The sounds were said to be reminiscent of those heard when a harpstring is overwound. The beauty of the sounds suggested to contemporaries a divine cause since clearly no simple mechanical structure could be so effective. The statue is depicted by Athanasius Kircher in the *Oedipus Aegyptiacus* (1652). Many of the animated devices of this period relied upon well-understood natural principles. For example, in the third century BC, Ctesibius is said (by Vitruvius) to have discovered many pneumatic principles: he 'devised methods of raising water, automatic contrivances, and amusing things of many kinds ... black birds singing by means of waterworks and figures that drink and move, and other things that have been found to be pleasing to the eye and ear'.

The invention of seemingly animate statues often helped priests to maintain their control over an ignorant populace. Statues built around 2500 BC contained trumpets through which the priests could address a gullible audience. However not everyone was convinced. Celsus, for example, one of the great sceptics of the ancient world, was keen to decry magic and animals 'not really living but having the appearance of life'. Over the centuries the engineers gradually took over from the magicians and priests, and later devices, based on obvious mechanical principles, evoked new superstitious awe.

In ancient China, five centuries BC, King-shu Tse was said to have described flying magpies made of wood, and a wooden horse worked by springs. Around the same period Archytas of Tarentum (*c*400 BC) invented a wooden pigeon suspended from the end of a pivot rotated by a jet of water or steam, and so simulated flight. (Archytas is supposed to have invented the screw and the pulley). In the fourth century AD, a golden Buddhist statue was revered by the pious. The construction was erected on a carriage, and accompanied by animated models of Taoist monks. When the carriage moved forward, the monks circled the Buddha, at the same time bowing, saluting, and throwing incense. Other Chinese records tell of an animated mechanical monk able to stretch out its hands, call 'Alms! Alms!', and put coins into a bag when they reached a certain quantity.

A wooden otter, built in China around 790, could supposedly catch fish; just as a wooden cat (*c*890) could catch rats and dancing tiger-flies. The Japanese Prince Kaya, son of the Emperor Kanmu, is said to have made a doll with a large bowl and set it in his rice paddy. When the bowl became full of rain water, the doll would lift it up and pour the water over its own face. The simple people of Kyoto were so fascinated by this contrivance that they kept filling up the bowl to watch the behaviour of the doll. In such a fashion was the rice paddy watered.

The Indian scholar Prince Bhoja of India (1018–60) described in the famous *Samarangana-sutradhara* many details about the construction of machines, and it was declared that some of the machines resembled animals. A contemporary text relates the machines (the yantras) to what were presumed to be the five elements of the universe: 'The yantras based on earth materials undertake activities like shutting doors; a water-based yantra will be as lively as living organisms; a fire yantra emits flames; an air yantra moves to and fro; the elements of either serve to convey the sound generated by these yantras.' In a more practical vein, *A Book of the Knowledge of Mechancial Contrivances* (1206) was written by Al-Jazari at Amid on the Upper Tigris to describe a wide range of hydraulic devices such as clepsydras and fountains. The 'Peacock Fountain', another remarkable Muslim achievement, was an early device for washing the hands. When water is poured into the basin, a small figure of a man emerges carrying a bowl of perfumed powder, followed by another with a towel.

Albertus Magnus (1204–72) is said to have built a functional robot servant, and there are several versions about its fate. One tale relates how it greeted Thomas Aquinas in the street, whereupon the worthy saint, thinking the device to be the work of the devil, smashed it to bits. In another version the robot was piously destroyed after Albertus had died. This automaton servant was reputed to be able to talk like a human being and to be able to open the door for visitors. Roger Bacon (1214–94) is also said to have constructed a talking head. Little is known of this device which is supposed to have taken seven years of labour to complete. René Descartes is supposed to have built a female robot, 'ma fille Francine', around 1640. Here the contraption was consigned to a watery grave. A nervous sea captain opened the case in which Francine was kept on a sea voyage: seeing the robot move, as if alive, the superstitious captain threw it overboard.

The eighteenth century saw a host of automata, often designed to resemble animals and human beings. A celebrated duck, contrived by Jacques de Vaucanson (1709–82), was made of gilded copper. It was claimed that this invention 'drinks, eats, quacks, splashes about on the water, and digests his food like a living duck'. A single wing was said to contain more than four hundred articulated pieces, and once the duck had fallen into disrepair it took more than four years to restore it to full working order. A contemporary report, cited by Chapuis and Droz (1958), observes: 'After each of the duck's performances there was an interval of a quarter of an hour to replace the food. A singer announced the duck. As soon as the audience saw it climbing on the stage, everyone cried: "Quack, quack, quack". Greatest amazement was caused when it drank three glasses of wine.' Another automaton from the same inventor was the flute player, able to play twelve different tunes by means of a current of air led through the complex mechanism. The name of Friedrich von Knauss (1724–89) is associated with the creation of a wide range of automatic writing machines, talking machines, and writing dolls. Baron Wolfgang von Kempelen (1734–1804) also invented a talking machine (Goethe commented: 'The talking machine of Kempelen is not very loquacious but it pronounces certain childish words very nicely').

By the end of the eighteenth century a number of European craftsmen were working to produce mechanical automata that could simulate many different types of human activity. Swiss craftsmen, for example, were building automata that could write, draw pictures, and play various types of musical instrument. Notable among such craftsmen were Pierre and Henri-Louis Droz. Their Scribe, built in 1770, was a mechanical child that could dip a quill pen in ink and then move the pen over a sheet of paper. This device used a complex array of precision cams driven by clockwork. The Draughtsman, built three years later, could draw various pictures, including a portrait of Louis XV. The Musician, able to play a miniature organ, had articulated fingers, a breast that moved to simulate breathing, a head that moved to the rhythm of the music, and eyes that glanced around from time to time.

Euphonia, in the form of a bearded Turk, was a talking machine exhibited in the Egyptian Hall, Piccadilly, in 1846. Professor Faber of Vienna spent twenty-five years constructing this device, which could produce sounds similar to those of a human being, laugh, whisper and sing, and ask and answer questions. The automaton contained keys, levers, a double-bellows, and a movable mouth in which were set a flexible tongue and an indiarubber palate; because Faber spoke German, Euphonia spoke English with a pronounced German accent. Other nineteenth-century automata were the celebrated games-playing machines (Kempelen had earlier manufactured a chess-playing automaton — including cogs, gears, levers, and moving cylinders, but also with a man inside!). Early in the twentieth century, Leonardo Torres y Quevado, President of the Academy of Sciences in Madrid, constructed an electromagnetic chess-playing automaton which could successfully conclude a simple end-game: the white king and rook mating the black king from any position. This machine, a triumph of classical mechanics, defeated the great cybernetician Norbert Wiener at the 1951 Congress of Cybernetics in Paris. This was seen as the last victory of classical mechanics over modern cybernetics: today all the most successful chess-playing automata are based on electronics. In fact it was the rapid development of electronics in the twentieth century that allowed robotic systems to evolve from the relatively simple mechanical machines of earlier times to the highly complex modern systems capable of purposeful and intelligent behaviour. In particular it was the emergence of the electronic digital computer, a mere four decades ago, that enabled robots to take a massive evolutionary leap.

It was inevitable that the earliest calculating machines were mechanically based. Hero of Alexandria is associated with various mechanical systems that used calculating principles, though it is the Spanish theologian Roman Lull (whose work and life are profiled in Gardner, 1981) who, working in the thirteenth century, is usually credited with the invention of the first mechanical device to serve as a logic machine. In 1642 the mathematician and philosopher Blaise Pascal built a mechanical calculating machine ('I submit to the public a small machine of my own invention by means of which alone you may, without effort, perform all the operations of arithmetic, and may be relieved of the work which has often times fatigued your spirit'). Doubtless aware of Pascal's achievement, Wilhelm Gottfried von Leibniz (1646–1716) constructed a device that could multiply, add, divide, and calculate square roots, and Jewna Jacobson, a clockmaker in Minsk, built a mechanical calculating machine in 1770. However it was the work of Charles Babbage (1782–1871), working with highly complicated mechanical systems — the 'difference engine' (1823) and the 'analytical engine' (1833–71) — that laid the basis for much of the computer theory that was to follow. While Babbage, working with Ada Lovelace, was pushing mechanical calculating systems to their limits, George Boole (1815–64) was formulating the algebraic system of symbols and postulates which, together with binary arithmetic, was to become so crucial to the development of the electronic computers of the twentieth century.

All sophisticated robots in the modern world owe their competence — their flexibility of response, their ability to handle sensory data, their ability to react with intelligence, etc. — to the fact that they are controlled by electronic computers. The earliest industrial robots were controlled by massive mainframe computers, the size of several wardrobes. However, with the development of solid-state electronics — from the transistor (first demonstrated in the US Bell Telephone Laboratories in 1948) to the densely packed integrated circuits of the 1970s and 1980s — it became possible to provide robots with local miniaturized computer power. Robots no longer needed to be linked to mainframes sited elsewhere: by the 1980s, robots could contain their own microcomputer brains.

The modern robot, already evolving many different anatomies for different purposes, can now be controlled by computer software embodying various types of artificial intelligence, i.e. programs that can variously solve problems, interpret visual and other sensory data, play games, handle — as do human beings — partial or uncertain ('fuzzy') information, and perform advisory and consultative functions in different fields (medicine, electronic fault diagnosis, geological prospecting, chemical analysis etc.). Robots are no longer simple mechanical automata, but highly sophisticated artefacts capable of intelligent multifunctional responses in the physical environment.

Our enlarged concept of the potential of the modern computer-controlled robot necessarily influences our attitudes to such phenomena as creativity and intelligent decision making. This in turn affects our attitudes to the doctrine of 'man as robot'. If we can conceive the idea of a creative and intelligent artificial robot, what are we to say about the creative and intelligent physical systems that we recognize as human beings?

What Can Robots Do?

People often feel threatened by the growing competence of intelligent machines, a circumstance that is encouraged by much modern fiction and film drama. The persistent cliché about 'machines taking over' — an idea explored by countless writers from Samuel Butler (in *Erewhon*, 1872) to Philip Dick in the twentieth century — seems less and less absurd with every major new technological innovation. Today computers can write poetry, compose music, out-diagnose (in certain areas) any human physician, and easily beat 98 per cent of the world's chess players. This is a rapidly evolving situation: whatever computer-controlled systems can do today, they will do better tomorrow. Faced with such dauntingly clever machines, people adopt a variety of strategies to protect self-image and sanity.

One ploy is to declare that computers and robots are 'nothing but' machines, dependent solely upon the behaviour of electrical pulses in complex switching circuits (as if human neuron networks in the brain did not depend upon equally mundane electrical potentials and chemical messengers). Another tack is to compare computer-controlled systems with lowly life-forms — to indicate thereby that computers are not about to encroach on *human* territory (as if it had not already happened in countless fields). Thus we have an article in a woman's magazine declaring that 'in manipulatory ability, robots are, at present, about as effective as the average crab'. In similar spirit, Lisa Mendelson (in *Computing*, 11 November 1982) quotes Dr David Grosman, of IBM's Research Division, to the effect that the smartest robot around 'is no smarter than the world's smartest grasshopper', and Leon Clifford (*Electronics Weekly*, 31 July 1985) is keen to point out that a slug (photograph included, in case we are not sure what a slug is) can match the power of a personal computer. So computer-controlled systems are unable to outstrip crabs, grasshoppers, and slugs — what a relief! In fact, as any AI buff knows, the situation is a little more complicated than that. When computers are beating International Masters at chess and finding mineral deposits overlooked by human beings, perhaps we should not be too scathing about the competence of artificial systems. It is instructive, and sometimes entertaining, to glance at what robots are up to in the modern world.

Most active robots in the world are involved with industry. This is not surprising. Robots are tireless, unlikely to get bored, and less than interested in trade union membership. Samuel Butler perceived the value of working machines more than a century ago. In *Erewhon* he wrote: 'Our sum-engines never drop a figure, nor our looms a stitch; the machine is brisk and active, when the man is weary; it is clear-headed and collected, when the man is stupid and dull; it needs no slumber, when man must sleep or drop; ever at its post, ever ready for work, its alacrity never flags, its patience never gives in; its might is stronger than combined hundreds...'. How can mere human beings compete with such prodigious industrial capability!

The early industrial robots had little programmability: they were often limited to set routines and specific ('dedicated') applications. Changing patchboards was often time consuming and in any case added little extra flexibility to robot performance. Today, however, with computer control, industrial robots are extremely flexible production units, suitable for medium or even small batch production which formerly could not be carried out economically by standard automaton techniques. Most modern industrial robots are involved in such tasks as painting, welding, deburring, diecasting, fettling, forging, etc. They can drill holes, sand-down workpieces, and assemble a wide range of units, such as electric motors, automobile alternators, electric motors, and electric typewriter subassemblies. Robots are even involved in assembling parts of computers. For example, Shugart Associates of California has designed a robot to perform the initial eight-step assembly process for a disk drive product. The GEC GADFLY (GEC Advanced Device For Assembly) system is used for assembling electronic components. The English Evershed Robotics company is supplying the Toshiba TSR-700H assembly robot which can — by screwing, inserting, and riveting — secure components on printed circuit boards. GEC Marconi has developed a 'reconfigurable' robot gripper (hand) that can manipulate a wide range of integrated circuits, resistors, capacitors, and the like.

The development of industrial robots has been stimulated largely by a variety of economic motives, with industrial managers interested in such factors as payback periods, labour costs, investment programmes, and kindred topics. There can be little doubt that robots have displaced large numbers of factory workers who were often engaged in boring and repetitive tasks. It is clearly desirable that people be spared soul-destroying and hazardous employment, though displaced workers are likely to have different views on the matter. As computer-controlled robots become ever more capable, we may expect a progressively more dramatic impact on traditional working practices, and we should not assume that professional employees will remain unaffected by robot evolution. It is clearly the case that robot performance will approach that of human beings in one field after another. It is useful to glance at some current developments.

We are accustomed to seeing references in the literature to newly developed robots senses (some details are given in Chapters 3 and 4), but we are still often surprised. Robots are able to exploit sensory possibilities unknown in the traditional biological realms, sometimes with unexpected results. For example, there is now a chemical-based visual-guidance system for use in many industrial applications. The Optical Engineering Group of the University of Dayton (Ohio)

Research Institute has demonstrated that a new optical scanner can react to chemical compounds in components and tools. This has suggested the interesting idea that robots will soon be able to react to industrial tools and components — by, in effect, 'seeing' smells — without the need for outside programming.

In another experimental project at Carnegie Mellon University, it has proved possible to issue commands orally to a robot using a microcomputer and a voice input system. This particular robot is little more than an animated arm, but it is equipped to recognize a set of one-word commands. If, for instance, you say 'up', the robot will raise its arm. Dr David Bourne, working on the project, has commented: 'What we're coming up with is pretty exciting.' Other experimental robots are skilled manipulators. The WABOT-1 robot, for example, built at Waseda University in Tokyo, is equipped with touch, sight, and hearing. You can tell WABOT-1 to find an item in its vicinity, whereupon it acknowledges the command, visually scans the environment to locate the item, moves to pick it up, and finally transports it to a specified destination. This robot can also pour liquid from one container to another. A famous precursor to WABOT-1 was the Shakey robot, developed at the Stanford Research Institute and launched on a surprised world as early as 1968. Shakey, 'the first complete robot system', was mobile (on wheels) and equipped with camera eye, a range finder, and a set of bump detectors. This device was skilled at assembling blocks and moving them from one room to another. But perhaps Cubot was one of the most remarkable manipulative robots of recent years. Developed by twenty scientists from Battelle's North-West Laboratories, Cubot is able to solve Rubik's Cube — both theoretically and practically, and in less than four minutes! You scramble the cube and give it to Cubot. The robot examines (visually) the disposition of the cube elements, decides what to do, and then manipulates the elements until the desired result is achieved.

It is commonplace for functional robots to have *one* articulated arm, but some have two. The Sterling Detroit Company, for example, has developed a two-armed Robotarm to cope with the industrial tasks of quenching and trimming, the two arms operating simultaneously. Yes-Man is a prototype two-armed robot made at Patscentre, Cambridge, for Prutec, the venture capital division of the Prudential. One aim is for Yes-Man, working with human beings, to take over a number of routine laboratory tasks such as assay work, culture transfer, and chemical sampling. In common with many species of factory robot, Yes-Man can be taught by taking it through the motions or by keying in the appropriate instructions. Possible factory applications are envisaged for this device. It could, for example, assemble gearboxes and electric motors. Interestingly enough, various safety devices have been incorporated: the robot screwdriver blades can have a retractable sheath or ultrasonic guard, and the robot arms are said to cringe when they touch human flesh! This is one of many robots being developed to perform a wide range of scientific and industrial tasks. Professor Yoji Umetani, for example, at the Tokyo Institute of Technology, has often drawn attention to experimental robots being developed in Japan for many different purposes. He has, for instance, highlighted a remarkable Hitachi robot that is able to look at an engineering blueprint, to understand what the sketch means, and then to assemble the various parts according to the specification. Here the camera eye would scan the drawing, the incoming visual data would be interpreted by the computer brain, and the eye would again be used — possibly in conjunction with touch sensors — as the robot hand manipulated the parts for assembly purposes. In a similar fashion a robot at the Autonetics Systems Division of Rockwell International (in California) is preassembling navigational gyros with 'humanly impossible' accuracy. This robot, able to work in a pressurized atmosphere of filtered nitrogen, can accomplish in about fourteen minutes what took human beings many hours or even days to perform. Few other robots meet the precision cleaning requirements demanded for this task (the new device has been dubbed 'My Super-Clean'). This is yet another clear indication that computer-controlled robots are achieving the dexterity once only associated with *human* fingers.

Robots are also being used to package chocolates at Cadbury's Birmingham factory in England. Pairs of arms, using vacuum grippers, pick up the chocolates and place them carefully in plastic trays. Each pair of arms is programmed to select just one kind of chocolate. The arms, supplied by the German company Otto Hansel, can pack sixty trays per minute, reducing the former staff of forty to twenty. Rowntree Mackintosh is also working to develop effective robot facilities. Once the chocolates have caused tooth decay you can meet another friendly robot in your dentist's surgery — if, that is, you happen to be treated by the American Ellis J. Neiburger. He has installed a robot in his surgery, which buzzes about vacuuming the floor and carrying patients' records up and down a 70-foot office corridor. A robot used for such purposes may, Neiburger admits, seem 'a little exotic', but other dentists are using robots for office security.

If robots are not yet used to extract teeth, they are already working as sheep shearers in Australia. There is current debate as to whether the sheep should be anaesthetized first, though it has been pointed out that the robot shearers draw blood less frequently than their human counterparts. Electronic sensors are used to measure the proximity of the sheep skin and so control the behaviour of the cutting edge. If robots can work in such a fashion with animals it may not be long before they learn to work with human beings, and to do more than to cut hair. In fact it has been reported (in *New Scientist*, 4 February 1982) that the Tokyo Institute of Technology was working to develop a slender flexible robot able to probe inside people's organs to carry out delicate surgical operations. In such applications, lasers may be used both as cutting devices and as a means of gauging distances.

Use is also being made of robots in Japanese university libraries. The user of a viewing booth in a library of the Kanazawa Industrial University punches in the number of a required videotape and then waits for the program to run. The video- and audio-tapes are stacked in layers, with ramps and runways set between the stacks. Videotape recorders and audio-cassette players are conveniently sited with respect to the stacks. Battery-powered wheeled robots — each the size of a shoe-box — shuttle between the stacks and the players. Each 'Intelibot' carries a 'magic hand' for pulling tapes from the stacks and for slotting them into the players. A central computer directs the robots, working out optimum routes, and ensuring that collisions are avoided. When not required, an Intelibot can sit in a parking bay for the lunch break (it charges up its batteries). There are more than three dozen of these intelligent robots at Kanazawa, fetching and replacing some 2000 video tapes and 1000 audiotapes for around 4500 students. Other types of robots, less industrious, are only interested in a game of cards. The Japanese firm Matsushita has manufactured a robot system that includes a camera eye, a computer for control purposes, and fingers containing pressure sensors. The robot can play cards, and it seldom makes mistakes as it physically manipulates the cards in its fingers. It is said to be an excellent bridge player.

In early 1984 it was reported (for example, in *Computerworld*, 13 February) that an American company, Denning Mobile Robotics, intended to develop mobile robotic systems for use as prison guards. The aim was for the robots to be used in tasks that were boring or dangerous: e.g. patrolling hallways at night. At that time the company had not yet produced a fully functioning prototype, but the plans were clear. The robot would stand about four-feet tall, weigh about 200 lb, and have various sensors — including 'ammonia sniffers' to detect smells given off by the human body. Also the device would be programmed to utter as many as ten different sentences: e.g. to warn escaping prisoners ('You have been detected'). Details of the prison geography could be included in computer memory. By late 1985 (see *Computerworld*, 7 October) Denning was ready to test a robot that could move, see, hear, and smell. The mobile security robot is equipped with ultrasonic sensors, video cameras, gas and fire sensors, an infrared tracking system, and a powerful microprocessor to handle incoming data and to control the system.

The aim is to sell the Denning security robot for between $45,000 and $65,000, and to run it at half the price of its human counterpart. The robot can constantly transmit a video picture back to a guard situated in a central control room and is able to indicate whether it has been tampered with by a prisoner. One estimate is that up to 10 per cent of security posts could be filled by robots incorporating existing technology — and this is early days.

What we see is a growing diversity of robot models, ranging from delicate devices for fine work to mighty machines for handling heavy castings. The diversity of robot systems is necessarily matched by a diversity of roles: we have seen that robots are now commonplace in industry (in West Germany, robots are even being used to fit wheels on cars), used in a wide variety of applications, and relatively insensitive to environmental hazards (extreme fluctuations in temperature, toxic gases, radioactivity, etc.) that would endanger people. Robots can also be used where a high level of atmospheric cleanliness is essential: e.g. in silicon circuit fabrication. Robots can obviously work in a partial vacuum and in darkness. They are more flexible than human beings in some respects, less flexible in others, but whereas human potential is known and more or less well defined, robot potential is evolving rapidly.

In such circumstances — in particular, where robots can be linked to computers using AI software — it is easy to speculate about how robots are acquiring characteristics that were once peculiar to people. Perhaps robots are becoming intelligent and creative. It is also possible to argue, perhaps more extravagantly, that computer-based systems are gradually evolving into new *life-forms* on earth. If this were so, it would obviously be a sign that robots (as one among many computer-based families) and biological systems were converging. Again, if robots were beginning to acquire 'life characteristics' it would be easy to see that human beings might be represented as a special class of robots.

Are Robots Alive?

It is obvious that robots often behave *as if* they were alive, but a system is not animate merely because it *appears* so. To mimic or to simulate life is not necessarily to be alive. Robots will have to do more than pretend to be alive if we are to accept them as actual biological systems. Are there ways in which robots can go beyond mimicry, simulation, and pretence? Is it possible that robots are evolving to the condition when they can make the first legitimate 'life claims' of any machine? First, an engaging piece of life mimicry....

In 1985 we saw the first case of a robot running amok in a restaurant. It was reported (*Daily Telegraph*, 26 June 1985) that a Danic robot costing £4887 had been purchased to serve wine to customers in the Kavio Restaurant in Edinburgh. Unfortunately the machine could not cope with the required tasks. When first tested, it merely spilled a glass of wine, but there was worse to come. It upset more glasses of wine, knocked over furniture, and frightened the customers. Finally the head of the robot fell into the lap of a customer, and the case was taken to court, with the robot, wearing a black hat and bow tie, the main exhibit in the court room. It was stated that the robot batteries had not been adequately charged, and that this omission would cause it to vibrate and to move in a jerky fashion.

Eventually the case was concluded ('Settlement in case of the mad robot') and 'Donic' was escorted from the court, still wearing black tie and homburg. It was decided to return the robot to London, presumably for repair and retraining as a wine waiter. In this example, customers were frightened but not fooled by the robot's antics into imagining that the machine was actually alive. A robot, after all, is only a machine. However there is more to be said about the possibility of machines developing as organisms in their own right — as *computer-based* systems that can reasonably be regarded as part of the *biological* world. Living systems need not necessarily be dependent upon hydrocarbon metabolisms: there are other biological possibilities.

I have argued in detail elsewhere (Simons, 1983, 1985a) that computer-based systems may reasonably be regarded as a family of newly emerging life-forms and I will not rehearse the arguments here. However it is worth highlighting some of the main considerations that are also relevant to the concept of 'man as robot'.

Where definitions of life are framed in systems terms, rather than in terms of chemical configurations, it is clearly possible in principle for electronic systems *of certain types* to qualify as alive. Such systems would, for example, be able to process energy and information in various ways and to carry out a suitable set of the behaviours that characterize acknowledged living systems. Thus we may expect living systems based on solid-state electronics to learn, to adapt to a changing environment, to take in energy (to 'feed') to sustain the life processes, to evolve, to take in information (to 'sense'), to reproduce, etc. There is nothing here that is outside the scope of modern computer technology. We need only to emancipate ourselves from the parochial view that living systems are necessarily based on impure carbon to see that a *systems* definition of life is perfectly adequate. It is, in fact, perfectly compatible with such obvious life phenomena as perception, thought, growth, evolution, death, and the restless search for survival strategies. Important discussions of the systems approach to biology can be found, for example, in Miller (1978), Riedl (1978), and Sommerhoff (1969). This approach highlights both the convenient analogy between, and the convergence of, machine and biological systems.

Comparisons between machines and human beings often occur as a metaphorical ploy. (We have already seen how the word *robot* can be used to *diminish* a person, to render him less than fully human.) Sometimes we are amused at metaphorical allusion. So a journal can run a heading, '*What next? Liability insurance for robots!*', over a description of new insurance cover being introduced for industrial robots in Sweden. A new 'personal liability' insurance scheme has been introduced by Skandia, the Swedish insurance company, to cover robots employed by manufacturers made more vulnerable, in the climate of increased automation, to expensive stoppages in production. The scheme is said to be comprehensive; in particular, covering all types of robot breakdown (an instance of comprehensive health insurance?). There are many other examples of how an anthropomorphic attitude to robots (and other computer-based systems) is coming to dominate the technological culture of the modern world.

New Scientist (12 April 1979) can exhort us to 'be nice to robots'; *The Guardian* and other newspapers periodically inform us about 'robot slaves' or 'the men who fall for their computers'; a woman's magazine asks: 'Could you learn to love a robot?'; and a General Electric advertisement for personal computers advises: 'Don't get married to a computer until you've had a meaningful relationship'. By 1980 the *Journal of Social Psychology* (vol. 108, no. 2) was able to investigate the extent to which computers could be regarded as people and, in February 1984, Don Nilsen (writing in *Educational Technology*) could ask, in connection with the use of metaphors in computer terminology, 'Who is more human, the programmer or the computer?'. Aart Bijl (1985), in an article about graphical input, asks: 'Can computers understand people?', and in countless other popular articles and technical papers we see discussion about computer-based systems that variously reverses, merges, confuses, or overlaps the traditional distinctive roles of machines and human beings. When A. Narayanan (1983) heads a research report, *'What is it like to be a machine?'*, we are encouraged to imagine a machine having consciousness, a world view, a sense of identity.

What we are seeing is a dramatic convergence — signalled in countless different ways — of man and machine. On the one hand, machines are acquiring startling new qualities, entitling us to ask whether computer-based systems can really be regarded as intelligent, conscious, alive; on the other hand, we are encouraged, for example, by increased knowledge of cybernetic brain mechanisms, by new insights into genetic programming, by fresh psychological awareness through such schools as transactional analysis, by progress in artificial intelligence, to analyse human performance and human nature in machine terms, to see human beings as robots.

We have, so far, suggested an attitude, a climate for enquiry. The doctrine of 'man as robot' has been stated, but has not yet been argued. The arguments will be given later (mainly in Chapters 3 to 7). First we need to identify the 'essence of the robot'. Exactly what does the doctrine of 'man as robot' entail?

The Essence of the Robot

We have glanced at many different types of robots — in myth, fiction and the real world. We have seen that robots can be trivial, absurd, clever, fearsome, and industrious. We have seen that, despite their frequent connections with the supernatural (in ancient tales and old religions), they have rarely been granted souls or the pleasures of an afterlife. Robots are essentially physical phenomena, with few paranormal or metaphysical pretensions. In the first place, therefore, a robot has an anatomy; more accurately, a robot *is* an anatomy. It is through its physical structure that the robot works to make an impact on the world, and it is through *behaviour* that the impact, of whatever scale, is felt by contemporary (machine or human) observers. So the robot is, in essence, a behaving anatomy.

The behaviour of the robot can be highly complicated, especially if man is a robot. This behaviour is enabled by complex programming, where the word *programming* signifies laid-down routines that allow the performance of significant and meaningful activities. If man is a robot, then he is a remarkably complex and intricate one, but this circumstance in no way tells against the basic thesis. Obscene graffiti and immortal literature are both prose, though having different features and different claims upon our attention. 'Man as robot' may well appear, to the rational person acquainted with the relevant arguments, as an unavoidable doctrine. However we will see that the idea need not *diminish* human beings: people will still be far removed from the robot artefacts, however impressive they may be, of the modern scientific and industrial world. We may even find that 'man as robot' is a paradoxically liberating notion, freeing us from false ideas and false expectations, stimulating a constructive approach to man's ethical and social predicament.

Hence the essence of the robot consists in an anatomy programmed for behaviour. If this is a reasonable observation, and if man as an entity can be interpreted *in toto* in such terms, then man is a robot. He may have a dauntingly complex anatomy and a dazzlingly complicated array of programs but if these two elements, considered with caution and circumspection, are adequate in principle to define the whole man, then man is a robot. Before discussing anatomy and programming — and such relevant notions as cybernetics and autonomy — in more detail, it is useful to profile some of the important *models of man* that have competed for attention, and that still do.

2   Models of Man

Preamble

The word *model*, used in connection with human beings, can have several different meanings, some of which we will ignore. It may signify a person who is a suitable subject for emulation: feminists, for example, may search for *role* models; or it may denote a way of looking at man, a means of interpreting his nature in society or the universe. Here we are largely interested in this latter meaning. What broad view of man can serve as a useful framework for identifying his essence? Is man both spiritual and physical, or neither? Is man a soul or a material system? Perhaps a soul is somehow 'glued' inside a lump of matter. Is man important? To what and to whom? Does he acquire significance through a divine plan or through a lengthy process of biological evolution? Is man a machine, an animal, a *robot*?

Some models of man are mutually incompatible. For example, it is difficult to see how man can be both a soul and a machine. If man is to enjoy eternal life he must surely be more than a mechanism governed by the laws of physics and chemistry. Perhaps man is no more that a fortuitous collocation of atoms, an intricate sociobiological system. Physical machines, we may safely assume, do not inherit eternal bliss, so if man is to be a machine, religious metaphysics may be totally irrelevant to his condition. Also, some models of man are mutually compatible: one view of man may complement or supplement another. Thus man may be animal *and* machine *and* system.

Whichever model we take as primary is often largely a psychological matter — a reflection of tastes, hobbies, and habits. This has always been true *mutatis mutandis* of our models (images) of God. The warrior fashions a warrior deity; the pacifist wants his god to be peace loving; Charles Babbage, we will see, wanted his divinity to be a writer of celestial programs. Our models of man (and of God) are not an arbitrary, subjective matter, however. There are often prohibitive rational constraints on models that we might prefer. The doctrine of an all-protective deity is a congenial notion, but one difficult to sustain in reason.

Different times favour different models of man, though a rich national culture — such as classical Greece or modern Britain — can simultaneously sustain a spectrum of different models. Where a number of different (incompatible) models cohabit in society, then one is likely to be a dominant 'establishment' model, with the others surviving as traditional remnants or because they serve some newly emerging subculture. Greece, for example, could sustain at once the notions of religious man and materialist man, and Ancient Rome could tolerate many gods and many schools of thought. Mediaeval and modern totalitarian states have found it harder to tolerate a diversity of incompatible man models.

Prevailing models necessarily signal the intellectual and ethical temper of the times. Some cultures can sustain multidimensional models, whereas elsewhere models are simple, inspired by a narrow perspective. Throughout history many different views of man have prevailed, serving a wide range of religious, political, and other purposes. So Aristotle saw man as essentially a rational citizen, though with a spiritual or metaphysical dimension. For Augustine, man was a creature to be saved, a soul threatened by temptation and in desperate need of divine grace. Erasmus, as a classical humanist, saw man as a social creature to be redeemed through education and enlightenment. For Rousseau, man was a natural spirit, constrained by social pressure and needing to escape. Marx saw man as a communal economic entity, chained and exploited by oppressors, needing to understand and use the dialectic of history. For Buber and the existentialists, man was essentially a free agent, able at every moment to reshape life. The rationalists and scientific humanists variously saw man as a social animal, a biological system, a piece of matter obeying natural law.

It is only in recent years that cyberneticians — information scientists, computer technologists, etc. — have been able to develop the framework for 'man as robot'. In this framework, for the most part constructed unwittingly, we see a linking of several traditional models. Here man can be simultaneously a social animal and a machine system. It may be difficult in such an approach to retain a religious dimension in man's nature, but it is clear that man had sacrificed immortality before the coming of the doctrine of robotic man. To treat man as, in some sense, a robot necessarily involves overthrowing some traditional models, but it reinforces others, strengthening a multi-faceted materialism that is quick to embrace social purpose, aesthetic delight and all the joys of human intercourse.

We need to glance at some of the historical (and current) models of man before considering in more detail the doctrine of 'man as robot'. First we may want to ask the following central question.

What is Man?

To promote a model of man is to declare a view of what man is. A model may, for example, serve to establish man's uniqueness by distinguishing human beings from other biological species. Thus man may be uniquely equipped to use language, to develop self-awareness, to use tools, etc. Since human beings are framing the definitions of man, many of the definitions are complimentary, but some are not: the doctrine of 'man as sinner' has a long history. Sophocles, as a Greek pagan, was impressed with *Homo sapiens*. For him, 'wonders are many, and none is more wonderful than man'. Here man is a great achiever, capturing birds and savage beasts and the 'sea-brood of the deep', taming 'horses of shaggy mane', and the 'tireless mountain bull'. Man is also adaptable and ingenious: 'And speech, and wind-swift thought, and all the moods that mould a state, hath he taught himself; and how to free the arrows of the frost, when 'tis hard lodging under the clear sky, and the arrows of the rushing rain; yea, he hath resource for all....' The Psalmist was able to ask 'What is man?' and reply 'a little lower than the angels, crowned with glory and honour'. When Benjamin Disraeli asked whether man was 'ape or angel', he was quick to declare himself on the side of the angels (Disraeli's question is one version of the *grand dichotomy*, discussed below). However, throughout, for reasons of vanity, there is the perennial search for the uniqueness of man.

Benjamin Franklin was one of the first observers to suggest that man was the only tool-using animal, though evidence was accumulating to show that many animal species were capable of using tools. Primates were the obvious example but there were many more: birds were observed to use twigs to extract insects from tree trunks and the Californian sea otter is adept at carrying stones under water to pound molluscs loose from rocks. Then it was decided that man was uniquely a tool-*maker*, if not perhaps the only tool-*user*. Again the evidence was inconvenient: birds, chimpanzees, and other species were observed to make tools for various purposes. Another ploy to underwrite man's vanity was to suggest that man alone could communicate in symbolic ways, of which the most obvious instance was the use of language, important not only for communication but also for thought. But then chimpanzees have been taught to communicate using American sign language, by arranging coloured discs and by pushing buttons on a computerized control panel. The feminists are keen to declare that man — and for once the male of the species is meant — is the only rapist, but such feminists have not read Zuckerman, and Ford and Beach, on rape among primates; Konrad Lorenz on rape among snow geese; and other biologists recording rape among insects, sable, and mink.

Man *may* claim mental activity as uniquely human. Aristotle wrote (in *Metaphysics*) that *all man by nature desire to know*. However it is obvious that curiosity and inquisitiveness are common in many non-human species — as are such mental phenomena as memory, deliberation (leading to decision making), affection, and an aesthetic sense (note the importance of colour display in mating rituals among many species of bird, amphibian, fish, etc.). Conceivably all human mental processes can be found, at least in rudimentary form, elsewhere in the biological world. In this view, man is only unique to the extent that he has developed particular mental traits far beyond anything that can be discerned in other animal species. Man is certainly unique, as far as we know, in framing the theory of relativity, composing elaborate symphonies, and plotting to ensure the total destruction of the human race.

One approach to answering the question *'what is man?'* is to cite an appropriate model, one that for us encapsulates man's essence. We may expect every observer immersed in a discipline to cite a model from the point of view of a particular perspective. Thus if a biologist is asked the question, we may expect the answer in terms of warm-bloodedness, cerebral competence, the capacity to suckle, etc. A physicist may be interested in human beings as heat engines, just as a biochemist may think in terms of metabolic pathways, enzymes, and the like. The economist is interested in such models as 'man as consumer', 'man as investor', etc., and the cynical politician may see people as nothing more than media fodder. There are as many models of man as there are disciplines.

In proposing that man is a robot, there is no suggestion that man is not also an animal, a consumer, an ecological force, an actor on the social stage. Man is obviously many things, but we will suggest that they can all be subsumed within the robot model. The idea that man is an anatomy of a certain kind, programmed in various ways for actions of certain types, is a comprehensive doctrine, and one that is surprisingly fertile in its ramifications. It is a model that can enlarge man's self-awareness, aid growth to maturity, and provide a framework for an understanding (and meeting) of social need.

The doctrine of 'man as robot' reinforces certain historical models (we will see which) and weakens others (mostly those already undermined by the cultural impact of science and technology). 'Man as robot' is surprisingly relevant to many of the ethical and philosophical issues that have run through history. In particular, the model of robot man is relevant to a persistent dilemma that is evident in every age, though defined in many different ways. We need to glance at the dichotomy that has always been apparent in man's scrutiny of his own nature. It is almost certainly the case that all the competing man models can sit easily on one side or the other of the grand dichotomy. Robot man is no exception, and the partisan nature of the robotic model has an important implication. If the model is sound, then the dichotomy is overthrown and a host of ancient and venerable man models evaporate on the wind.

The Grand Dichotomy

Two views of man have run through history from the earliest times. On the one hand man is in some sense free, an autonomous creature, a unique link betwen natural and supernatural worlds. On the other, man is a product of cause and effect in a physical universe governed by discoverable law. The first view is traditionally relevant to conventional morality and to such religious doctrines as salvation, redemption, the Fall, and divine grace. The second view finds it easy to regard man as a complex system, a cybernetic organism, a machine. In this view, notions such as free will and moral responsibility need to be redefined if not, according to the nihilist, abandoned altogether. For it is difficult to sustain conventional attitudes to 'ought' and 'should' once it is admitted that all human actions are totally constrained by the properties of matter. What, in such circumstances, becomes of moral obligation and social order (more is said about this in Chapters 6 and 8)?

Hence at one level the dichotomy is between mechanistic man and spiritual man or, as in Hollis (1977), between *plastic man* and *autonomous man*. Put another way, is man *passive* or *active*? *Plastic man* is seen as a 'programmed feedback system' where the inputs, inner workings, and outputs can be interpreted in many different ways.

What we find here is an effective model of machine man, a valid precursor to the robotic man of the modern age. Feedback is a much studied element in conventional cybernetic theory (see Chapter 4) and programming is an obvious requirement for the computer systems that provide modern robots with purpose and intelligence. The idea of inputs being accepted and subsequently worked upon to generate outputs according to the character of the mechanism is a commonplace in computer theory. It also has some relevance to the 'black box' theory of neobehaviourism, and is essential to a systems analysis of machines, human beings, organizations, societies, and many other dynamic and complex entities.

By contrast, *autonomous man* is closely related to religious man. Some people embrace the idea of human autonomy because it seemingly saves human dignity. Here man is active, imposing his will on the external environment, demonstrating that human beings are more than mere passive components in a materialistic universe. In autonomous man we may expect to find a *self*, albeit a somewhat nebulous phenomenon, capable of moments of creative initiative far beyond what the narrow mechanist may anticipate. And *self* is akin to *soul*. Autonomous man is more likely than his 'plastic' counterpart to tolerate such doctrines as immortality, the transmigration of souls, redemption through suffering, and such like. The idea of being 'active' rather than 'passive' is more comforting to those people who want to influence events, to imagine that there is some constructive purpose behind human life.

Hollis observes that the idea of plastic man suggests that we are 'natural creatures in a rational world of cause and effect', a view from which few modern observers would dissent. We are like other objects in nature, only more complex. La Mettrie (of *L'Homme Machine*) is quoted: 'Man is not fashioned out of a more precious clay; Nature has used only one and the same dough in which she has merely varied the leaven.' So there is only one basic stuff in the world, but it can be arranged in countless different ways. In this view we are right to see the importance of such contributing notions as naturalism and determinism. We are talking about a cause-and-effect environment in which man has responded through biological evolution to arrive at his present state. We need not pursue this matter (more is said below, in 'Man as Machine', and elsewhere). The present aim is simply to contrast the two basic ways of interpreting the nature of man.

The same *grand dichotomy* is sometimes expressed by talking of *humanist* (for autonomous) man and *mechanist* (for plastic) man. For example, this usage runs through the papers of a 1979 conference, 'Models of Man', held in Cardiff under the auspices of the Welsh Branch of The British Psychological Society (see Chapman and Jones, 1980). Here it is suggested that the humanist psychologists tend to concentrate on human values and purposes whereas the mechanists aim to study our limitations and resources. We may expect the 'humanist' to be more interested than the mechanist in self, creativity, autonomy, with the mechanist more disposed to the influence of traditional materialisms and the influence of such modern disciplines as computer technology and information science.

We have seen that Disraeli asked whether man was ape or angel — yet another version of the dichotomy, and one replete with religious overtones. He asked the question in 1864, stimulated to do so by the controversy over Darwin's claims about the mutability of animal species. It is significant that psychological schools influenced by biology tend to have a mechanistic flavour. For example, behaviourism is often reckoned to have much in common with aspects of nineteenth century evolutionary theory. Thus Reid (in Chapman and Jones, 1980) observes that 'phylogenetic shaping by contingencies of survival is echoed in the shaping of individual behaviour by contingencies of reinforcement'. It is also significant that behaviourists and evolutionists have been accused of undermining morality, a charge that is quickly levelled against mechanists. If people are simply animals, responding systems, machines, etc., will they not be indifferent to spiritual or ethical demands?

The dichotomy was clearly discernible in the classical world, where the natural science of Archimedes, Aristotle, and Lucretius could co-exist with polytheistic religion and gross superstition. In the later Christian Dark Ages, strenuous efforts were made to promote an orthodox piety linked to a divinely justified monarchical succession. Attempts to promote a naturalistic model of man were branded heretical and were discouraged by torture, mutilation, and execution. We need not be surprised that, in such circumstances, the grand dichotomy was all but submerged for several centuries. However, despite the rigours of religious absolutism, a positivistic science managed to emerge — to give rise to the science and technology of the modern age.

Today the dichotomy can be seen in the religious (or religion-linked) schools of thought, on the one hand, and the naturalistic (or scientific) schools, on the other. However there are often intellectual confusions, aberrations, paradoxes. A naturalistic existentialism can promote the doctrine of autonomous man: atheism can embrace notions of free will traditionally associated with theological sanction. In addition a minority of scientists still strive to save a place for God at the naturalistic table (with the soul, for example, seen as a technical specification laid up in some solid-state heaven!). There is often a strong impulse to abolish the dichotomy by showing the compatibility of different models: both autonomous and mechanistic man have traditionally made strong claims on our commitment. But it is a mistake to imagine that a new synthesis of models can be achieved without embarrassment to some devotees.

Robotic man is a model well rooted in the mechanistic tradition, making few concessions to competing models that refuse to acknowledge its claims. At the same time it is not insensitive to the appeal of such notions as self, freedom, autonomy, creativity and individual worth. But such notions cannot be secured within the framework of an inadequate model. If man is a robot it is necessary to sustain his values and truths within the framework implied by such a model. We will find that robotic man can still laugh and joke, exult and despair.

We may also find that the perennial Grand Dichotomy will yield to a new modern synthesis, but this time one erected on firm foundations. Before embarking upon an examination of robotic man, it is worth looking at some of the competing man-models in more detail.

Man as Soul

This model has a rich history and many dimensions. It is intimately connected with the schemes of priests, popes and kings — and survives in the modern world for a variety of reasons. Some readers may quibble that man *has* a soul rather than *is* a soul, but the assumed identity of man and soul in this model is quite intentional. All advocates of the soul doctrine are quick to argue that soul is superior to flesh, that immortality in some infinite realm is immeasurably more important than a brief existence on earth. Soul, in such a view, is what counts.

The soul theory appeared in simple communities — partly as explanation, and partly as hope. It was argued that if the self could wander in dreams it must have an independent existence: sleep liberated the self from the body, just as it would be liberated one day in death. And there was always the terrifying threat of individual extinction. The body was manifestly mortal. Hopefully the soul would escape, one way or another, from the ravages of ageing and decay. However the soul could not be expected to exist *simply as soul*. It soon became necessary to set the soul in a broader context, in an evolving eschatology of purpose and destiny. A spirit world was invented and imbued with many of the pressing circumstances of human life: for instance, good and evil were not unknown in the supernatural realm — angels could be good or bad, and ethical decision making could meet its just desert. It is not always realized, in our more secular times, what the Christian mythology (for example) actually proposed.

The teaching of St Paul gradually evolved into a framework containing elements of Aristotelian science and the theology of St Augustine. A key event in this scheme was Satan's rebellion against God in the supernatural world. This cataclysmic event led to bad angels — 'demons' — being thrown out of heaven into some darker spiritual province. A consequence was that the ranks of the angels in heaven were depleted, an unfortunate circumstance in the perennial battle between Good and Evil. God's answer was to create Adam and Eve, apparently as adults, with the idea that their offspring would restore the number of angels depleted by the satanic revolt.

Satan, evidently alarmed at this strategy, managed to induce Adam and Eve to disobey the command of God that they were not to obtain knowledge. So the first human being fell from righteousness and handed on a corrupted nature to all succeeding generations. Hence all human beings were depicted as sinners, destined for damnation — unless God could think of a way around the problem. The solution was to send his 'son' in the form of a human being to serve as a sacrifice for human sin. The institution of the Church evolved to explain to sinners how they could avail themselves of the divine sacrifice in order to achieve eternal salvation.

We need not explore this tale in detail. Merely to state it is to show how uncomfortably it sits in modern technological culture. Even within its terms the myth raises many questions that are impossible to resolve. How did God and Satan coexist for the eternity before the revolt? How did the eternal angels — and their leaders — acquire their 'good' and 'bad' natures? Will the struggle continue in the supernatural realm for all times? Is it possible that an 'Almighty' god will be defeated? What would the universe be like in such circumstances? We do not expect serious answers to such questions.

We are told, in any case, that the myths are *symbolic, allegorical, signposts to greater truths*. In short, conveniently enough, we are not expected to enquire whether the myths are literally true or false.

In this framework the souls of human beings may be expected to become the new angels of heaven — providing individuals work on earth to achieve righteousness and so salvation. To the modern ear this may seem an extraordinary notion, as indeed it is, and we would not dwell on it were it not for the fact that much of the soul model lingers on in modern attitudes to man. For example, the soul model helps to sustain a belief in 'free will', without which it would have been historically impossible to sustain the notion that sinners would be tortured for all eternity. It is worth reminding ourselves what the traditional Christian view of man actually entailed.

'Man as sinner' meant that human beings were wretched creatures. As well as praising man, Pascal was able to declare him a *monstrosity*, the *excrement of the universe*. This was a common theme to run through the writings of the early Christian Fathers, and because they were male they saved particular invective for women. So Tertullian saw woman as 'the gateway of the devil.... You should always go dressed in mourning and in rags', and he remarked, perhaps gilding the lilly, that woman was 'a temple built over a sewer'. In this spirit, St John Chrysostom declared: 'What else is a woman but a foe to friendship, an inescapable punishment, a necessary evil, a natural temptation, a desirable calamity, a domestic danger, a delectable detriment, an evil of nature....'

Where human beings could be viewed in such a fashion it is hardly surprising that attitudes to their possible supernatural fate should be equally perverse. This is shown vividly in many of the historical depictions of Hell, clearly an essential element in the historical eschatology of mainstream Christianity. Owen (1970), for example, draws our attention to a wide range of images of Hell in mediaeval literature. Thus in the *Vision of Gunthelm*, the work of a Cistercian novice, we read of how certain women in Hell are occupied thrusting blazing brands through the entrails of sinners; men are stretched for torment on a great wheel; and devils beat people's heads with massive sticks. In the *Vision of Tundal*, sinners in Hell burn like bacon in a pan until they melt, then pass into a great fire, where they are then renewed for yet more torment; devils with blazing iron forks impale sinners and toss them about; people find spikes lacerating their feet and are driven to rend their own cheeks in agony.

The nineteenth century saw more of this type of material, though there has been less in the twentieth, despite its bloody course. In 1856 the Reverend C.H. Spurgeon delivered a sermon in Southwark on 'The resurrection of the dead', in which he observed that God prepares the body of a sinner so that 'it will burn for ever without being consumed ... body and soul shall be together, each brimful of pain ... suffused with agony ... limbs cracking like the martyrs in the fire ... all thy veins becoming a road for the hot feet of pain to travel on...', and so on and so forth.

We would not spend time on such bizarre material were it not an important element in the soul model that has run through theological attitudes from the earliest times. Today it is conventional for believers to propose a moderte religious creed that has little to do with hell fire and eternal torment, but a belief in Hell is still an important part of Roman Catholicism, statistically the most typical branch of Christianity. It is this same religion that elevated the most appalling masochistic practices into a virtue (see G. Rattray Taylor, 1954). This suggests that perhaps the worst element in the soul model is that it allows the grossest denigration of the flesh, and in consequence encourages a perverted antihumanism.

The soul model — and various related models — have historically been amongst the keenest opponents of mechanistic man. It is frequently said that the soul model elevates human beings whereas mechanistic theories degrade them. In any comprehensive historical perspective this is obviously untrue, but the soul model remains associated with notions of human autonomy, free will, voluntarism, etc. — ideas that are supposed to enhance human dignity. Perhaps it is the peculiar perversity of the soul model — based as it is on an old-fashioned 'substance' metaphysics — that has led to such ethical confusion in the modern world. Other models propose a more rational approach to the human essence. Perhaps one of these in the doctrine of 'man as animal'.

Man as Animal

This may seem a simple matter. Today we are well aware of our evolutionary roots, and our kinship with the rest of the animal world seems self-evident. Historically, however, there has been much confusion. From one culture to another we have never been quite sure whether to torture animals, to regard them as honorary humans, or to worship them as gods. It is inevitable in such circumstances that our own relationship to the animal world should be uncertain.

We all know of the sacred animals in ancient Egyptian religion, in Hinduism and other belief systems, and of how, in primitive folklore, a god can be deemed to reside in a particular species. The Buddhist 'reverence for life' — as in the thoughts of Albert Schweitzer — succeeded in elevating all animal species to the point where their rights should be taken seriously. In enlightenment thought we are exhorted, by such writers as Tom Paine, Voltaire, Bentham, and Mill, to be humane in our behaviour to animals. There is much here that is relevant to the struggle of the modern antivivisectionists, and one thing they have to combat is the notion that all non-human animals are less than conscious.

Descartes identified the human soul (or consciousness) with the rational faculty, and so concluded that non-human animals could not be conscious. In fact, interestingly enough for our purposes, he regarded all animals as *automata*, as unfeeling systems akin to machines. This of course is to downgrade animals. (Our strategy is a different one — to suggest that automata, e.g. human beings, can be conscious and capable of feeling. We upgrade animals without downgrading *Homo sapiens*.) It is obvious that various enlightenment thinkers were worried by the automata view of animals. Thus Voltaire asked the vivisectionist, 'You discover in it all the same organs of feeling that are in yourself. Answer me, mechanist, has nature arranged all the means of feeling in this animal so that it may not feel?'

Sometimes we may feel it eccentric to view animals in excessively anthropomorphic terms, to ascribe to them the full spectrum of rights that we may reasonably afford to human beings. This attitude is often condemned as being too sentimental: animals, we may be told, should certainly be treated humanely, but they are still nonetheless merely animals, less than human. There is another disturbing side to the observer who persists in regarding non-human animals as equivalent to human beings in their sensitivities and consciousness.

In earlier times it was fashionable to regard animals as morally culpable, even to try them in courts for their transgressions. According to the old Mosaic code an ox should be stoned to death if it had killed a man, and if a man committed bestiality, both man and beast were to be executed, as if they equally shared the guilt. In 1456 a pig in Rhine killed and ate a small child, and the pig was sentenced to be burned. Another pig died at the stake in 1463 at Amsens for the same offence. In some cases the animals were first tortured, according to one interpretation, so that their grunts and squeals could be interpreted as confessions, and according to another because torture had become a necessary part of many legal proceedings in mediaeval Christian courts. Under the *lex talionis* a man bitten by a dog was allowed to bite it back and a man whose leg had been broken by a horse was expected to break the horse's leg.

Sometimes anthropomorphic attitudes were carried to bizarre lengths: an animal might be dressed in human clothes and secured in a sitting position for the duration of the trial. A pig that had torn the face of a child in 1386 in Falaise, Normandy, was dressed in clothes, tried in the court, and then sentenced to be maimed like the child. In 1685 a wolf was tried in Ansbach for killing several people. First its snout was cut off and the animal was then dressed in clothes, wig, and beard, before being hanged.

Sometimes animals were allowed to have lawyers to defend them in court, and testimony as to 'previous good character' would be allowed to influence the severity of the sentence. In 1750, for example, Jacques Ferron was arrested in Vanvres for having sexual relations with a she-ass. Character witnesses were allowed to testify, a convent prior testifying on behalf of the animal. It was pointed out that the ass 'had always been virtuous and well-behaved and never given occasion for scandal'. In consequence it was decided that the she-ass had not been an accomplice to the crime, and so only Ferron was hanged. However it was commonplace for court decisions to go against animal defendants. For example, in 1712 an Austrian dog was sentenced to a year in jail for biting a man.

These examples highlight a rarely cited aspect of anthropomorphism. Where animals are held to be morally responsible, much in the way that people are, they can be punished cruelly for transgression — especially, as in mediaeval Europe, where harsh penal sanctions are in force for human culprits. The examples also highlight a point of relevance to our enquiry. What is the nature of responsibility in a behaving system? It may be that animals *are* automata in some unusual and unexpected way. Indeed, if man is a robot we can reach no other conclusion with regard to non-human animals. For the reasons that man is a robot, animals too (*mutatis mutandis*) are robots. Descartes was right but for reasons that he never imagined.

'Man as animal' and 'man as robot' are perfectly compatible models. There is nothing in the idea of an animal that is incompatible with the notion of an anatomy of a certain type programmed in specific ways for particular types of behaviour. It is easy to see the biological and evolutionary continuity between *Homo sapiens* and the rest of the animal world. It was Charles Darwin, building on the evolutionary notions of countless predecessors, that finally established man's kinship with other animals. The mutability of animal species was at once seen as allowing an evolutionary route from lower forms to man. Man is an animal but one with many remarkable features. He is no commonplace animal — just as we may find he is no commonplace robot.

Man as Humanist

The humanist, by definition, is man-centred, but within that broad commitment there can be a host of other beliefs and allegiances. The pagan Greeks were humanist, as were many later clerics and the scientific humanists of the modern age. The Christian humanist may have little in common with the scientific humanist, the one still able to contemplate supernatural worlds whereas the other will profess a naturalistic agnosticism. To be a humanist is to think that people matter: it is to embrace a system of values.

We have seen (in Chapman and Jones, 1980) the on-going conflict in psychology between humanist and mechanist views of man. Perhaps the conflict is apparent rather than real. In psychology the conflict often relates to topics of interest, academic approaches to be adopted, and it can be suggested that the different approaches are equally legitimate but in different ways. There is, however, a broader conflict between humanism and mechanism, and we have touched upon it already. It concerns how people are valued — how the worth of human beings is to be estimated.

Many humanists — from Erasmus to Thomas Henry Huxley — have been interested in how people may be improved in society, not necessarily as a means to some supernatural salvation but as a route to the enrichment of human life and the intellectual and emotional fulfilment of the individual. It is hardly surprising that education has been such an important thread in humanist thought, and with education in the modern world has come an increasingly secular view of man's place in society and in the universe. The education espoused is not simply a matter of book learning. Huxley himself was suspicious of narrow book-based education, believing that merely to peruse scientific works and to memorize formulae was totally inadequate. Instead people should feel the 'pull of nature', cultivating a sensitivity to the real world, its mysteries and possibilities. We find similar thoughts in writers such as Einstein and Russell, sceptical thinkers not quite able to dismiss the mystic sense of awe evoked in contemplation of the world.

We may cite humanism — in particular, scientific humanism — as an antidote to the barren mechanism that may downgrade human beings to 'robots' *in the old sense*. Humanism is, in one interpretation, an evocation of values, an exhortation to a set of ethical and personal values. Therefore, 'man as humanist' is not a model in the sense that 'man as soul' or 'man as machine' are models. Many models declare, rightly or wrongly, that *this* is what man is. 'Man as humanist' is a plea for what man might become.

The humanist, like some schools of psychology, is keen to celebrate the unity of man's body and mind: the unity is sometimes *argued for*, in opposition to the dualism of Christian orthodoxy, but more often the unity is *assumed*. The humanist is also keen to celebrate the full earthly life, suspecting there is no other. Kit Mouat (1963), a committed humanist, is keen to pay tribute to 'abundant life', in which 'an active ability to serve' is blended with 'an appreciation of contemplation and solitude'. There is no paradox in exhorting people to a humanist perspective and promoting the doctrine of robotic man. Indeed in most humanisms of the modern age there is a discernible secularized systems view of *Homo sapiens* that is nicely compatible with the 'man as robot' approach. At the same time the typical humanist, rightly anxious about any creed that demeans human beings, may doubt that robotic man can embrace aesthetic appreciation, ethical sensitivity, and proper awareness of human values. How can a robot think, feel, create, and make decisions? We shall see.

The humanist is also interested in what may be termed *spiritual nourishment*. The life of the spirit, suitably conceived, is not alien to the concerns of the modern humanist, but *spirit* is necessarily subsumed under a panoply of mental abilities and experiences that does not imply an immortal life in a 'spiritual' realm. This approach, perhaps, accords well enough with the notion of robotic man. Man is manifestly concerned with what may be dubbed *spiritual* sustenance. The idea of 'man as robot' does not deny this obvious truth but insists that it be interpreted in the context of mortality — in the context of inevitable extinction. The humanist is keen to celebrate earthly life. If man is a robot, there is no problem here. Robots are nothing if not mortal. Robotic man can celebrate the potential of human life without any prejudice that it will last for ever.

Man as Scientist

Man's social evolution, as opposed to his biological evolution, is in some sense the history of 'man as scientist'. Here scientist is a broad concept, associated with a variety of traits such as curiosity, restlessness, and the desire to predict and control. Now such traits are highly relevant to many of the man models that might be proposed. So 'man as scientist' — regarded as a thinking being taking in data in order to comprehend and to control — may be seen as a general model equally relevant to any field where information is relevant and problems need to be solved. Hence 'man as problem solver' is closely related to 'man as scientist': both models are concerned with data acquisition and manipulation in order to resolve practical or theoretical difficulties in the environment.

There is also a paradoxical linkage between the man-scientist model and other models that are seemingly not compatible with it. Even 'man as soul' rears its head here. Some people suggest that the natural theologists were the first true scientists, piously striving to comprehend God's creation: there are certainly many scientific names associated with important stages in scientific progress. Even 'man as astrologer' and 'man as alchemist' have kinship with 'man as scientist': astronomy and chemistry cannot gainsay their superstitious roots.

It can also be suggested that 'man as problem-solver', linked to the man as scientist model, is a concept of great power. It has moreover gained considerable modern support by work in artificial intelligence (AI) where computer programs are devised to solve problems in many different fields (in games, linguistic analysis, perceptual comprehension, decision making, theorem proving, etc.). Howarth (in Chapman and Jones, 1980), for example, argues that the problem-solver model bears on the pragmatism of such thinkers as William James, John Dewey, and George Herbert Mead: 'Ideas must be evaluated in terms of their effectiveness, and are only truly known when they have been evaluated.' With evaluation seen as essentially a social process, problem solving can thus be seen to have relevance to the organization of social structures.

'Man as scientist' is thus a multidimensional model. It is concerned with personality traits such as curiosity and investigation; with intellectual elements such as concept formation and problem solving; and with the evaluation of practical activity in the real world. Is such a multifaceted model compatible with the doctrine of robotic man? How, we may ask, can a robot be inquisitive or formulate concepts? Can a robot effectively solve problems? Such questions can be tackled in various ways. If, for example, it can be shown on other grounds that man is a robot, and since man is manifestly a formulator of concepts, then a robot can form concepts. There is much in this that is relevant to modern progress in artificial intelligence.

The man-as-scientist model is particularly useful since it links a range of personality and intellectual elements that can be found in human beings, but it says little about how man is to be valued or about how man functions as a physical system. It is largely the modern approach to physical systems that has enlarged our doctrine of robotic man. The scientist and the problem-solver are active in the physical world, but it seems likely that their activities could be nicely simulated in AI-linked software — and there is nothing here of bodies, anatomies, physical structures. It is conventional for some AI specialists to disparage hardware — Margaret Boden (1977), for example, has a 'tin-can' theory of electronic computers — but man is more than merely a set of programs (man is *partly* a set of programs). Any adequate model of man must say something about anatomy, and this is why the robotic model has such potential.

We have seen that even the animal model of man is confused since the status of animals has always been uncertain. So we need to link the manifest anatomical focus of 'man as animal' to the intellectual elements to be found in 'man as scientist'. Any adequate model of man must be able to talk about bodies and minds, without any implication of a metaphysical dualism. Two more models that are essential to this new approach should be mentioned before 'man as robot' is considered in more detail. 'Man as machine' and 'man as system' are both central to the doctrine of robotic man.

Man as Machine

The machine model of man has been attractive to intellectually robust observers from the earliest times. For one thing, it suggested that man was inherently comprehensible, though the knowledge for a full understanding may be temporarily lacking. For another, it dispelled a collection of obscure and inconvenient notions — such as spirit and soul — that appeared to be nothing more than useless gap-fillers, creating an illusion of understanding but explaining nothing. With every scientific advance — in such areas as thermodynamics, biochemistry, neurophysiology, and computer science — the machine model of man became more attractive. The more that was understood about the workings of man's body the more reasonable it seemed to search for mechanistic explanations of the working of the human mind. And the behaviour of neural circuits in the central nervous system seemed nicely analogous to the behaviour of silicon-based circuits in the modern electronic digital computer.

There are many examples in literature and elsewhere of the doctrine that man can profitably be regarded as a machine. In 1872 Samuel Butler was able to wonder, in *Erewhon*:

Whether every sensation is not chemical and mechanical in its operation? Whether those things which we deem most purely spiritual are anything but disturbances of equilibrium in an infinite series of levers, beginning with those that are too small for microscopic detection, and going up to the human arm and the appliances which it makes use of? Whether there be not a molecular action of thought, whence a dynamical theory of the passions shall be deducible? Whether, strictly speaking, we should not ask what kind of levers a man is made of rather than what is his temperament? How are they balanced? How much of such and such will it take to weigh them down so as to make him do so and so?

In the same spirit, Somerset Maugham (in *The Summing Up*, 1938) remarked of the great many medical books that 'told me that man was a machine subject to mechanical laws; and when the machine ran down that was the end of him'. When he saw men die at the hospital 'my startled sensibilities confirmed what my books had taught me'. The machine model of man may not always be the most heartening but for the honest person it is very persuasive.

Perhaps the most celebrated historical description of the machine model is *L'Homme Machine*, written by Julien Offray de La Mettrie and published in 1747. As we may expect, this work has great scientific limitations — it is of course constrained by the physics and physiology of the time — but it has nonetheless great philosophic importance. It is one of the first attempts to portray man as a wholly mechanistic system.

La Mettrie was born at Saint-Malo, Brittany, in 1709, the son of a wealthy textile merchant. For a while, having been educated in Paris, he turned towards the Church, but his intellectual development soon turned him against theology and in the direction of the man-as-machine model. It has been suggested, however, that he never fully emancipated himself from his early contact with religious thought. For example, in the 'physiologic predestination' of the human machine, it is easy to detect an echo of the inner compulsion that characterized Jansenist belief. His celebration of the sensual has been portrayed by some observers as a reaction against the severe austerity of clerical attitudes.

In 1725 La Mettrie began the study of philosophy and natural science at the famous Collège d'Harcourt, the establishment which was to educate Diderot into some similar views. After further study at the Faculty of Medicine in Leyden, La Mettrie began professional practice in the region of Saint-Malo. When in due course *L'Homme Machine* was published, the publisher not sharing the materialist thesis, the book stimulated a wave of criticism and abuse. The young publisher, Elie Luzac, was summoned before the Consistory of the Eglise Wallonne de Leyde where he was ordered to deliver all available copies of the book for destruction, to reveal the identity of the author, and to promise not to commit such an offence again. In fact Luzac surrendered some copies of the book but distributed others, at the same time professing ignorance of the author's name. La Mettrie himself sought refuge in Berlin, taking up a fortunate invitation from Frederick the Great. The atheist writer died in 1751, having consumed a vast quantity of 'pâté de faisan aux truffes'. Rumours that La Mettrie had turned to the Church in his last moments may be assumed to be false. Such tales have often been told of unbelievers to discredit their unpopular philosophies.

La Mettrie was encouraged to write *L'Homme Machine* because of the manifest failure of alternative metaphysical explanations of the nature of the human mind. He was clearly unimpressed with the dualism of Descartes, the Leibnizian monadology, and Locke's idea that somehow God had added thought to matter. No such ploys were seen as genuine explications of the nature of mental phenomena. Like the many sceptics that were to follow, La Mettrie was unimpressed by theological explanations. His central task was to present the problem of mind as essentially a problem of physics: here man is seen as a purely mechanical entity in which all mental events are produced by bodily changes. This was a rigorous psychological approach that rested boldly on the idea that man was a machine. Like all great intellectual innovators, La Mettrie was heavily influenced by the intellectual tenor of the times, keen to draw on contemporary knowledge in the areas of physics, chemistry, and medicine.

He notes, for example, the psychological effects of organic disease, fatigue, and stimulants; and records how mental states can be conditioned by hunger, pregnancy, sexual desire, ageing, and the climate. He was able to draw on the rather meagre stores of information in such fields as neuropathology and brain anatomy to demonstrate that differences in behaviour — both between species and between same-species individuals — could be occasioned by differences in brain structure. He maintained that the man-machine model could serve as a comprehensive theory of mental phenomena, including purposeful activity. The necessary link between purposive intent and subsequent motion was taken to be one of the central difficulties that had to be overcome by eighteenth century materialism. La Mettrie solved the problem, not entirely satisfactorily, by identifying muscular irritability as a source of purposive motion. The discovery of nervous activity within the organism was taken as adequate refutation of the various soul theories: the obscure and ill-defined soul was no longer needed as a means of animating the physical frame. In a sense, of course, Descartes had already suspected this by suggesting that animals were merely automata. La Mettrie extended the automata theory to embrace human beings — and in an important fashion that prefigured the neurophysiological theories of mind that were to emerge in the twentieth century.

La Mettrie knew little of the biochemistry that today is so obviously a part of any understanding of animal species. He relied, like Samuel Butler after him, on the science of mechanics to give an explanation of the machine character of the human body. We will see that mechanics is still highly relevant to an understanding of robotic man — as are biochemistry, cybernetics, and systems theory. La Mettrie was important in showing systematically that traditional metaphysics was no longer required in an elucidation of the human species. Like animals, human beings could be described adequately in terms of automata. Once audacious thinkers had ventured on this path, the route to robotic man was clear, but to describe human performance and mental states in terms of Samuel Butler's '*levers*' or the *muscular irritability* of La Mettrie was clearly insufficient. It was necessary to broaden the machine view of man by drawing on scientific disciplines in addition to those of mechanics and chemistry. The new disciplines — those of systems theory and information science — were born in the nineteenth century and then rapidly expanded in the twentieth. They are essential to any comprehensive view of robotic man.

Man as System

The notion of a system does not depend upon a physical framework. In this sense, *system* is akin to *software*: it sets out a functional sequence without the assumption that the sequence (or procedure) is implemented by this or that material structure. Of course many systems are physical: animals, human beings, machines, societies, organizations — all are difficult to imagine without a physical substratum. However the notion of system can be set out with no preconceptions about how it is instantiated in the world.

In the most general terms, a system takes in inputs, operates on them, and generates outputs. The sequence from input acceptance to output generation defines the type of system — though we do not always know how it works in detail. Typically a system takes in *information* or *data* and manipulates it according to operators that characterize the system, whereupon an output is produced. This generalized description implies that a system has an interface with the external world — to allow the *input* of external data and to *affect* the external world by in turn providing an input (the system's output) to it. A system therefore usually operates in an environmental context and in ways that are discoverable and amenable to abstract description (the ways of working may be regarded as 'systematic').

A systems description of man need say nothing about biochemistry, though it is likely to say much about information. The idea of man as a *biochemical* system is contingent: we could conceivably replace part of his biochemistry by electronic devices that would allow his essential information-processing tasks to continue. In this view, however, the idea of man as an *information-processing* system is necessary rather than contingent. It is not even conceivable how a man could cease to process information and remain a human being: the spectrum of cognitive and conative functions that define the mental apparatus of a person are irrevocably associated with the procedures of information processing. However, a human being also exists in a physical dimension, though we need not assume a particular type of chemical substratum; there is a sense in which an *electronic* system capable of thought, joy, anguish, expectation, learning, panic, etc., would partake of the human essence. Even when human nature is instantiated we do not need to assume a particular chemistry (or, for that matter, a particular electronics).

What this means is that a systems view of man is essential to any adequate understanding of *Homo sapiens*. In fact we see a hierarchy of systems and subsystems arranged to allow functions to be carried out at different levels in the total individual. Some of the systems are best understood in terms of their biological and chemical features; some are purely mechanical in their operation; yet others are best approached through a comprehension of information processing.

The doctrine of robotic man depends heavily on an outline of 'man as system' but requires also an assumption about anatomy. Systems man may even be construed as compatible with 'man as soul': one may imagine, fancifully no doubt, ethereal substances processing information in ways that preserve various human concerns — perhaps this is how the angels manage it! Such a doctrine, albeit true to abstract systems theory, is akin to a mathematical dimension that has no real existence. We can scarcely doubt man's existence in the physical world, though we may debate about the models that best depict and convey that existence. We need a machine model working in conjunction with a systems model to capture the essence of *Homo sapiens*. The result is robotic man.

Man as Robot

We have suggested that man is an anatomy of a certain type programmed in specific ways for behaviour of a particular sort. Until an effort is made to define *certain type*, *specific ways*, and *a particular sort*, the definition is too general to be wholly accurate. In its generalized form it would apply equally to various sorts of machines, animals, and non-human robots, but despite its blanket coverage of many different types of working systems it is still an evocative description of man.

First we may glance at anatomy (considered in detail in Chapter 3). We often neglect the simple truth that man is a physical system, entirely dependent upon physical laws in mechanics, dynamics, chemistry, physics, etc. (Samuel Butler knew we relied upon levers;

we also depend upon the strength of materials, upon ball joints, pneumatics, lubrication, and a host of other 'engineering' principles.) When we look at anatomy we see an adapted and adaptable structure, remarkably intricate and complex, but one solely dependent for its worldly success upon the effectiveness of its programming.

We will find (in Chapter 5) that man is programmed in many different ways for many different purposes. This much would be acknowledged by even the most hostile opponent of robotic man. But we say more: that *human beings can pursue no task, attempt no endeavour, strive for no creative insight, feel no emotion, make no decision – without using relevant programming.* All insight, all understanding, all love, all human achievement and experience — all these depend upon programming. In the beginning was the program, and nothing has been achieved without it ever since.

The uniquely human tasks performed by members of *Homo sapiens* are possible by virtue of species-linked programs. This is so whether we are talking about the suckling of the human infant or the profoundest speculations in mathematics or philosophy. It is in this sense that man is a robot: he is a programmed anatomy functioning solely according to his programs. If the observer finds such a view depressing then the scope of programming has not been appreciated. If man is a robot, he is still lover, poet, scientist, inventor, teller of jokes, spinner of tales. If this is so, why does it help to call man a robot? For one thing it may be true — in the terms we have indicated. For another, there are many ethical and personal implications in such a view (see Chapters 7 to 9). If we once acknowledge that man is a robot, then it is inevitable that our image of man will change; it is inevitable that we will see human beings in a new light and that we will evaluate human conduct in a new way.

Robotic man is still a flexible and capable performer. He is still the familiar biological system that we know and love and resent and cherish. But our perspective on his nature and his potential will have altered. We will see new possibilities, a new dimension for 'man as robot'. People will still regret the new image, sensing lingering connotations from decades past. However if robotic man is still perceived as a demeaning image, as an antihumanist approach, then it has not been fully understood. The simple truth remains: if man is a robot then it cannot be helpful, it cannot serve humanist purposes, to deny the fact.

Choice of Models

This is a pregnant subtitle, not least because robotic man has much to say about the phenomenon of choice (see Chapter 6). In fact people are *caused* to choose their models, just as they are *in some sense* caused to perform any other act in their daily lives.

The cultural times influence choices of models. Few people who lived in mediaeval times were able to choose the man-as-system model: not much work had been done on system theory. Today we have broader choices with the climate — or our own subcultures — impelling us in one direction or another. It may be more difficult today to embrace the idea that people are on earth so that the depleted ranks of heavenly angels may be restored. Historical periods inevitably impose constraints. Today we are conscious of computers and a proliferation of computer-based systems (including robots); this awareness shapes our choice of models and our reaction to competing views of man. The doctrine of robotic man is an offspring of the computer age, though we have noticed machine-man models in earlier times. Apart from the cultural climate, individual personality also imposes constraints. Are we tough- or tender-minded? Advocates of robotic man are probably toughish in their opinions, relatively uncompromising in their philosophy.

The man-as-robot model may be a purely contingent phenomenon, a product of personalities of a certain type responding to aspects of the modern world. If this is true then all models are equally contingent, equally shaped by the accident of history and personal temperament. There is a pregnant point in this also. Perhaps we are not free, in any useful sense, to choose our models (Chapter 6): they will compete in the philosophic marketplace, with some succeeding through reason and others for other reasons. However among the various models only robotic man can smilingly observe that this must be so. The world, like man, is subject to the omniscience of programs. To mix our models — God said, 'Let there be a program, and there was....'.

3 The Physical Frame

Preamble

It is a commonplace fact that human beings, like non-human robots, have anatomies. This is of course of some importance to us all, but of particular interest to certain actors on the social stage — such as lovers, dressmakers, physicians, and robot engineers. Nor is it surprising that non-human robots have anatomies. In a way it is inevitable since robots are machines made in the image of man. But there is a paradox in the common attitude to the human anatomy, a paradox occasioned by human vanity. For example, we are aware of our kinship with the rest of the animal world and we are well aware that animals have anatomies, but we still like to imagine that human anatomies are in some way fundamentally different to those in the bestial world — not simply because of a unique physical appearance, but because it is hoped that the human anatomy harbours refined sensitivities, a rational intellect, spiritual awareness.

This will not do. Our anatomical and mental links to the animal world cannot be broken or ignored. *Homo sapiens* is an animal species. To confirm the fact we need only look at comparative anatomy, comparative embryology, and genetic phenomena (how significant that we share more than 90 per cent of our coded DNA with a gorilla!). There is worse to come. We do not only have kinship with animals, we also have kinship with machines. We have already looked at the power of the man-machine model, but there is more to be said. We are, for instance, surprisingly dependent upon a complex of technological principles that appear to be of more interest to engineers than to biologists. We are well aware of how chemistry is at the heart of most biological functions in the human being: we are accustomed to the biochemist making a substantial contribution to our knowledge of why we work as we do, but our existence as a mechanically engineered system receives less exposure. La Mettrie tried to describe the human system solely in terms of mechanics, and chemistry scarcely figured; today chemistry is usually at the heart of biological explanation. We need to look again at mechanics if only to underline our kinship with machines. Many technological disciplines are relevant to the operation

54

of robotic man, and a full understanding requires attention to them all. Non-human robots are often essentially mechanical systems. To draw attention to aspects of mechanics, as part of the human robot, is to highlight our kinship with the rest of the evolving robot world. It is important to appreciate that human beings are variously cybernetic systems (Chapter 4), chemical systems, electrical systems, mechanical systems. A complex of systems, operating in concert, defines every individual person.

Biological Engineering

General

The biological world exploits a host of engineering principles. Countless plant and animal species have kinship with machines. For instance, one writer (Paturi, 1976) has dubbed plants 'masters of hydraulics', pointing out that a full-grown birch tree can carry forty gallons of water up almost sixty feet on any warm summer's day. Here the trick is a simple one, the tree required to do no work itself: evaporation from the leaves causes a compensatory suction of water. In such a fashion plants and trees use the energy of the sun for water haulage, and they have evolved an effective architectural structure in order that this can be achieved. Plants also use electrostatic effects, principles of thermodynamics, and pneumatic procedures to accomplish various tasks necessary for life.

Many animal species exploit obvious engineering principles to move, capture food, and adapt in a changing environment. Insects adopt different bodily postures to absorb solar radiation. The basking postures of butterflies, for example, are species linked: the wings may be extended (like those of an aeroplane) for dorsal basking or they may be held together over the body for lateral basking. Colour is also important for thermal regulation in butterflies, since surface colour determines which wavelengths of radiation are absorbed. Robert J. Moffat at Stanford University has used an engineering approach to develop mathematical models relating the physical characteristics that govern temperature regulation, such as wing colour, to the various weather conditions in which a particular species of insect can fly. The relations can be shown graphically using the concept of a 'flight space'. On a plane having coordinates for air temperature and wind speed, the flight space for a particular species is the area including all the conditions under which the species can warm up enough for flight to occur. The flight spaces for different species can be compared to observe how wing colour helps to determine the range of weather conditions in which the butterfly, for example, can become airborne. The mathematical model made successful predictions about limitations on low-elevation species. This helps to show that animal performance can be studied using engineering principles that at first do not appear to have biological relevance.

One scientist, Joel Kingsolver, has observed that the mechanisms underlying butterfly feeding and thermoregulation rely on 'physical principles that can be observed *in the operation of many machines*' (my italics). However flight modes in insects are usually quite different to those used by aircraft (though the early aircraft builders often tried to imitate bird behaviour as a means to flight). Some butterflies and dragonflies use a 'flap and glide' technique in which one type of behaviour can follow another repeatedly and to good effect. Gliding, of course, is well understood because it is involved in the behaviour of the classical airfoil. The wings of an insect can generate lift much as do the wings of an aircraft, but the flapping motion of the butterfly wing is less understood. It has even been suggested that some animals — humming birds and bumble bees, for example — should not be able to fly: discussed in engineering terms such creatures should not be able to achieve lift and forward motion (we may conclude in such circumstances that the engineering information is incomplete and that an adequate theory would account for the various aspects of flight performance). In fact the wing of an insect, bird, or bat is both an effective aerofoil and a propulsion unit. There is a nice analogy here with the helicopter, which uses its main rotor both as a wing to provide lift and as a propulsion unit.

These few examples — from the fields of hydraulics, thermodynamics, and flight propulsion — show how recognized engineering principles are central to an understanding of many aspects of biological behaviour. This is a circumstance that is highly relevant to the notion that man is a robot. We are, in some important sense, *engineered systems*. However before any student of natural theology rushes to see in this a version of the classical teleological argument for God's existence, I hasten to add that we are engineered by biological evolution, not by some mysterious deity with mischievous purposes of its own. We can be seen to be engineered systems by virtue of the physical phenomena that we exploit. Our structures and our mechanisms are similar in many respects to those employed in, say, mechanical or civil engineering. We are physical systems working *as if* an immensely talented — but not infallible — engineer had designed us. This is shown in many ways, not least in the character of the materials out of which we are constructed. Any materials specialist will be able to discuss, in terms of stress and strain, durability and elasticity, etc., the various substances and structures out of which the human being is built.

The Strength of Materials

The two most commonly used measures of strength are tensile strength and compressive strength: tensile strength determines how much a material can resist stretching while compressive strength determines how much a substance can resist compression. These types of tests are highly relevant to the performance of biological systems, just as they are essential in building bridges, tanks, skyscrapers, and (non-human) robots. There is a complex mathematics to describe such aspects as theory of fracture and stress concentration, and again this is important to the durability and behaviour of animals and plants. It is informative, for example, to glance at the use of composite materials, highly effective in the design of boat hulls, aircraft wings, etc.

Many biological structures exploit the juxtaposition of disparate materials and other aspects of composite theory in order to achieve strength and durability. For example, mollusc shells comprise crystals of calcium carbonate embedded in a matrix of protein. A typical shell material is nacre (mother of pearl), used as an inner layer in some shells and the whole thickness of others (e.g. the pearly *Nautilus* and the pearl oyster, *Pinctada*). The crystals of nacre are staggered, which means that a crack travelling through the matrix has to take a long path, and the longer the crack the more work needed to produce it. In short, the crystals are oriented in such a way that only a relatively strong force can drive a crack through the thickness of the shell.

Bone is another type of composite material. About two thirds of the mass of bone (about half its volume) is inorganic bone salt which contains calcium, phosphate, hydroxyl ions, and various other ions in different proportions. Much of the rest of bone is organic collagen. The bone salt crystals are sited between the collagen fibrils, attached to them in a parallel array, though the actual disposition of the fibrils varies from one type of bone to another. In mammalian bone, for instance, the fibres are often laid down neatly in lamellae, but can also be tangled (in woven-fibred bone). The fibres in adjacent lamellae are almost at right angles to each other, so providing added strength by exploiting an important principle of composite materials.

Researchers have shaped a wide variety of bones, using machine tools, to carry out tests for strength, much as man-made engineering materials would be examined. Bone must be machined with care since overheating (and moisture) can affect its tensile and compressive properties. The channels for blood vessels may weaken bone seriously by acting as stress concentrators, but cavities may also strengthen the material by preventing cracks from spreading. The blood vessel canals may help in this way but are often further apart than the bone cell cavities, and so less effective in preventing the spread of cracks.

Bones are usually protected by skin, fat, and other materials that serve to diminish the effect of sudden impact. In work on the metatarsal bones of rabbits it was found that the mean energy needed to break bones padded with furry skin was 37 per cent more than the mean energy necessary to break the bare ones. Other structures — e.g. spider frame silk — can be enormously resilient, though seemingly delicate. The thinness of the struts of a spider's web means that very little protein has been used for construction purposes. Here the protein structure is an obvious example of where architectural specialization has occurred through biological evolution to achieve a particular objective.

It is obvious that stresses, strains, compressions, etc., can be studied in the artefacts of biological systems as well as in the systems themselves. A wide range of engineering principles can be used to examine the properties of spiders's webs, beavers' dams, termites' nests, etc., as well as to investigate the articulations in a spider's leg, ball-joints in the mammalian skeleton (see below), and the sensory equipment of communal insects. Again we can look at the skeleton of a human being to appreciate how many of the mechanisms for stability and durability would also be used in a mobile artificial robot.

It is possible, for instance, to see how balancing loads and braces can be used in a biological system to reduce the stresses in a structure. For example, we can explore the disposition of forces acting upon the human skeleton, and show how classical principles of mechanics can illuminate aspects of structure in biological systems. Thus, a man taking a step relies on muscles to keep the femur in place; at the same time the stresses in the femur are reduced by tension in the iliotibial tract, a sturdy array of collagen fibres. This fascia of fibres can be seen to reduce the stresses in the femur in much the same way that a crosspiece in an architectural structure can reduce the stresses in a supporting member. Similarly, muscle action (in this case, contraction in the brachioradialis muscle) can support the bones of the forearm much in the way that a guy rope supports a flagpole.

Engineering and mathematical principles developed for non-biological purposes can be seen to have surprising relevance to many biological phenomena. Finite element analysis, for instance, where a complex shape can be viewed as an assemblage of smaller geometrical shapes, can be used to investigate bone performance (the shafts of bones can often be seen to resemble simple geometrical shapes such as cylindrical rods and tubes). In this way, an equation can be produced to show that tall sea anemones are liable to a particular kind of buckling: the theory of elastic stability can be applied to biological structures — including robotic man — just as it can be applied to a host of problems in non-biological areas of engineering. Where materials *are* found to be strong and durable — in animals and machines — other problems, amenable to engineering investigation, are likely to arise. If a substance — bone or metal — is hard, it will probably have an abrasive effect on neighbouring materials. Human engineers have an answer for this — lubrication. Not surprisingly, nature has resorted to the same device to protect hard materials (e.g. bone) that need to come into contact.

We all know that human hip joints run into problems from time to time. Put in anatomical terms, the difficulties may arise when the articular surface of the femur slides over the surface of the acetabulum — when, for instance, a person takes a step. It is particularly interesting that in fact the force on the head of the femur is greater than the weight of the body: the body mass is not immediately above the joint, so the muscles lateral to the joint are obliged to contract to balance the moments. Here it is necessary to do work against the frictional force at the joint, which would represent a considerable amount of work if the coefficient of friction lay in the usual range for solid surfaces moving against each other in the absence of lubrication, the heat generated may damage the surrounding tissue, including the muscles doing the work. It is well known that proteins can be damaged by heat. These difficulties can be overcome by the provision of natural lubrication in mammalian joints.

The end of each bone is covered by a type of cartilage; a membrane encloses each joint and the associated cavity is filled with synovial fluid. This fluid can be squeezed out of the sponge-like cartilage, allowing a form of lubrication unknown in man-made engineering. This type of lubrication, usually dubbed 'weeping', can be demonstrated using sponge rubber that contains bubbles of air. Where soapy water is used as a lubricant, nearly all the load is carried by the water when the sponge is pressed against a piece of glass. It is difficult for trapped water to seep out sideways, and the coefficient of friction rises gradually if the sponge is kept pressed against the glass. The coefficient of friction is much higher if a plain piece of rubber is used. It has been suggested by various researchers that an articular cartilage soaked with synovial fluid behaves like sponge rubber soaked in soapy water. The coefficient of friction between a pig's humerus and glass has been explored to verify this type of theory, and one conclusion is that weeping lubrication may be a common natural device to minimize the wear of bones that come into contact in mammalian joints. It is suggested, for example that the large molecules that comprise synovial fluid tend to remain trapped: when they are compressed, they tend to form a gel which acts as an effective lubricant. Lubrication is important in the world of man-made artefacts — as any motorist faced with the cost of an oil change is aware. We are usually less conscious of the fact that effective lubrication is also vital in the durable working of vertebrate animals.

Heat Regulation ￼

We have already mentioned heat regulation in connection with insect performance. It is worth saying something about the same mechanism as it operates in the case of human beings and many other mammals. Thermoregulation is a useful example of control in the physical world, not least because it exemplifies a number of cybernetic principles: e.g. a 'loop' system relying upon various types of feedback to achieve an optimum 'steady state' (i.e. homeostasis) is a familiar cybernetic mechanism evident in many biological and artificial systems (the household thermostat embodies many of the principles that can be found in the more sophisticated thermoregulation systems of the biological world).

A human being needs to achieve a balance between the heat generated and the heat lost. In fact the body has little control over the amount of heat generated since this depends upon the type of activity being undertaken; so regulation has to be achieved by controlling the heat lost. To achieve the required balance the peripheral areas are allowed to cool or to warm as necessary by adjustment of the thermal insulation of the tissues, the blood flow, and the constriction or dilation of the surface blood vessels. One result is an adjustable temperature gradient from the centre of the body towards the limbs and within the body tissue and the limbs themselves.

A principle device to achieve effective heat loss is the mechanism of sweating, though — like all biological devices — it can easily be overstressed. Once the body surface is wet, the amount of heat that can be evaporated is limited by the latent heat of evaporation of water. It has been calculated that a fit young man can evaporate as much as 4.5 litres in four hours, but this is a rate that cannot be maintained indefinitely. If the body temperature is caused — for whatever reason — to rise too much, the metabolic rate will progressively increase to the point of thermostasis failure and heat stroke. When the temperature reaches 42°C (108°F) in the brain, the nervous centres can no longer function and death occurs. We are not surprised to learn that if heat loss is greater than heat production in the body, sweating will cease and the surface blood vessels become constricted to maintain the existing temperature. Shivering is one compensatory mechanism, but this ceases at around 27°C (80°F); as the blood becomes progressively more viscous the heart has increasing difficulty pumping it around the body. The person becomes sleepy and is likely to die at around a temperature of 25°C.

The mechanisms of heat control in human beings and non-human animals are well understood: they exploit many of the principles known to, for example, heat and ventilation engineers. Again it seems manifestly obvious that the human body, like the body of non-human mammals and other species, is an engineered system which aims to function and adapt in the constant search for survival.

Butler's Levers

The suggestion of Samuel Butler (in *Erewhon*) that man may be a system of levers, some too small for inspection by the naked eye, is of obvious interest to robotic man. We do not need to believe in a *hierarchy* of lever systems to maintain nonetheless that levers are extremely important in human anatomy. In fact the body can be portrayed as an effective system of levers, all working in different ways to achieve different purposes.

Three types ('classes') of lever systems can be found in the human body, according to how the three elements of the lever — force, fulcrum, and load — are distributed. For example when a person pulls a chain down, the force may be in the upper arm with the load acting via the hand, the elbow being the fulcrum; when a foot braces on the floor to lift a body, the point of contact is the fulcrum, the load acts through the bone, and the force through the associated muscle. The direction of pull of a muscle and the rotation of a bone can effect the mechanical advantage achieved through a particular disposition of elements.

The mechanical advantage of a biological lever system is not the only factor that can effect the magnitude of the force being exerted: e.g. the position of the joint can also influence the tension in the muscles. In some limb positions more of the composite fibres are contracting than in others; in fact as a muscle becomes shorter its contractile power increases. So we may expect less force to be applied at the end of a contraction when a muscle becomes short than at the start when a muscle is longer. Such considerations are important when estimating, for work or leisure purposes, what types of activity may be reasonably expected of healthy (or unhealthy) human beings. Again there is the simple point to stress: that human performance can be investigated using the principles of mechanics (statics and dynamics) that are commonly employed in the study of machines. A scrutiny of Butler's levers is one approach to the doctrine of robotic man. There are many others.

Summary

This section has concentrated on the idea of man being an *engineered system*. We have glanced at some of the technological considerations that are relevant to an exploration of behaviour in the biological world. We need not be surprised that the principles of thermodynamics, stress and strain, compressive loading, strength through composite materials, hydraulics, pneumatics, etc., provide clues for an understanding of living systems. It is important for our purposes to emphasize the broader point that man, as a robotic system, is not separate from the machine world. By virtue of the fact that he has to function, as do machines, by exploiting the properties of physical materials, he has obvious kinship with all types of artefacts.

Any full evolutionary theory should be able to account for the emergence of the various devices that enable physical biological systems to operate with success in a changing environment: e.g. it should be possible to describe how composite materials came to be used in bone, how fluidic principles came to be exploited in human organs (e.g. the penis, also involving intriguing telescopic features), how cybernetic feedback came to feature in many biological control systems (e.g. thermoregulation and the maintenance of blood sugar level). It is likely that evolutionary theory can account for the emergence of some of these mechanisms but not of others. One thing, however, seems clear: it is unlikely that our understanding will increase unless we assume as a working hypothesis that man is an engineered system, a mechanical structure subject to the same physical laws that govern any working artefact, any robot. Robotic man is more complex than any artificial robot, but in his total reliance upon natural physical law he is set squarely and unambiguously in the robot world. This is manifestly true of anatomy, which we tend to view at the 'macro' level. We will find that it is also true at the 'micro' level, at the level of the cells in the central nervous system (see Chapters 4 and 5).

It seems clear that man is an engineered anatomy, irrespective of the physical level at which we describe his attributes and performance. We have glanced at some elements of this anatomy; we need to look in more detail at particular anatomical features, with particular reference to their connection with the emerging anatomical features that are becoming well known in the burgeoning world of artificial robots.

Some Anatomical Aspects

Skeletons and Structures

We have touched on bones, but so far said little about skeletons. With the skeleton we are approaching some of the structural considerations that are relevant to the building of artificial robots for industrial and other purposes. The strength of bones is one thing; how they are linked is another. The linking of bones is analogous to how rigid components are connected in machines to provide structural stability and to allow the performance of necessary tasks.

Any reasonable biology book tells us that the average human being has 206 bones, though 5 per cent of people enjoy a thirteenth pair of ribs, mongols often have only eleven pairs, and a baby is born with 350 bones, some of which fuse as the baby develops. Bone provides a mineral reservoir to allow proper metabolic functioning, as well as providing a strong framework for the support of muscles, organs, and other bodily items. The bones are unevenly distributed throughout the human body. Each arm has thirty-two bones, each leg thirty-one; surprisingly there are twenty-nine bones in the skull, more than the spine which has twenty-six — seven cervical vertebrae, twelve thoracic vertebrae, and five lumbar vertebrae, as well as the sacrum and coccyx (or tail). It is interesting that the spine is nicely engineered for strength.

The spinal column is effectively constructed out of a number of components — vertebrae and other elements — securely linked and only allowing a small amount of movement between any two adjacent pieces, though the whole can move to a considerable extent. The individual vertebrae are articulated closely together, making it unlikely that sprains will be severe: a degree of violence sufficient to tear the ligaments would be more likely to cause fracture or dislocation. The spine is also a curved elastic column which will bend before it breaks. Of particular interest for our purposes are the intervertebral disks which act as buffers to protect the spinal column from sudden jars and shocks. It is also worth recording in passing that the spinal marrow, an important substance for metabolic purposes, is unlikely to be affected by most forms of fracture. Talking of the marrow, Mr Jacobson observed, in Holmes's *System of Surgery*, 1883, that

...being lodged in the centre of the column, it occupies neutral ground in respect of forces which might cause fracture. For *it is a law of mechanics* that when a beam, as of timber, is exposed to breakage and the force does not exceed the limits of the strength of the material, one division resists compression, another laceration of the particles, whilst the third, between the two, is in a negative condition (my italics).

The provision of disks between the vertebrae has a nice analogy in at least one modern design for artificial robots. In 1983 a novel design for a painting robot was introduced by Spine Robotics of Molndal in Sweden. Most traditional arms for artificial robots are akin to the human arm, i.e. they comprise a number of rigid members articulated at joints. However, the new design from Spine Robotics featured an actuation and control system similar to that of the human spine. Here the robot comprises two arms, or spines, bolted together in a serial manner, with each arm carrying a hundred disks connected together by four steel cords. The 'spinal' arms are caused to move by using hydraulic actuation to pull the cords in a mathematically well-defined way.

The spinal design has a number of advantages over many conventional robot manipulators. For example, the robot has a long reach: it can extend to a height of 4 m, and horizontally 2.4 m in any direction through 360 degrees. What is termed the 'working envelope' of the robot is almost a pure hemisphere. Moreover the robot has a remarkable seven axes of movement, which means, for instance, that a tool can be held stationary at the end of the spinal arm while the rest of the arm is able to move! Thus the arm can access difficult places by bending round obstacles and awkward corners — a much greater degree of flexibility than the human arm can manage. This means that the spinal arm can reach into places where it would be quite impossible for the human arm — or the manipulator of a conventional robot — to operate.

The spinal concept was conceived by Ove Larrson in the mid-1970s, and he was helped by mathematical professors at Chalmers University in Sweden who worked out the algorithms for the type of automatic control that was required. Projects that focused on the spine concept have so far yielded well over a dozen Masters degrees, with work continuing on various associated aspects. The spinal robot has been tested in many different ways, including in the manufacturing environment at Volvo.

It is interesting to compare the engineering of the human spine and of the spinal robot. There are obviously superficial similarities but also many profound and important differences. The human spine is highly complex in mechanical terms and also important for metabolic chemistry; the spinal robot has novel mechanical features but no chemical significance. What *is* important is that these are analogous structures, concerned with the exploitation of mechanical principles for effective operation in a physical environment. Both are unable to function without intelligent control (by brain or computer); both are subject to the tensile and compressive forces experienced by complex mechanical structures that operate in the real world. There are lessons here for robot design in the future.

The artificial robot is necessarily an anthropomorphic phenomenon ('made in the image of man') but its particular features may or may not be analogous to specific equivalent features in human beings. So the traditional robot arm has often resembled the human arm. Now there is an artificial *spinal* structure that functions as an effective human *arm*, suggesting that analogous anatomical features can be developed in unexpected ways. This highlights the immense potential for flexibility in robot design. Robotic man — by the accident of a particular ecological evolution — has only one possible anatomical structure. Non-human robots, however, labour under no such constraints: their designs can be conceived, using computer simulation and other methods, in imaginative and unprecedented ways. The designs will be influenced by what we know of human anatomy, but their anatomical scope transcends such considerations.

We have seen that the robot manipulator can be an articulated linkage or a stack of disks pulled by wires. We find a similar flexibility in other aspects of robot design, making it easy to see robotic man as a mundane stereotype compared with his anatomically diverse robotic brothers. This circumstance is well illustrated by glancing at robot hands and grippers.

Give Me a Hand

Efforts to establish human uniqueness in the animal world have not ignored anatomical features. Thus the opposed thumb has often been cited as giving *Homo sapiens* a remarkable advantage over other species. However other primates seem to do quite well in this respect, and so perhaps the thumb is not the dramatically significant feature that has been suggested. Anthony Smith (1968) has drawn attention to another important feature of the human hand: namely, that it possesses two distinct grips. For example, two billiard balls can be held simultaneously by the same hand — one between the last two fingers and the palm, the other between thumb and forefinger. This interesting circumstance may do little to underwrite human vanity.

It has also been pointed out that confusion exists as to what constitutes a finger. Does a person possess ten fingers or eight? This semantic peculiarity is of little importance to the world of non-human robots since many of them, though having highly sophisticated 'grippers', have dispensed with fingers altogether, and this may be regarded as another sign of design flexibility in the robot world. The human hand is regarded as comprising three segments: the carpus (or wrist-bones), the metacarpus (or bones of the palm), and the phalanges (or bones of the digits). By contrast, non-human robots are also interested in a wide range of gripper features — some relying on suction, magnetic, or piercing elements — used to secure tools or workpieces for manufacturing or other purposes.

It is obvious that without grippers of some sort the robot is effectively rendered inoperable in a wide range of physical activities, and the same is largely true of robotic man (though various other parts of the human anatomy can be used to work equipment). This notion was nicely portrayed in Bernard Wolfe's *Limbo '90*, a novel in which men agreed to have their limbs amputated to protect peace (there could be no 'demobilisation without immobilisation'). However artificial limbs were soon fitted, equipped with levers and linkages to perform the work of the original muscles and tendons. Electrical energy supplied by an atomic energy capsule was translated into mechanical energy, allowing the new limbs to perform feats that would be impossible to ordinary men.

The possibility of effective artificial limbs represents an important theoretical bridge between the world of non-human robots and the world of robotic man. To date, many artificial adjuncts to the human body (e.g. the walking equipment being developed for the police constable Philip Olds) have been impressive but have not surpassed the competence of the original human body. What *is* important is that artificial and natural bodily parts clearly inhabit the same functional world, the realm of practical physical accomplishment in striving after particular objectives. It is easy to see that artificial anatomical adjuncts have long been seen as a way of preserving or renewing human operational effectiveness in physical activity. This is as true of the human hand as it is true of other bodily parts.

In 1509 an iron hand was made for Goetz von Berlichingen, a knight immortalised in Goethe's *Goetz*, a dramatic drama. The hand, including gears for fingers and thumb, had limited use, and even Goetz himself was forced to admit: 'My right hand, though not useless in combat, is unresponsive to the grasp of affection. It is one with its mailed gauntlet — you see, it is iron!' In fact many of the artificial limbs of the period (for instance, those devised by the famous military surgeon Ambroise Paré, 1510–90) were made of heavy metal and were difficult to use. Nonetheless it was not uncommon for artificial hands to be made, with fingers extended by springs and flexed by ratchets and levers. There are clues here to the kinship of robotic man to the world of artificial anatomies.

Efforts have also been made to manufacture hands that do not have the obvious disadvantages of heavy metallic structures. For example, the hand devised by D.W. Collins in 1961 is made partly of metal but also of transparent plastic and with a soft covering for the fingertips. The result is that it feels like a real human hand when shaken. This device comes in different sizes and can exert varying degrees of pressure when grasping objects. More recently a flexible three-fingered hand has been manufactured by the Automatic Control Division of the Electrotechnical Laboratory in Japan. Here the three fingers are able to extend, bend, and pinch under the control of electrical power. Another hand and arm prosthesis, from Waseda University, is powered by a hydroelectric system with a miniature oil pressure pump, while the XI hand from Chuo University has five fingers with a sense of touch based on 384 contact points to allow the hand to recognise the shape, texture, and size of objects.

There is now a feeling among robotic designers that the human hand, quite admirable for many purposes, should not necessarily serve as a model for artificial grippers. We have already seen that artificial robots can play the piano, take part in a card game, and manipulate Rubik's Cube, but such performances are intentionally anthropomorphic: they do not lead to versatility or to specific task performance that is useful in the real world. To some extent, human-like robot hands are inappropriate at the moment since few robots can sense in detail what they are doing. We may, for example, expect complex manipulative fingers to be accompanied by an effective sense of sight. The Cranfield Institute of Technology in Britain has developed the prototype of a hand with five fingers, but it is clear that for many manipulative purposes this device is not particularly useful. The human hand is limited in many tasks — e.g. picking up large sheets of metal or bales of straw — and non-human robots may be expected to evolve alternative manipulative mechanisms. Sheets or metal, glass, or plastic can best be handled by magnetic or suction grippers: the 'grip' is secure and can be made to release simply by flicking a switch. Some robots can be conceived with a giant hand instead of two arms and yet others may have two hands on a single wrist. An advertisement for automation equipment from Hitachi shows a three-fingered hand driven by metallic tendons and able, with its 'humanlike dexterity', to carry out a wide variety of assembly and maintenance tasks. The anthropomorphic and non-anthropomorphic routes to robot hand design are proceeding in parallel.

Some robot grippers have only two fingers, like a pair of pliers, and they may be controlled by pneumatic or hydraulic actuators: hydraulics enable the grippers to exert more clamping force, but pneumatics allow for the applied force to be more closely determined. There are now also electrically operated 'proportional grippers', able to close to a specified position. Gripper pads, designed to ensure adequate suction when a part is being handled, are often made of polyurethane bonded to steel. The polyurethane material has the interesting feature that it can be machined to any shape, provided that it is frozen first. Some delicate objects may be handled by means of an expandable bladder or balloon, and vacuum, adhesive, and puncturing grippers are also well known.

One intriguing approach to gripper design is to use conventional artificial fingers — usually three — padded with a loose lining filled with granular powder. In operation the padding moulds round the object to be grasped, whereupon the granules are locked by applying a vacuum or an electromagnetic force (to iron granules). This approach, seen as 'passive' manipulation, has the disadvantage that it is difficult to sense where the grasped object is relative to the robot wrist. This problem can be overcome to some extent by the Omnigripper developed at Imperial College, London.

This device has two parallel 'fingers', each consisting of an array of 8×16 closely spaced pins which can move vertically up and down independently of each other. When the gripper is powered over an object some of the pins are pushed up out of the way, with the effect that the fingers are shaped each time to fit the individual part. The two fingers can be brought together to grasp objects, so achieving an external grip, or they can be moved slightly apart from a closed position to achieve an internal grip.

The Omnigripper is also remarkable in that it has a sensory capability. Information feedback from each pin provides physical details about an object, which allows objects to be recognized, compensation to be made for inaccurate part positioning, and sensing of external features (pins not holding an object will still be pushed up if they encounter an obstacle). The device is also remarkably versatile: it can, for example, pick up more than one object simultaneously, and can select and separate overlapping parts.

Hence we see an intriguing spectrum of robot hands and grippers. The hand of robotic man, with its four digits and a fifth opposed one, has served as a model for hands for non-human robots — though often the artificial hands have two or three, not five, articulated fingers. With Omnigripper the finger are not articulated, to exploit a versatile concept not to be found in the natural world. With vacuum cups and electromagnets, robot grippers can work effectively with a precise on/off action — the grippers can be rendered inoperative by simply switching off an air supply or an electric current. Other grippers, as we have seen, can adhere to an object or pierce it for manipulation or transportation purposes and an expanding bladder can, like Omnigripper, be used to assume the contours of awkwardly shaped or delicate items.

The hands of robotic man lack the design flexibility to be found in the world of non-human robot grippers but make up for this lack by a surprising versatility of performance: the human hand can variously serve the boxer, the pianist, the artist, the craftsman, etc. There are many similarities between the use of human hands and the employment of artificial grippers. Both types of mechanisms can accommodate to objects of different shapes and sizes, using information feedback via visual and tactile sensing and by applying appropriate gripper pressures and positioning. Human hands and artificial grippers are both concerned with the manipulation of objects in the physical environment for the achievement of particular goals. They are both subject to intelligent control by complex information-processing systems (brains or computers). Hands and grippers, of whatever type, are sited equally in what, for our purposes, we may regard as the broad robotic realm.

Arms and Wrists

The typical human arm, wrist, and hand carry between them — if we include the collar bone and the shoulder blade — no less than thirty-two bones, including humerus, radius, ulna, eight wrist bones in two rows, five metacarpals in the palm, and fourteen phalanges (three in each finger and two in the thumb). Artificial robots tend to avoid this degree of structural complexity, though they manage to achieve complications in other ways.

In one classification there are five types of robot arm. Each type is designed to move in a different way for a different type of physical activity. The jointed arm robot, based on the human arm, is the most common design, and it can function in various ways. Again robot operation is often modelled on a scrutiny of how a person works in the physical environment. For example, we can typically think of the human arm swivelling about the waist and the shoulder allowing the arm to tilt up and down. Together the waist and the shoulder ideally allow the arm to reach any point within the volume of a sphere — this is the aim in the design of 'spherical' robots, though it is rarely achieved in practice (there is usually some unreachable zone). In one interesting survey of teaching robots, Dave Futcher (1984) surveyed eighteen different devices ranging up to £2000. The various models illustrate well the various approaches to the design of artificial arms.

The robot arm necessarily helps to define the competence of the system to which it belongs. Some artificial arms can do no more than raise a chess piece, while others can carry a motor vehicle from one factory site to another. The Unimate Series 4000 industrial arm can achieve a maximum reach of nearly 3 m, a horizontal sweep of 200 degrees, and a vertical sweep of 50 degrees. An arm developed by the British United Shoe Manufacturing Company can rotate and move up and down on a vertical pillar, as well as having a rotatable wrist at the end of the arm. Sometimes, as we have seen, two arms can be mounted on the same central pedestal (or torso): e.g. the two-armed robots designed by the Sterling Detroit Company to carry out the operations of quenching and trimming in steel plant. Again there is a significant anthropomorphic element in the idea of a two-armed robot. There is also variation in the materials used for robot arms. We have already noted that human bone is a composite material and composite materials are now being used in a number of experimental robot arms. The Locoman robot, for instance, developed by the Wolfson Industrial Unit, has a three-dimensional pantographic arm constituted out of carbon fibre reinforced rods (described in *Machinery*, 21 April 1982, p. 15).

The main purpose of the robot arm is to allow the hand to move to a required position, and this objective can be achieved in various ways. We have already met the spinal robot with its uncommon flexibility of movement, but other methods can also be adopted to provide a versatile positioning facility. A simple robot arm may be designed to operate along the classical Cartesian coordinates — up and down, side to side, and in and out. Or a robot arm may move on cylindrical coordinates, where the side-to-side movement is replaced by a rotational one. A robot operating on polar coordinates achieves up and down movement, as does the human shoulder, by tilting.

One elaborate — and highly anthropomorphic — system of arm

geometry can be based on revolute coordinates. Here an elbow articulation is used but — from the human perspective — in an upside-down position, like an anglepoise table lamp. This is a highly versatile arrangement but one that introduces all sorts of control problems: e.g. movement at the elbow has to be coordinated with movement at the shoulder, and the wrist will have to move if the gripper is to remain in the same alignment. The wrists of artificial robots have a certain advantage over the wrists of robotic man: they can, for instance, rotate through 360 degrees, not needing to allow the gripper to leave go (and then regrasp) when using, say, a corkscrew or a screwdriver. Wrist flexibility clearly enhances robot competence when working with a mobile arm structure (see, for example, the discussion in Stackhouse, 1979, of a particular approach to wrist flexibility).

The arms of robotic man, like his other anatomical bits and pieces, are for the most part well defined. There are of course genetic oddities and tragic mishaps, as with the victims of thalidomide, and in such circumstances efforts may be made to provide prosthetic devices to supplement inadequate limbs or to serve in the place of totally absent ones. Human beings, like other mammals, are unable to regrow a severed limb: a spider or an axolotl can grow a new leg, but a human being is required to make do with an artificial substitute if he loses an arm or leg. Again we may remark that the development of prosthetic devices serves as an important bridge between the natural and artificial robotic worlds.

Artificial arms can obviously be of great importance to amputees or to those unfortunate individuals who are born without any limbs at all. The scope for appending an artificial limb depends to some extent on the amount of surviving tissue that remains in the appropriate region. Thus if an amputee retains the original arm muscle intact in the upper arm he can be fitted with an artificial limb such as the Boston Arm developed by Dr Melvin J. Glimcher, a professor of orthopaedics at Harvard University, in collaboration with Professor Robert W. Mann of MIT. This mechanical limb, first introduced in 1969, can be controlled by messages from the brain: the pulses are amplified and fed to the artificial arm. Here the applied voltage determines the speed of movement of the limb, with strain gauges indicating to the individual the size of the load being manipulated. An amputee can raise objects of up to 10 lb in weight using this device. An artificial arm from the Stanford Research Institute is controlled by computer to enable the user to comb his hair, eat, and scratch his back. This device has seven joints and an embedded integrated circuit to allow as many as twenty different coordinated movements. Quadriplegics have been helped to greater mobility and control of their environment by means of computerized systems controllable by minimal movements on the part of the patient. There can be plenty of ways of controlling the movement of a door, the operation of a typewriter, or the switching of a light without the need for a fully fledged prosthetic limb.

In this area, as elsewhere, we see three overlapping worlds — that of robotic man (with his bones, joints, information feedback systems, etc.), that of the non-human robot (with articulated limbs, computer control, etc.), and that of the prosthetic device, where a human being is linked to artificial limbs and other devices to enlarge his scope for activity and communication. There is obviously a sense in which this is a unified world with the various areas conveniently subsumed under different heads. The arms, wrists and hands of robotic man have their obvious counterparts in the world of artificial robots, though the different systems achieve versatility in different ways.

There are many ways in which robotic man is a flexible, highly adaptable system. One of these relates to his mobility — to date a superior facility to that found in any non-human robots. Already artificial systems are evolving to challenge man's supremacy in this field. The mobile robot is commonplace in fiction but comparatively rare and unimpressive in the real world, but for robotic man and for his robotic siblings and cousins there is a pressing need for mobility.

The Need for Mobility

It has been obviously beneficial for biological systems to be able to move purposefully round their environment: e.g. to search for mates, food, and security. There are a host of problems associated with movement that have required the evolution of specialized mechanisms of anatomy, information processing, sensory discernment, etc. In coping with the need for movement, human beings — like other animals — have again demonstrated the fact that they are effective engineered systems. Robotic man has exploited many principles of mechanical and electrical engineering, physics, and information science to develop the capacity to explore his world in an intelligent and mobile fashion.

One problem is friction (and we have already glanced at the

provision of natural lubricants in biological systems); another is the question of balance in straight-line or curved motion (these aspects are well discussed by Tricker and Tricker, 1966). In general, questions of stability, balance, friction, momentum, etc., can clearly be discussed in terms of classical scientific theory. Man, as an engineered system, is well described by the spectrum of considerations that focus on the movement of systems in a physical environment. It has been suggested, for example, that physical instability is not necessarily a disadvantage to a living organism (we are invited to consider the resting flamingo which, in terms of gravity constraints, resembles a pencil standing on end). An unstable animal will quickly fall into a swerving mode, and so avoid predators more easily. Such observations say little about non-human robots but help to account for movement characteristics among various animal species. Tricker and Tricker consider a wide range of movement aspects — hydrodynamics, rotation, work, energy, the conservation of angular momentum, etc. — to show how such matters are directly relevant to the behaviour of animals in the world. Animals, human or not, are self-evidently engineered systems, akin to artificial robots in their necessary observance of physical law.

As with hands and arms, concerned as they are with movement, legs can also inhabit the three perceived worlds of robotic man, artificial robots, and prosthetic devices. The first mention of an artificial leg can be found in the *Rig-Veda* which dates to the end of the Veda period in India (1500–800 BC), and Herodotus cites an artificial foot which Hegisistratus of Elis made for himself after cutting off part of his own foot to escape from the stocks. There is also mention of artificial limbs in the Talmud, the Nordic sagas, and other ancient texts. Peg legs, supposedly a common accoutrement of pirates, have featured in tales from the earliest times, and there is one shown in a Roman mosaic at Lescar in the French Pyrenees. Here thin bronze is nailed to a wooden core and lined with leather, a square piece of iron added at the foot to provide strength.

Artificial legs made by Ambroise Paré included a movable knee and tarsal section of the foot, and a knee lock to provide rigid support at the appropriate time. Such contrivances were often akin to items of armour, though wooden peg legs were also made for the poor: a 1568 Bruegel painting shows beggars wearing wooden legs. A celebrated leg (once nicely depicted in a television programme) made for the Marquis of Anglesey included a steel knee joint and a wooden ankle joint with cords from the knee controlling the motion of the ankle. This leg, in common with many similar designs, made a clapping sound when used, and so became known as the 'clapper' leg; later versions were known as the American leg.

It is generally recognized that bipeds are not particularly stable, a circumstance not improved by alcohol or fatigue. In this regard mobile artificial robots are more likely to learn from four-legged animals and six-legged insects, rather than from robotic man. In fact we learn that a variety of multilegged artefacts — walking tractors and mechanical horses — have been in use for agricultural purposes since the 1940s, though with varying degrees of success. In the Soviet Union, stepping excavators have been used to clear forests. It is found that walking vehicles can demonstrate a number of advantages over wheeled machines or trucks with caterpillar tracks. Artoboleskii and Kobrinskii (1977) have described a four-legged *mechanized horse* weighing $1\frac{1}{2}$ tonnes and powered by a 90-horsepower automobile engine.

Other walking devices have been built by General Electric for the US Army; by the University of Wisconsin to study problems of locomotion, stability, and control; and by various medical researchers to provide amputees with mobility. It has been known for some time that legged locomotion systems can adapt well to rough terrains, and a theory of adaptive walking machines has been evolved (see, for example, Orin, McGhee, and Jaswa, 1976, McGhee, 1977, and McGhee and Iswandhi, 1979). A hexapod robot that has been operating at the Paris VII University since November 1980 has been described by Kessis, Rambant, and Penne (1982).

Today a theory of *generalized gaits* has been developed to aid the design of mobile robots. Possible gaits have been enumerated and attention has been given to the relative stability — not necessarily an overriding option — of the various gaits. Six-legged gaits are reckoned to be best when they have *symmetrical wavy* features and a number of different gaits have been found to possess such characteristics. Microprocessors can be included in the design of walking machines to control the sequence of leg movements, i.e. to organize the effective gait in different environmental circumstances. (This is akin to how microprocessors can be used to control prosthetic upper limbs — see Nightingale, 1985 — and is nicely analogous to how insects, for example, might have local processing power to control the movement of individual limbs.) Sensors can also be incorporated to provide information on the progress of a mobile system and to allow it thereby to modify its gait in order to progress in an optimum fashion. Such concepts can also be adapted to aid human mobility: e.g. in allowing the development of a mobile frame for amputees and paraplegics. Such a frame was developed at the Department of Mechanical Engineering at the University of Wisconsin in 1976.

The provision of such mechanical frames — to supplement or renew human mobility and strength — have a long history in human imagination. Thus Hieronymus Fabricius ab Aquapendente (1537–1619), a famous Italian anatomist and embryologist, introduced in his *Oper a Chirurgica* a section about surgical instruments which included two exoskeletons that could fit and support a human being. It has been suggested that the supporting frame was inspired by mediaeval armour, and refers to the notion that man is composed of replaceable parts. This is obviously highly relevant to the notion of robotic man: man is more than the sum of his parts, but there is a clear sense in which the total number of parts in an individual is all that there is to that person. (Reductionism is both true and false, depending upon what is claimed: neither a molecule of hydrogen nor a molecule of oxygen are characteristically wet, but a wet molecule of water is nothing more than oxygen and hydrogen.)

Again we see a complex of prosthetic and supplementary devices that can link to an individual to enhance human strength or human mobility. A spectrum of independent walking machines are being developed to allow non-human robots to explore their environments and to take adaptive action in an intelligent fashion. For example, a walking robot was on display at the September 1985 International Conference on Advanced Robotics held in Tokyo. This adaptive suspension vehicle (ASV) was developed with $5 million from the US Defence Advanced Research Project Agency. In the words of Bob Johnstone (*New Scientist*, 26 September 1985), the ASV looks like a 'cross between a three-humped camel and a praying mantis'. The device is nonetheless seen as a highly sophisticated walking machine, able to stride across ditches 3 m wide and to step over obstacles 2 m high. The ASV itself is 5 m long and weighs 2.72 tonnes; driven by a modified 50-kw motorcycle engine, it can carry 90 kg and move at 8 km/h. An optical radar tells the vehicle where it is going, and use is made of infrared and other sensors. Displays above the operator's head show the position of all the ASV's legs which are on the ground and which are in motion. Well over a dozen single-board computers are used to analyse sensor data, to control leg movement, to read commands from the operator's joystick, and to carry out other tasks. Once the machine has been perfected it will be able to operate in various modes — under operator control or autonomously for rapid progress over rough terrain.

Development in the design of mobile robots will inevitably bridge the gap between robotic man and non-human systems, and such development will be achieved by greater insight into various subject areas — gait theory, biological control mechanisms, the physics of friction and stability, etc. In all this there will be the underlying acknowledgement that mobile robots — human and non-human — obey physical laws, the laws that govern the progress of physical objects in a physical environment. Mobile robots are obviously engineered systems and as such they are subject to characteristic engineering constraints. One of the consequences of research into artificial robot systems is to realize that robotic man is subject to the same constraints.

The Mechanics of Joints

The articulated sections in animals, human beings, and non-human robots require connective regions of one sort or another. It is obviously necessary for the sections to remain joined but to be able to alter their relative positions, so that prey can be chased, food grasped, mates secured, etc. Without the complex of articulated lever systems, all animals would have to depend upon the caprice of wind and water.

In insects, for example, the main types of joint are simple strips of flexible cuticle that join one section to another: e.g. the various parts of a locust's leg. Here the primitive joint can allow rotation and linear movement in any direction, limiting the extent of possible movements but not their variety. Arthropods also make use of hinge joints, e.g. to link the femur and tibia of a locust. Buttresses extend either side of the axis of the hinge and are connected by flexible strips of cuticle. The strips bend when the joint is moved. Put more technically, the joint is operated by means of a flexor and an extensor, each of which includes an apodeme carrying flexible joints.

Muscles are distributed in various ways according to the type of joint they are expected to operate. Typically we find a pair of muscles for each degree of freedom of relative movement that the joint can accomplish: e.g. the hinge between the insect tibia and femur has one pair of antagonistic muscles — one of the muscles is used to straighten the joint, the other to bend it. Muscles are disposed in a characteristic way to operate the ball and socket joint between the thorax and coxa of the typical insect. Here we may expect three pairs of antagonistic muscles to control a joint allowing three degrees of freedom, but in fact two more muscles on either side of the socket supplement the action of the three muscle-pairs.

The joints in mammals, like those in insects, exploit a variety of hinge and ball and socket principles. The spherical head of the human femur fits neatly into the acetabulum and is secured by ligaments surrounding the joint. Thus the hip joint is a typical biological ball and socket joint allowing three degrees of freedom. This means that a leg can be swung laterally, forwards and backwards, and can be rotated — with different ligaments becoming taut in different positions and limiting the amount of travel.

A simple hinge joint is set between the ulna and humerus, mainly allowing rotation about a specific axis when the elbow is bent and extended. In some circumstances, without restraining ligaments, the ulna could also slide from side to side. However, as the articulating surface of the humerus is grooved — like a pulley wheel — the ulna fits it neatly, so sliding is prevented. The radius has a short cylindrical head which rotates against an articular facet on the ulna, allowing a degree of motion within constraining limits.

Not all articulating surfaces fit closely together. In the human knee, for example, the lower end of the femur rests on the flat upper end of the tibia, the bones held together by ligaments. When the knee bends a ligament pulls the femur posteriorly relative to the tibia; another ligament is used to operate the knee in the opposite direction. The loose fit of the articular surfaces means that only small areas of the articular cartilages are touching at any one time, the areas changing with the movement of the joint. This can be important for the weeping lubrication of mammalian joints (considered earlier).

The various human joints or articulations can be classified in various ways (we have hinted at one approach already when talking of hinges and ball and socket joints). One breakdown (in *Gray's Anatomy*) discusses articulations under three headings: synarthrosis (immovable articulations, such as the joints in the cranium), amphi-arthrosis (mixed articulations), and diarthrosis (movable articulations). It is emphasized that movable articulations represent the greatest number of joints in the body, 'mobility being their distinguishing character'. The range of joints in this class is determined by the types of motion associated with each. Four basic types of joint movement are recognized: gliding, angular, circum-duction, and rotation. Many joints manage to combine these various types of motion in order to provide great flexibility of behaviour.

There are obvious similarities between biological joints and machine articulations using pivots, hinges, and ball and socket mechanisms, and the fully articulated arm of the non-human robot clearly resembles a mammalian limb. At the same time there are many differences between joints in robotic man and in his artificial counterparts. The biological ball and socket can allow great flexibility, often more than in an analogous artificial joint: the shoulder, for example, relying on a ball and socket articulation, can achieve two degrees of freedom with a single joint, whereas a mechanical arm needs two joints to accomplish an equivalent range of movement. This evident advantage of the familiar ball and socket is only part of the story. This type of joint can easily be dislocated: it relies on muscles to hold it in the correct position and it can only move effectively when the muscles flex and relax in highly complex coordinated patterns.

The human engineer cannot aspire to accomplish anything so sophisticated. For a start there are immense difficulties in trying to duplicate muscle tissue. All materials are elastic to a degree, but the peculiar elasticity of muscle fibre presents particular problems. Therefore, for the most part, robotics engineers have been content to rely upon simple joints that allow movement in one plane only and upon a rotation capability that can be based on the familiar turntable principle. For this reason non-human robots have evolved without a requirement for muscles to provide leverage to a skeletal structure. Instead artificial robots have relied upon gearing, powered typically by electric motors, to provide a rotational force directly to a joint. Electrical (or hydraulic) power is used to provide the effective muscle force to cause a robot limb to move in a controlled fashion. But the question of control is also complex.

Where an artificial robot limb is provided with a separate articu-lation, rotation, or telescopic movement to each degree of freedom, it is necessary to provide also a separate drive for each: therefore six degrees of freedom will imply six drives, each linked to a controlling computer. Furthermore, most movements will require at least two drives working in close conjunction with each other. In consequence, the effective robot muscle is required to supply power and to operate in a precise way in conjunction with other artificial muscles. If a single drive in a multidrive system becomes inoperable, or even faulty to a small degree, the movement of the robot limb becomes unreliable, unpredictable, and even hazardous to any human robots in the environment. We may regard such an eventuality as strictly analogous to cases where a human robot runs amok, in circumstances where some (cerebral) control centre has ceased to function in the proper manner.

Some artificial muscles used for non-human robots are simply rams acting directly on skeletal limbs: they can be used to activate, for example, telescopic devices designed to work in difficult environments. However rams, activated by hydraulic pressure, are not always the most suitable types of artificial muscle for non-human robots. Electrically powered stepping motors, activated by pulses amenable to computer control, are very suitable for robotic applications requiring a precise positioning of artificial limbs for particular purposes. A computer can control electrical pulses much more easily than it can start and stop a flow of hydraulic fluid through a valve.

We have seen a wide range of strategies for joint mechanics in animals, non-human robots, and robotic man. The various systems are all required to move with precision in the physical world, and to position tools, workpieces, food, and other items to achieve specific objectives. For this reason a variety of joints — ball and socket, hinge, pivot, fixed, etc. — have evolved in artificial and natural systems to behave in a controlled fashion. Again we stress the *engineered* status of robotic man: his hinged articulations have plenty of parallels in the mechanical world and his unique biological muscles have obvious counterparts in the electrical and hydraulic mechanisms devised for non-human robots. His evident engineered articulations are only useful if they can be controlled effectively for the accomplishment of particular tasks. Non-human robots require analogous control facilities, provided in the main by electronic digital computers. Control is achieved in robotic man by means of the brain.

Brains for Control

The human brain is the most remarkable anatomical feature of robotic man. It provides him with whatever intelligence or creativity he may possess, and is also capable of generating mythology, mistakes, illusion, and confusion in vast quantities. We are rightly accustomed to regarding the brain as a prodigiously capable information-processing machine (Marvin Minsky's 'meat machine'), but we should occasionally reflect on the fact that robotic man typically labours under a host of perplexities, lacking psychological security and the wit to operate in an optimum fashion to maximize satisfactions and self-fulfilment. It is of little help to our efforts to understand our own brain operations that most cerebral activity proceeds in ways that are not amenable to conscious scrutiny. Just as we cannot directly witness the functioning of the spleen or the kidneys, so we cannot survey in any immediate fashion the operation of the cortex or the hypothalamus. The brain of robotic man provides a host of control functions for his physical articulated frame, but usually does so in mysterious and perplexing ways. The brain is an anatomical component governed by natural law: we will see that it reinforces, rather than discredits, the doctrine of robotic man.

In a typical reckoning the human brain has around 14 thousand million cells (neurons) distributed through two cerebral hemispheres that sit on a section of tissue that comprises about 10 per cent of the total brain mass. The brain controls all thought and imagination, all movement and emotion, all the searching and striving undertaken by human beings in the constant quest for survival. The control is exercised, using a hierarchy of information-processing modes, by means of a complex of cybernetic processes (see Chapter 4). It is possible to localize particular brain functions (e.g. those connected with muscle control or speech), but facilities such as intelligence or creativity cannot be associated with a particular region of the brain: instead they are properties of the brain as a whole, somehow encapsulated in the complex network of 14 billion neurons, each having hundreds or thousands of connections to its neighbouring cells.

The spinal nerves in humans are much more complex than in most other animals, though the spinal cord does not run the full length of the backbone. At the end of the spinal cord there is an untidy cluster of fibres, tracts, and other nervous complexes. The entire spinal cord, about half an inch wide for most of its length, weighs about an ounce, around a fiftieth of the weight of the brain. Typically, an energy source (chemical, thermal, osmotic, electromagnetic, or electric) in the environment causes an energy transmission in a nerve, for example from the skin along a nerve pathway to the spinal cord and so upwards to the brain. A neuron gives an electrical pulse as output when certain electrical input conditions are satisfied (this is strictly analogous to the behaviour of logic gates in the circuits of digital computers). Chemical messages in the brain influence the diffusion of ions across cell membranes, so generating a requisite potential change that can carry to the next neuron. The brain cell is essentially a go/no-go device: when the chemical and electrical conditions are right it will 'fire' and when they are not, it will not. This is essentially a binary approach to information processing, again strictly analogous to the binary basis of all computation in electronic digital computers.

The effective control offered by the 'meat machine' based on hydrocarbons has no direct chemical equivalent in the world of artifical robots. However there are many control facilities, usually relying on binary arithmetic and electronics, that allow artificial physical frames — the anatomies of non-human robots — to behave purposefully and with intelligence. The evolution of control mechanisms in artificial anatomies already nicely parallels the evolution of brain tissue in the progressive emergence of the higher biological species. Some theoretical investigations have focused on the analyses of biological behaviour as a means of gaining insight into potential robot systems. Thus Powers (1979) used a computer subroutine to explore controlled variables in an experiment involving a human subject. In this way it is possible, for example, to investigate sensory systems — to test controlled variables involving intensity, sensation, change, strategy, and systems concepts relating to visual, tactile, auditory, kinesthetic, and other sensory phenomena. This is clearly relevant to the design of robot systems intended to exploit sensory data to operate purposefully in the real physical world.

The simplest types of robot control are achieved by means of *physical set-up*. For example, a stepping drum may contain reprogrammable cams to operate electrical switches to control, via hydraulic actuators, a robot arm. Some solid-state reprogrammable controllers are little more than high-speed electronic analogues of simple physical stepping systems. The Auto-Place SPM-4 unit, developed in the 1970s, is a typical pneumatic stepping system designed to control a sequence of robot actions in the performance of a task. Such systems, based on physical set-up or pneumatics, do not allow for intelligent discrimination in the control of a process: for this, effective computer supervision is required.

In one research project initiated to develop a control facility for AMF Versatran devices — robotic and other automated systems — it was soon acknowledged that a computer was necessary for most of the design objectives. The options included selecting an appropriate microprocessor facility, choosing a minicomputer, or designing a special-purpose computer for the tests to be performed. In due course a Digital Equipment Corporation LSI-11 microcomputer was selected.

Before microcomputers, based on microprocessors, became available it was common for robots to be controlled by minicomputers. A minicomputer could supervise a single robot or a complex of robots in an industrial environment. This meant, for example, that the robot could be sited at the place of work and its brain — the minicomputer — could be sited elsewhere, some distance away or in a protected room to avoid environmental hazards. Today the operational flexibility of minicomputer-based robot control systems has been realized in many working situations. However there are many advantages in being able to design local processing capability into robots. The robot does not need to be linked by lengthy and cumbersome cables to its computer supervisor: it can carry its own brain around with it, and moreover have the benefits of processing power sited in conjunction with articulated limbs, sensory facilities, and other items of robot anatomy. One consequence has been that it is easier to view robots in anthropomorphic terms: a robot that keeps its brain in some distant room does not appear akin to human beings!

Today it is commonplace for robot brains to be provided by microprocessor-based facilities. For example, the Metal Castings Company (Worcester, England) is now using a complex of Unimate robots with their own effective microprocessor brains. Here work can be rapidly reprogrammed for the production of different parts. The computer defines the required sequence of operations and also controls the various safety provisions (an increasingly important consideration where robotic man is required to work with his artificial brothers): the computer examines various sensors to check that there are no guards open and no obstacles to prevent the operation from being performed. Microprocessors can be used to interpret the information supplied by, say, visual sensors, much in the way that parts of the human brain interpret visual data taken in by the human eye and passed down the optic nerve.

The use of microprocessors in robotic systems is one of the main developments that are progressively expanding robot intelligence and decision-making capabilities. It has long been recognized that information processing is performed in various parts of the brain for different purposes. For example, Garrett (1978) has commented that 'the human brain is organised as a distributed processing system' — an arrangement that is increasingly common, using networking, in the realm of the computers used to supervise non-human robots. Again it is possible to highlight the similarities between data processing in artificial robots and in robotic man.

Data are selected, collected, processed, and stored — and reprocessed whenever necessary — in both animal brains and artificial computers. Program sequences can be modified in the light of new and worthwhile experiences, and unexpected contingencies can be handled by means of decision facilities that can draw on relevant stored data. We have seen that different parts of the human brain are assigned to different human subsystems, much as different 'on-board' microprocessors can be dedicated to different activities in non-human robots. The brain — whether based on hydrocarbons and other chemicals in the cranium of robotic man or on the solid-state silicon circuits of an electronic computer in some segment of a non-human robot — is the effective control centre, responsible for the purposeful organization of all behavioural and cognitive responses. Without an effective brain, a physical anatomy can accomplish no more than at best a few repetitive programmed procedures. Brains, of whatever sort, allow a spectrum of mental attributes — intelligence, creativity, insight, intuition, imagination, decision-making competence, etc. — to be encapsulated in higher-order programs (see Chapter 5).

The design of brains for non-human robots will continue to be influenced by what we know of mammalian brains and of the nervous systems of less complex non-human (but animal) robots (insects, fish, reptiles, etc.). It is likely that we will find it useful to model the control hierarchies of non-human artificial robots on the control hierarchies to be found in the central nervous systems of human beings. In such circumstances it will be possible to arrange for a central on-board microcomputer to control the spectrum of distributed processing units assigned to specific subsystems in the artificial robot. In any event it is the brain that allows flexible behaviour and creative initiative. It can only do this, in a changing physical environment, by relying on the information supplied by the various sensory systems.

Sensory Systems

The senses of robotic man, of other animals, and of artificial robots are the working interfaces between the central controlling computer or brain (and any distributed information-processing units) and the outside world. Computers and brains need data to work with: the senses are the data suppliers. Again there are similarities between the sensory systems of robotic man and the various analogous mechanisms designed for robotic and other purposes. The human eye, for instance, resembles a camera: it includes a lens, a stop (the iris), and a photosensitive area upon which the image falls. At the same time there are many physical differences between human and artificial eyes. The lens in the human eye, unlike the camera, is fixed in relation to the photosensitive area: change of focus is not achieved by moving the relative distance but by altering the curvature of the lens. Also the photosensitive region of the eye is curved and varies in sensitivity, whereas a camera makes use of a flat film equally sensitive over its whole area. Moreover the eye can cope with great variations in the intensity of illumination: the scope of a camera, using a particular type of sensitive emulsion, is comparatively limited. Apart from such differences, the biological eye and the camera are governed by common optical principles: in this sense they both rely equally on the laws of physics.

The adult human eyeball weighs about one-quarter of an ounce and is about one inch wide. It is interesting that the eye of a baby is nearer to its adult size that the baby's brain or any other part of the baby's anatomy: the body increases its volume as much as twenty times after birth, the brain 3.75 times, and the eye only 3.25 times. Light entering the eye passes first through the cornea, then through the anterior chamber, then through a gap between the iris diaphragm, then through the lens and the posterior chamber, before landing on the sensitive retina. The lens grows flatter and harder with age and is almost totally surrounded by liquid. The light-sensitive cells of the retina are the millions of rods and cones which feed signals along the optic nerve to the brain. There are well over one hundred million retinal cells, and the relatively narrow optic nerve carries 800,000 fibres. The 'blind spot' is an area devoid of receptors and caused by the exit of the optic nerve (this area was first noted in 1668). Rods tend to be used for night vision (detecting mainly shades of grey), with cones used for day vision (to sort out colours). This can be shown by comparing the proportions of rods and cones in noctural and daytime animals: paradoxically, however, daytime man has more rods. The eyes of robotic man are more effective than in many mammals but less effective than in some birds (for example, the hawk and the falcon). It is hardly surprising that efforts should be made to equip non-human robots with sight, a most effective means of collecting data about the environment.

The idea of sighted robots is of course commonplace in mythology and fiction, but was first considered as a practical technological possibility in the 1950s when the US National Aeronautical and Space Administration (NASA) was contemplating landing robot vehicles on the moon and the inner planets. At that time few working vision systems were designed. Even as late as the 1970s, unmanned planetary vehicles were obliged to transmit pictures back to the earth before the machines could be given fresh instructions: there are immense problems in designing effective artificial vision systems. The main difficulties are associated with the vast amounts of data contained in a visual scene and the need to process this body of data in a speedy fashion.

One approach in these daunting circumstances is to estimate whether parts of a scene can be ignored: are they crucial to the purposes of the person or the non-human robot? By ignoring shadows, 'irrelevant' light effects, and other phenomena, it may be possible to appreciate the significance of a scene — constructed as akin to a line drawing — so that appropriate operational decisions can be taken. There is evidence in fact that human beings employ just such a strategy. The visual cortex receives information from the optic nerve, but then carries out a discriminatory function to store essential information. In this way a complex image can be reduced to, in effect, a few significant lines. What is true for the visual sense is also true for the other senses of non-human robots and robotic man.

Artificial robot systems now possess a wide range of sensory facilities: including sensitive skin, tactile probes, ultrasonic devices, voice-recognition facilities, and even an ability to detect gases in the atmosphere (i.e. to smell). Dr Paul Clifford at the Carnegie Mellon University is currently developing an effective robot nose by combining simple sensors with sophisticated computer interpreters. The sensors — tiny elements of tin oxide, iron oxide, and zinc oxide — are heated by a coil embedded in an electrode; each of the oxides gives a different reaction to the gases passing across them, allowing subsequent interpretation by a microcomputer. The robot nose, using pattern-recognition methods, will be more discriminating than conventional gas-detection systems. Here there is little physical resemblance between the artificial nose and the analogous part of the human anatomy. Nor does the typical voice-recognition unit resemble the human ear, though both may contain a vibrating diaphragm and be governed by the same acoustic laws.

We may expect artificial robots to evolve a wider range of senses than those to be found in robotic man and in other animals. The common five senses will be evolved for artificial systems, but it is likely that other senses will also emerge. Some robot senses may be based on capabilities found in animals but not in humans, but first it is necessary to recognize all the relevant animal senses. It was, for example, a long time before bat 'radar', relying on acoustic principles, was understood by human beings. The influential biologist Cuvier in 1800 dismissed the careful experiments of Spallanzani and Jurine which showed that bats could 'see with sound'; instead Cuvier preferred to believe, without carrying out any useful experiments of his own, that bats navigated using only the sense of touch (though coating the wings with varnish and flour paste had not affected the navigational ability of the bat!). Here the problem was in recognizing that there were sounds that could be heard by bats but which were inaudible to human beings. It is likely that other animal senses exist which, when fully appreciated, will form the basis of additional sensory systems in non-human robots. It is already possible to use infrared light for such purposes, and it may also be practical to use magnetic and other physical phenomena in appropriate circumstances.

The various anatomies of the sensory systems will be directly determined by the physical principles that they are designed to exploit. The various sensory components of the human ear, for example, are all engineered to detect and interpret small mechanical forces. For instance, the semicircular canals of the inner ear act as a receptor system to detect rotational movements of the head: sense can be made of head movements by detecting and interpreting the various accelerations and decelerations of fluid within the canals, a matter of orthodox dynamics. Similarly the saccule and the utricle contain the otoliths — groups of hairs and chalky particles — which are sensitive to gravity, so enabling a person to know his disposition relative to the earth. The mechanical complexities of the middle ear are engineered to cope with complicated sound waves, and so to make a vital contribution to the sense of hearing.

Sound waves enter the ear and cause the tympanic membrane to vibrate, the complex oscillations of the membrane then being transmitted to three small bones (the malleus, the incus, and the stapes) and then from these bones to a further (smaller) membrane, the organ of Corti, that converts the vibrations into nerve impulses that can be fed to the brain and interpreted as meaningful sound. Thus vibrations in the air can be conveyed through a complex mechanical system — the outer, middle, and inner ear of the human being — for translation into the electrical potentials that can feed through a neuron network for interpretation as the sound of music, voices, or rain. Non-human robots are already evolving their own anatomical organs for hearing, but they are likely to be less complex than the analogous organs in robotic man.

It is again obvious that the anatomical constraints on the sensory organs of both human beings and non-human robots are determined by the laws of orthodox science. The lens of the human eye, the tympanic membrane of the human ear, etc., each have a character directly determined by the laws of optics, the mechanical laws of elasticity and momentum, etc. The sensory organs of robotic man are as directly engineered, in a purely physical sense, as are the analogous sensory units in industrial and other artificial robots. The *agency* of the engineering is different for the two cases. Robotic man is engineered by biological evolution; non-human robots by robotic man (often with computer assistance). In both cases, however, we see engineered systems, working configurations programmed for behaviour in a physical environment.

Man–Machine Systems

The place of man in the broad robotic world is emphasized by the evolution of man–machine systems, functional complexes in which man and machine are parts of a broader operational unit. Here efforts are made to collect ergonomic data that is relevant to the design of machine configurations in which man also will play a part. So it is important to know about human posture, average limb length, visual acuity, information assimilation rate, etc. Armed with such knowledge the ergonomist can provide data that are relevant to the design of machine-based systems that will operate in conjunction with human operators. In this way we can envisage the evolution of complex man–machine systems in which the human role is determined solely by an estimate of the competence of human beings and the competence of non-human machines in task performance. Many observers will see this as a bleak vision of man's future, but the trends are manifestly clear and cannot be denied.

An initial decision will be taken as to whether a man or a machine performs a particular task more satisfactorily. It may be that a man should supervise other men and computer-based systems; or perhaps a computer would make a better supervisor in certain circumstances. The fact that such a question can be posed emphasizes the purely functional and operational roles of robotic man. When his place in the overall system is defined, efforts will be made to structure all the system components in ergonomically optimum ways: so account will be taken of how to site man in the system, of the limits on his concentration span, and of how well he is likely to respond to the demands that will be made upon him. Robotic man is a component in such an operational environment. Pessimists will declare that he will be an increasingly superfluous component — with all functional tasks, from routine manufacture to high-level decision making and judgemental activity, progressively transferred to computer-based systems.

Efforts have been made to evaluate the role of man as a functional element in a man–machine system. Murrell (1965), for example, explores the place of 'man as a system component'. Here it is suggested that a man–machine unit has three basic functions:

1. an input function which conveys information to the man's senses;

2. a control function carried out by man in the central mechanism;

3. an output function achieved by the activation of man's motor system.

The absence of a direct link between the input and output means that the unit is an open loop; where the output can have some influence on the input, the unit operates as a closed loop in which the man acts as a control element (this is a familiar cybernetic concept — see Chapter 4).

In a simple closed loop the man is supplied with immediate information about the effect of his action; he can then respond accordingly to achieve a defined objective. Where the human response is continuous he is said to be performing a *tracking* function. Tracking may be *compensatory* (where an index has to be maintained at a predetermined position) or *pursuit* (where a control index needs to be kept aligned with an index that is moving in a random fashion). Such considerations are highly relevant to the study of man as a controller in a complex man–machine system.

Human limitations and strengths should be appreciated in estimating how robotic man can be deployed in a functional con-figuration. For example, people are better than (simple) machines at sensing minimum stimulae, improvisation, pattern recognition, translation, inductive reasoning, judgements, making decisions, etc., whereas even simple machines are likely to be better than human beings at computation, high-speed response, precise repetition, and short-term information storage. As soon as we consider *complex* machines, however, a more alarming picture emerges: we can discern a progressive transfer of functions from human beings to machines. For example, with the development of computer-based artificial intel-ligence, judgemental activity is no longer the prerogative of robotic man (more is said about this in Chapter 6).

The existence of man as a physical component in a man–machine complex can be studied at many different levels. For example, society as a whole can be interpreted as a vastly complicated cybernetic system (Chapter 4) in which a host of active programmed systems strive to achieve survival and other contributory objectives. In such a view ethics and politics become amenable to exploration in cybernetic terms (Chapter 8). First it is necessary to explore the interpretation of robotic man as a cybernetic system.

Summary

This chapter has explored man *as a component in an engineered world*, as a physical element in a realm governed solely by natural law. Man is not an angel, a demon, a wraith, a disembodied spirit floating through the void. Man is a physical structure, an anatomy — with programs for performance laid up in genes, nervous pathways, and brain cells. Of course when pressed we invariably admit as much, but because of the accident of historical circumstance — our cultural evolution from relatively ignorant prescientific times — we rarely allow our awareness of 'man-as-anatomy' to inform fully our consciousness. To perceive man as a purely physical engineered system is to move to a new concept of what it is to be human; it is, in fact, to embrace the doctrine of robotic man.

We need to emphasize the engineered aspect of human reality. First we are all built of chemicals, organized in startling complexity to achieve the necessary functions. Metabolic processes allow chemicals to be absorbed, processed, and then distributed via the bloodstream to maintain the functioning and health of organs. Such activity is performed in conjunction with other physical processes carried out in the engineered anatomy. Composite materials, ball-joints, levers, lubricating substances, lenses, vibrating membranes, elastic materials, hinges, thermoregulators, gravity detectors, fluidic pumps, stabilizing structures, electrical generators, shock absorbers — this is all the stuff of engineering, and it is the stuff of robotic man.

4 The Cybernetic System

Preamble

The idea that we can view man as a *system* should not surprise us. We are already familiar enough with the notion that the human being is made up of a number of *sub*systems: e.g. the blood system, the lymph system, the temperature control system, etc. So already we are acquainted with the possibility that a human being may be *nothing more* than a bunch of cooperating sub-systems that together define the whole. (Again we can stress that we are not seduced by a simple reductionism: there is an obvious sense in which the whole is more than the sum of its parts, but also a sense in which the whole has no other elements than its parts.)

If man can be represented as a complex system — comprising a hierarchy of contributing subsystems — then several inferences can be drawn. For a start, man can be studied according to classical systems theory in which a dynamic entity can be analysed in terms of inputs, outputs, adaptation, information processing, and the like. With this approach life can be seen as a *systems* phenomenon — not as one in which a hydrocarbon metabolism is a logical necessity — so our view of a *living* system becomes divorced from the parochial acquaintance with one broad class of animate entities (namely those based on organic chemistry). Perhaps more importantly for our purposes, a systems view of man implies that the behaviour of human beings is at least influenced by discoverable systems rules (for instance, consider the implications of the notion that a human being at all times acts *systematically*). This in turn nicely complements the doctrine that man, both as an individual and as a species, is governed by natural law. Physics, chemistry, biology, and systems theory (plus the engineering considerations sketched in Chapter 3) conspire to set man in a deterministic frame, a complex universe having no time for caprice or physical lawlessness. There can be little doubt that systems theory, properly viewed, underwrites the doctrine of robotic man.

It is also significant that classical systems theory has been greatly enhanced and strengthened by advances in computer science. The emergence of cybernetics, as a unifying discipline for biological organisms and machine artefacts, aided both the development of increasingly versatile computer-based systems and the growth of the idea that man is a computer of sorts, an information-processing mechanism, an adaptive system.

The dramatic announcement of cybernetics in the 1940s (see below) represented, above all, an expanded programme for systems theory. We should remember that important work had been carried out in this field in the decades before the Second World War (we need only cite the work of such specialists as Roux in Berlin, and Cannon, Hill, and others, working in the United States). Such researchers were already helping to frame — in terms of biology, physics, etc. — the cybernetic principles that would be made explicit after the War. When Cannon (1932) declared that 'the constant conditions which are maintained in the body might be termed *equilibria*' (his italics) and in proposing the word *homeostasis* to denote 'steady states' in the organism, he is already talking cybernetics. It was Norbert Wiener in the 1940s who was to provide the focus for such ideas in their relevance to biological and machine systems.

It is easy to see the gradual evolution of systems theory up to the emergence of the electronic digital computer in the immediate post-war years and its rapid development thereafter. Wiener, fortified by a prodigious mathematical competence and an intimate awareness of machine systems, advertised the notion that machines and living systems could be discussed in the same 'cybernetic' terms: the processes of control and communication could be regarded in the same way for both animate and inanimate systems. Immense impetus was given to the age-old dream that a common discipline could be established for the rigorous discussion of animal and machine systems. This is a central idea in the doctrine of robotic man.

Systems Theory

General systems theory is a set of related rules, definitions, assumptions, propositions, etc. — all of which relate to the behaviour of organizations, of whatever type. Computers are amenable to investigation by systems theory, as are primitive tribal groups, modern corporations, ecological environments, and human beings. Two obvious subsets of systems theory are those dealing with *animate* and *inanimate* systems, but common to both subsets are the general propositions and principles that bear equally on machines and robotic man.

There are many definitions of the word *system*, mediated to a large extent by the subject area in which the definition is expected to operate. So we encounter different definitions of *system* in the fields of mathematics, law, biology, and management. In all areas, however, a system is commonly taken to be a group of interacting elements with relationships amongst them. This implies that the various interacting elements have something in common or they could not affect one another — the number 2 cannot affect a volt. The corollary is that the elements in a system are somehow linked — conceptually or physically — to allow the interaction to occur. So another division of systems theory is apparent: systems can be *conceptual* or *concrete*, with both types of importance to robotic man.

It is often declared that human beings are remarkable in their ability to manipulate symbols, and it is obvious that this facility is intimately associated with the notion of concept formation, the building of abstract systems. At the same time, human beings — as anatomies in a physical environment — are individually a complex hierarchy of systems and subsystems. (Miller also proposed the idea of an 'abstracted system', where relationships can be selected by an observer in the light of specific interest, philosophic bias, prejudice, etc.) It is also apparent that the conceptual or concrete systems are subject to analogous environmental constraints, whether these are interpreted literally or in some metaphorical sense. Consider, for example, how Miller (1978) explores the idea of *space*.

The features of physical space affect the operation of all physical ('concrete') systems. Thus the number of different nucleotide bases in a DNA molecule affects how many bits of information the molecule can carry; people tend to interact more with people who live near them than with people who live far away; the diameter of a fuel line affects the amount of fuel that can flow, and so the logistics of an advancing army. (I owe these examples to Miller.)

It is obvious that physical space is a common constraint on all concrete systems. Moreover scientific researchers exist in physical space and collect all their data in it. Thus Miller notes: 'This is equally true for natural science and behavioural science.' At the same time there are *conceptual* spaces, usually linked to the conceptual systems (already mentioned), that are characteristic of living systems. (We will not digress into the intriguing question as to whether concept formation — which may occur in computers — is a sufficient or necessary condition for living systems.) Thus concepts of social distance, the spectrum of political parties, the distance between opposed opinions (e.g. between supporters and opponents of robotic man) — all are examples of conceptual space.

Here space is a metaphor, a way of conveying the idea of difference or separateness. *Time* can be explored, to some extent, in the same fashion. It has reality as part of the space–time continuum, but a different sort of significance in such symbols as *The Day of the Triffids* and 'nothing has power like an idea whose time has come'. Time, in its physical role, also has links with entropy and information (see below): a system tends to increase in entropy over time, so nicely conforming to the second law of thermodynamics.

The space and time constraints on abstract and physical systems may be regarded as ubiquitous limits, bounds from which no type of system can escape. However the character that these constraints assume are also determined by the type of system in which they apply: e.g. the laws of metallurgy will govern the operation of an internal combustion engine but not the working of the cerebral cortex. Apart from the specific focus of such localized constraints, it is useful to highlight other broad concepts in general systems theory: in particular, those of *process, structure,* and *steady state* (homeostasis, considered later under 'Elements of cybernetics').

It is characteristic of systems that they change over time: they are essentially dynamic enterprises, responsive and adaptable in their typical environments. The notion of change (movement, alteration, evolution, modification, etc.) is intimately associated with the idea of process. Change is commonly achieved by virtue of a process, and change (and the associated processes) can be of many different types. Change can be reversible or irreversible: within a small section of space or time it may appear to run against the second law of thermodynamics; i.e. it may seem that there is a decrease in local entropy. When a broader space–time segment is surveyed, however, it can be seen that change invariably results in an increase in entropy. Change is often identified with process. Thus history, a type of change, is also a process: such life changes as birth, growth, maturation, and dying are obvious processes — as are the (sometimes reversible) changes associated with learning and loving. The concepts of change and process are also linked to the idea of structure. It is hard to imagine change in a physical system without also assuming the correlates of a structural alteration, a new relationship between subsystems and (possibly) the initiation of a new range of processes, leading to further change and further structural modifications.

The idea of change is also associated with the idea of programming, the notion that a process can be accomplished by performing a number of discrete steps, usually in a sequential fashion (see Chapter 5). This suggests the further pregnant possibility that once the character of a program is understood, it is possible to describe in detail the course of change in a system. It can be argued that efforts to interpret human behaviour have not yet been sufficiently influenced by the programming model, one of the most precocious children of the computer age.

Where change occurs in a system by means of programming or via some other mechanism, it is possible to imagine in various ways how structural changes could occur. A building hit by a bomb is structurally altered, as is an impregnated woman or a cancerous brain. If a program achieves new knowledge, the structure of its data base has assumed a new and unprecedented shape. Change in a system involves a degree of structural change determined by the nature of the change and the character of the system. Systems themselves, before being subjected to change, can have many different types of structure. They may have few elements linked in simple relationships (like a manual paper punch) or they may have a complex of subsystems linked hierarchically or in some other complicated fashion.

Hierarchy is a common concept in social systems, relating as it does to rank, status, pecking order, and similar notions. It is even arguable that hierarchy is a natural state of social and biological systems: efforts to establish 'real' democracy often result in a few dominant individuals leading the rest — by one means or another. Miller and others have been quick to recognize that the biological world is an effective hierarchy of systems, beginning with the simple cell at the bottom and finishing with the complex worldwide social order at the top. It is of course possible to be even more fundamental: the cell itself may be regarded as a complex whole (see below) comprising a number of subsystems at various lower levels.

The recognition of hierarchy in a complex system depends in part upon a scrutiny of the various component elements and their modes of interaction. In an army, officers will talk in one way to fellow officers and in another way to ordinary soldiers; a corporate board meeting shows modes of interaction which are rarely evident when a manager addresses his department. Close observation of such disparate activities provides clues for interpreting a complex system in terms of hierarchical concepts.

There may also be structural or functional similarity between the components at a particular level in a hierarchy. Thus all brain cells may be regarded as similar, as are all muscle cells or all liver cells. But a liver may not be thought to resemble a spleen or a kidney. Similarity of structure or function may suggest that components exist at the same level in a hierarchy, but dissimilarity does not necessarily indicate that they do not. There are many advantages in having similar components at the same level in a hierarchy: the strength or competence of a single element — a soldier or a white blood corpuscle — can be magnified in simple numerical proportion to the number of members. There are also advantages in having dissimilar members in a hierarchical level: consider the contribution of different lecturers in a university, of the different parts of a domestic appliance, and of the different organs in the human body. Diversity can mean division of labour and flexibility of response, obvious advantages in a system aiming to survive.

It may be suggested that the structure of a system, whether hierarchically organized or not, is the arrangement of its components and subsystems in space at a given time. This emphasizes that systems are dynamic affairs, constantly shifting and evolving according to ecological pressures. A particular social system may seem 'rigid' or 'firmly based', but it is inevitably undergoing constant change. The broad framework may be sustained but it is likely that the survival strategy is evolving according to economic, technological, financial, and other pressures. The English class system, for example, once unambiguously supported by the established church, can no longer rely on unfailing support from that quarter, and there is greater reliance on the media as a multifaceted device for social control. The components of systems evolve, and so structures are forced to change.

The dynamic character of systems is important to the doctrine of robotic man. We tend to think of robots as boringly repetitive, with well-defined but highly predictable behaviour patterns. It is interesting in this context that robots are becoming more flexible in their responses, more capable of discrimination in a working environment. The seeming unpredictability of man, as one level in a complex hierarchy of life systems (cellular, organic, individual, social, national, etc.), cannot be taken as evidence that he is not a robot. It is easy to see that systems (man, etc.) change *in systematic ways*, according to rules that are characteristic of the systems and the broader hierarchies. Again systematic and lawful change supports rather than undermines the notion of robotic man. A system is no less mechanistic and predictable because it is complex. It is certainly more interesting, but it is no less amenable to robotic interpretation.

The concept of the *changing* system is also linked to the idea of programming (Chapter 5). To say that a system is changing may also be to say that it may be changing its programs. Where a system has changed, its responses to the same stimuli will be different: until it changes again, its behaviour patterns will have settled down into new modes. The programs that govern its performance may be unprecedented, creating the impression that the system is operating *with initiative* or *in a creative way*. However if initiative and creativity are nothing more than obeying new programs, then there is nothing here to threaten the doctrine of robotic man. An anatomy governed solely by programs is clearly, in some sense, a robot. (The programming notion is explored in more detail in Chapter 5.)

Systems theory leads naturally to the notion of cybernetics (see below). The discipline of cybernetics — with its implications for man, machines, and other adaptive systems — was an obvious seed in early systems theory. Today systems theory is often viewed as synonymous with cybernetics; put another way, cybernetics may be regarded as systems theory 'come of age'. Before glancing at some elements of cybernetics, we need to profile one of its key features — information.

Aspects of Information

Information is of central importance to the doctrine of robotic man. It is information that defines the character of change in human and other social systems; it is information that gives significance to programs (of whatever sort), that gives meaning to communication, and that defines the degree of complexity of systems. It is the recognition that man is essentially an information-processing system that has given emphasis to the idea that man is basically a mechanism for computation; i.e. that the various human functions — thought, visual recognition, problem solving, language, mood, emotion, intuition, decision making, etc. — are *computational* activities. The implication is that the specifically human functions, whatever they are, can be modelled (simulated) or duplicated in artificial information-processing systems (computers, robots, etc.). This means that there is a growing family of information-processing organisms — some based on hydrocarbon chemistries, others on silicon circuits. The capacity to collect, process, and disseminate *information* is the link between these various systems. Computer-based systems may evolve into a new life-forms (Simons, 1983, 1985a) and man may be seen as a computer-controlled anatomy, a robot.

There is a popular view of information which, alas, does not always resemble how it is viewed by information specialists. To the specialist, information is a technical communications matter. Here the researcher is interested in *amounts* of information (e.g. what is the information capacity of a communications channel), not in what particular items of information *mean*. Thus the technical view of information is indifferent to semantics where, for example, the electronics of communications is being considered. The semantic view of information entails technicalities of a different sort. It is significant that human beings are interested in the two types of information: viewed quantitatively in communications terms and viewed as an effective mechanism for communicating meanings in the real world.

The idea of complexity — in, for instance, biological or social systems — is intimately related to the quantitative aspect of information. *Amounts* of information help to define the complexity of a DNA molecule, the complexity of the United Nations Organisation, and the complexity of the Andromeda Nebula. 'Amount' is insufficient to define the reality of a system, whether simple or complex. The complexity of the respective DNA molecules in two human beings may be identical, but the two people are likely to be very different. Moreover, there are many practical reasons why a biological organism should be interested in the semantic aspect of information: it is important to be able to recognize food, potential danger, and possible mates. Surviving organisms in the real world therefore have a considerable vested interest in both the quantitative and semantic meanings of information.

One of the consequences of the development of computer science in recent years has been to focus attention on the importance of information to organized systems. This means that the capacity to process information, obviously crucial to computer performance, is also central to the various activities and functions of biological systems, at whatever level (cellular, human, social, etc.). For our purposes, this is a central idea: the notion of man as an information-processing organism is nicely compatible with the interpretation of man as a robot. After all, a robot may be regarded as an anatomy programmed for behaviour in the real world, and this behaviour is invariably accomplished by means of computer-based information processing.

It is important to appreciate the daunting scope of this approach. It implies more than the obvious idea that man *uses* information processing, much in the way that he uses words or oxygen or trace elements. Instead it implies that man is, in his functional aspect (so important for definitions of *Homo sapiens*), nothing more than an information-processing system. Of course the information is processed at different levels and for different purposes; the information is held and processed in different ways. All functions can, it may be argued, be interpreted in terms of the collection, processing, and distribution of information — to control reproduction, birth, growth, maturation, ageing, dying, thinking, feeling, choosing, etc. In this spirit, Lindsay and Norman (1977) have commented: 'We believe our extensions of the area of information processing research show how the scientific analyses of this book [*Human Information Processing*] can help illuminate many *if not all* human phenomena' (my italics).

It is obvious that at one particular fundamental level — biochemistry — organisms are interested in information processing. In recent decades the growing knowledge of genetics (specifically, new insights into the structure of RNA and DNA) has clearly established to specialists and laity alike the importance of biochemistry as an information concept, not only as a chemical affair. The language of servomechanisms and computers suddenly seemed dramatically appropriate in application to the processes discernible at the molecular level. Terms such as *feedback, steady state, control,* and *coding* were quickly adopted by a new generation of biochemists, keen to see how DNA *patterns* could *program* the emergence of the next biological generation. It was recognized that the biological cell, under the control of the DNA molecule, was able to regulate its own internal working according to what were seen to be generalized cybernetic concepts. The concept of the *program*, ubiquitous in all biological functions, was seen to be applicable, with singular significance, to DNA-sponsored activities at the molecular level and subsequently at the cellular level also. For instance, DNA *instructions* are used to supervise the making of protein, essential to robotic man and to all other living systems. The whole of the biological world can be viewed, at one level, as a complex manifestation of DNA-sponsored programs, an information-processing exercise of staggeringly complicated proportions.

It was in 1953 that Francis Crick and James Watson, supported by various co-workers, mapped out the double helix model of DNA. The classic paper in *Nature* began with the remark: 'We wish to suggest a structure for the salt of deoxyribose nucleic acid (DNA). This structure has novel features which are of considerable biological interest.' This much-quoted understatement launched a dramatic new field of enquiry, one that would quickly support the notion that biological systems are concerned, perhaps above all, with the processing of information.

The key element in the new discovery was that the two threads in the double helix are mirror images of one another, each strand containing enough information for the construction of a complementary strand. Crick and Watson were quick to notice that the pairing of the complementary strands 'immediately suggests a possible copying mechanism for the genetic material'. It was soon clear that DNA could copy itself, as well as supplying all the necessary instructions for the building of a new living system. The DNA molecule was variously seen as a template, a blueprint, or a program: in any event it was obvious that it contained information — and in prodigious amounts. Thus DNA was soon regarded as the repository of specifications for every living species: reproduction, growth, and many other life processes were quickly seen to be exercises in information processing. It became possible to define the complexity of an organism by determining the minimum information content of its genetic material. It is reckoned, for example, that a typical DNA molecule in a human being carries about five billion pairs of nucleotides: less complex creatures, not surprisingly, carry smaller quantities of genetic information. One estimate suggests that the Viking landers that arrived at Mars in 1976 carried a few million bits of preprogrammed instructions. Carl Sagan observed in consequence that Viking had slightly more genetic information than a bacterium, but significantly less than an alga. Such a comment advertises the fact that even relatively complex man-made machines are primitive in comparison with the higher animals.

It is now obvious that biochemistry and information processing are intimately connected in all living systems, including man. In this way, life itself can be interpreted as an information-processing phenomenon, with the corollary that evident disorders in life-forms can be interpreted as a coding error, as a mistake in some information-processing program. So we are not surprised when we read of well-known diseases suddenly being related to anomalies in DNA, to aberrant or absent genes. Health in organisms, like life itself, is a programming affair, and the impact of a virus or a bacterium on a formerly healthy organism can similarly be interpreted in ways that depend upon information content (e.g. in the modes of replication of a bacterium).

Information is used by organisms in many different ways and at many different levels. Information storage at the molecular level is the most basic form: from information storage at this level all the higher biological functions flow. The performance of organs in the biological system depends upon how a specification for the growth of a liver or a brain, say, is laid up in the DNA molecule. Once the internal or external receptors start to interpret information in their own characteristic ways they do so in a *species-specific* way, in a way defined by species-specific DNA. We know that the internal receptors stimulate a variety of cybernetic mechanisms to regulate the metabolism of the system, and the receptors — biological devices for collecting and responding to information in various forms — enable the various sensory systems to operate in ways that are essential for the survival of the organism.

The human brain processes information in countless ways, most of which are only partially understood, if at all. Information processing at the cerebral level is related to such activities as sleep regulation, attention giving, decision making, intuitive reasoning, aesthetic response, and falling in love. It may result in movement (flight, eating, copulation, etc.) or in on-going mental activity (imagining, fantasizing, deducing, etc.) where there is no stimulation of the motor system. Much, probably most, of the mental activity is likely to remain unconscious: only a small proportion of information processing at the cerebral level is amenable to introspection — and with what accuracy it is difficult to say. Information processing at the cerebral level is often regarded as nicely analogous to what goes on in the circuits of a digital computer, and it is easy to point to obvious similarities between brains and computers.

Such similarities are of some significance in exploring the doctrine of robotic man. Few people would doubt that the human brain is the most complex organ known, the most complicated biological component. If this impressive device, in which all human claims to uniqueness lie, can be shown to be closely akin to an electronic digital computer, then the doctrine of robotic man is not far behind. In fact there are many surprising resemblances between the electronic artefacts of the computer age and the remarkable organ of which human beings — not blessed by prodigious speed, mighty strength, or insect-like procreative abilities — are so proud.

The neuron 'fires' in a binary fashion, just as the computer uses effective on/off switching in all its information-processing circuits (brains and computers can also make use of analogue functions but in general they enjoy less publicity). There is an intriguing similarity between the physical inputs and outputs of neurons (the axons and dendrites) and the inputs and outputs of logic gates in silicon circuits. We also find analogous modular structuring, with particular sections of brains and circuits assigned to specific functions: neuro-physiologists can identify neuron networks 'dedicated' to particular well-defined cerebral activities. Such phenomena as buffering of information, retrieval from long-term memory, and multiprocessing (where several tasks are performed simultaneously) can be found in both organic brains and the processing circuits of electronic computers. The constraints on organic information processing are analogous to the constraints that bear on the equivalent activities in artificial digital systems. Robotic man is equipped with an information-processing mechanism that is analogous to, though prodigiously more complicated than, the information-processing devices to be found in all current types of non-human robots.

It is obvious that the capacity to process information lies at the existential centre of man: it is this capacity that allows him to think, feel, love, invent, fight, flee, talk, procreate, and sing. 'Man as an anatomy' must be supplemented by the notion of 'man as an information processor'. In fact man is an anatomy built to process information in characteristic ways, in ways that define his membership of the species *Homo sapiens*. It is through information processing that man can be recognized as a human being. All else is secondary, derivative, partial.

The idea of man as an information processor is a strong thread in modern cognitive psychology, an important modern school much influenced by the development of computer science. One very general definition of cognitive psychology (in Mayer, 1981) is that it is 'the scientific analysis of human mental processes and memory structures in order to understand human behaviour'. This does not take us very far, but at least we see a link to the world of the computer (memory structures, concerned with the storage and retrieval of information, are of central importance to modern computer systems). We obtain a fuller picture of cognitive psychology by appreciating some of the trends that have been influential in its development.

In the 1950s the computer was beginning to have a profound effect on many schools of thought — in biology, psychology, philosophy, etc. It was quickly becoming obvious that computers could do many things that had formerly seemed to be the prerogative of human beings (or at least of the more highly evolved biological species). For example, computers could collect data, store it, process it for particular purposes, and make it available when required. In anthropomorphic terms, computers were evolving to *remember, think, feel, decide,* etc. This was a highly stimulating circumstance for many researchers who felt that the traditional psychological models were yielding few adequate research programmes. It was soon recognized that the computer model of the human mind was immensely fertile, suggesting attitudes to enquiry that enabled a whole new spectrum of investigation to be initiated. If, in some sense, man was a computer then the rapid evolution of computers themselves would surely throw light on human mental processes.

A second influence on the newly emerging cognitive psychology was the linguistic work mainly associated with Chomsky (see, for example, his *Syntactic Structures,* 1957). Here efforts were being made to investigate possible structures that were important to the various aspects of language usage: e.g. sentence formulation, comprehension, the creation of a spoken utterance, and the interpretation of words by a hearer. This approach encouraged an enquiry into mental structures, against the prevailing behaviourism that tended to regard the human mind as a 'black box', as essentially unknowable in its interior structures.

The new interest in structures was also supported by the work of Jean Piaget (1954) who focused on how the growth of internal structures and the associated processes could be shown to underlie the developmental changes in human behaviour. It is significant in this context that the biological orientation of Piaget was closely linked to methods of information processing. Hence such trends as the rapidly emerging computer technology, a new and rigorous focus on linguistics, and an epistemological approach to human development were combining to encourage a new psychological orientation that was highly relevant to the doctrine of robotic man. Computers in particular were influencing the philosophic climate in ways that were to have wide-ranging implications for every discipline.

The changing philosophic atmosphere was signalled by many new articles and books in the 1950s and beyond. For instance, a book by Miller, Galanter, and Pribram (1960) emphasized the idea of the *plan*, a behaviour-generating system analogous to the rapidly developing electronic computer. In such a scheme use is made of feedback loops (see below), a common mechanism in cybernetic systems. Subsequent work (for instance, Neisser, 1967) developed further the notion of a general information-processing model for the human mind. Here there is much discussion of memory stores and the associated processes, an approach heavily influenced by computer science. Increasingly it was being recognized that information-processing models could assist in analysing a wide range of mental processes — perceiving, remembering, learning, reasoning, comprehending, etc.

Again it can be stressed that cognitive psychology, perhaps the dominant modern school, is highly sympathetic to the doctrine of robotic man. The central information-processing model states that human beings are processors of information collected by the senses, though the processing is not necessarily *passive*, as was suggested by some of the more simplistic schools of behaviourism. Robotic man is an *active* processor of received information, though we cannot imagine how such activity can be conducted in the absence of 'plans' or 'programs'. (We will discuss further how *active* and *passive* processing may be interpreted in this context — see Chapter 6). We can see that the information-processing model is based directly on an analogy with computers. Human beings, like computers, are engineered to collect information, to process it, and to make it available for retrieval when required.

A central objection to this model of the human mind was that human beings were more than simple processors of information: they also came equipped with attitudes, personalities, feelings, emotions, strivings, and objectives. Perhaps, it was argued, the information-processing model only applied to the human intellect, interested as it was in information in its many aspects. Perhaps a different model was needed to cope with the *conative* (willing and desiring) side of man, and perhaps such a model could supplement or supplant the *cognitive* interest in information processing. The cognitive model showed itself to be remarkably robust. It was suggested, for example, that the information-processing model could be enlarged to cope with such matters as feeling and emotion: a cognitive element in emotion was quickly proposed (see Chapter 7). Perhaps man was also an information processor in his emotional moments, when he was being responsive to music or affection. Robotic man has many talents: we are learning to see that he is a multifaceted phenomenon.

The cognitive model offers more than simple analogy. It also suggests how particular mental processes can be investigated and understood (e.g. how arithmetic is performed). It also indicates how knowledge (verbal knowledge, factual knowledge, etc.) may be structured in the human brain. Here it is interesting to remember how *knowledge representation* is of crucial importance to computer-based 'expert systems', perhaps the largest subclass of artificial intelligence (AI) products in modern technology. Ways of storing and handling knowledge is a central research interest in modern psychology and computer science. The cognitive model also suggests how plans or strategies ('programs') can be developed and implemented by the individual to achieve particular objectives. One common research ploy has been to set people problems and to ask them to describe what they are doing when they set about solving them. This approach, however, is open to the common objection (met before) that only a small proportion of cerebral processing is open to introspection, and personal testimony is notoriously subjective. What *is* particularly useful is the idea that a knowledge of processing structures in computers can give clues for an understanding of cerebral processing networks. This is a pregnant possibility in which robotic man is particularly interested.

The information-processing model is also nicely consistent with many current research programmes in biology, neurophysiology, genetic engineering, etc. One important area, for instance, focuses on how sensory experience can modify the development of the brain or structures within it. The behaviour of neurons in the cortex and elsewhere is immensely sensitive to many different kinds of chemicals; chemotransmitters are essential, along with the generated electrical potentials, for information transfer from cell to cell. Sensory experience can influence the structure and disposition of key chemicals, an obvious circumstance that is relevant to information processing in the brain.

The handling of information in various ways is essential in any cybernetic system (see below). Man is such a system, and it is becoming increasingly possible to describe his nature, to define him, in information-handling terms. Computer-based systems — for example, robots — are also information-handling mechanisms. In such circumstances, it is just one small step to robotic man.

Life as Systems

We have already suggested that life can be interpreted as a systems concept and that this approach may be preferable to viewing living organisms solely as chemical phenomena, as essentially hydrocarbon metabolisms. Before exploring some elements of cybernetics in more detail, it is useful to restate the systems view of life, for it is this hurdle that often proves too high for those observers newly acquainted with robotic man. Once it is recognized that man is not some mystical figment in a divine imagination but a physical system obeying cybernetic and other laws, the route to robotic man is unobstructed and well signposted.

Briefly, systems theory can be effectively applied to organisms (we will see that cells, organs, and organisms nicely exemplify a range of cybernetic features). In one version (Miller, 1978), all living systems in a seven-layer hierarchy are individually composed of nineteen 'critical subsystems' (variously concerned, in a directly physical way, with handling matter, energy, and information). Aspects of the various subsystems can be discussed without reference to hydrocarbon chemistries (though organic chemistry is invariably the substrate of the various subsystems); i.e. the subsystems can be explored in cybernetic terms, in ways that show their kinship with the growing range of computer-based artefacts.

The main advantage, from our point of view, of a systems view of life is that it advertises considerations that apply equally to biological and machine systems. When we see that animals, human beings, computers, robots, and other complex mechanisms are all equally interested in 'feedback', 'steady state' (homeostasis), and adaptation — and also in the all-important provision of plans and strategies ('programs') — we recognize that many traditional distinctions between living and non-living systems cannot be sustained. The 'feeling' computer, a commonplace of fiction, has perhaps not yet arrived upon the scene, but such an entity can clearly be imagined and described — in systems terms (there are human systems for feeling and emotion controlled by the hypothalamus). If this is so, then we need to be more circumspect, more subtle, in drawing distinctions between natural and artificial systems. Perhaps in the future the main difference will be their means of generation (procreation) rather than their existential behaviour in the real world. We may come to find that the living computer is the imperfect reflection of robotic man.

We need to glance at some central cybernetic notions before profiling some key aspects of biological cybernetics. We live in a systems world and we are systems ourselves; we are engineered to behave, as are all the other systems in our environment. The central fact is the complex ecology of systems — which is itself a system.

Elements of Cybernetics

General

The emergence of cybernetics as a new phase in systems theory is associated with the name of the mathematician Norbert Wiener. It is worth giving a brief indication of how *cybernetics* — the word and the topic — broke upon the world.

In the 1930s and 1940s there was growing interest, particularly in America, in the idea of applying some of the principles of engineering to living systems. Immediately after the Second World War, Warren McCulloch at the Massachusetts Institute of Technology decided to organize a meeting of about twenty interested scientists from several disciplines. The conference was entitled *Mechanisms Underlying Purposive Behaviour,* and it was attended by experts in psychiatry, psychology, neurophysiology, sociology, mathematical engineering, and other subjects. The discussions took place on 8 and 9 March 1946 at a hotel in New York. It is recorded (for example, by Steve Heims, 1980) that John von Neumann and Norbert Wiener were the star performers. Von Neumann spoke much about the current state of computer design and Wiener considered 'purposive' behaviour in mechanisms and how feedback and information were crucial to their operation (whether the mechanisms were artefacts or biological systems). The group of experts, after planning to meet regularly, first called itself the Conference for Circular Causal and Feedback Mechanisms in Biological and Social Systems, but Wiener favoured the Greek word *cybernetics* (meaning helmsman), and so the group became known as the Conference on Cybernetics.

Efforts were made to develop mathematical models of nervous systems, but the complexity of biological systems brought great problems. Thus von Neumann remarked that the difficulties 'reside in the exceptional complexity of the human nervous system, and indeed of any nervous system'. At the same time, it was clear that progress could be made. Wiener and others had already developed formal models to describe aspects of communication and control in simple nervous systems, and work on the primitive bacteriophage was attractive to von Neumann, as such organisms, though simple, had the ability to reproduce. Max Delbrück, an expert on bacteriophage, attended one of the meetings of the group but thought that the deliberations were not of immediate relevance to his own work. (It is interesting that later workers, building on the research of Delbrück, were to discover the structure of the DNA molecule and how genetic information was coded.) Norbert Wiener remained the dominant influence at the meetings. (He was later to become involved in the development of cybernetic machines to help the disabled, whereas von Neumann became committed to weapons research.)

Wiener was interested in interpreting physiological data in ways that were relevant both to a theoretical exposition of cybernetic principles and to the practical development of aids for the crippled, the blind, and the deaf. He is worth quoting:

...why can an artificial hand not feel? It is easy to put pressure gauges into the artificial fingers, and these can communicate electric impulses to a suitable circuit. This can in turn activate devices acting on the living skin.... Thereby we can produce a vicarious sense of touch, and we may learn to use this.... Moreover there are still sensory kinesthetic elements in the mutilated muscles, and these can be turned to good account.

This is a good illustration of how Norbert Wiener was one of the leading heralds of robotic man. It is recognized that there is continuity between machine and biological systems, that engineering — viewed in a particular way — is equally relevant to both.

His work on medical technology began in 1947, and one of his aims was to develop ways of building artificial limbs to replace lost arms and legs. In 1962 he was hospitalized after a fall, and his work gained a new impetus! The hospital discussions led to collaboration between orthopaedic surgeons, neurologists and engineers to develop a limb prosthetic device, eventually dubbed the 'Boston arm'. Wiener remained devoted to the idea that technology should be used to help people rather than to destroy them by producing ever more powerful weapons.

In 1948 he published the seminal work, *Cybernetics: Control and Communication in the Animal and the Machine*. The basic idea was that a level exists at which animals and machines can be explored by a common theory, and it is precisely in connection with control and communication functions that this can be done. It had long been obvious to Wiener and his co-workers that this approach had far-ranging implications. Communication, in both its popular and technical aspects, is intimately linked to the notion of information handling, and so relates directly to the cognitive model of human mental processes. Cybernetics, with its biological and engineering connections, was able to give real substance to the systems theory approach to analysing human beings as functional automata. Wiener's status as a profound humanist at least suggests that there is nothing demeaning in the doctrine of robotic man. Human beings *may* be controlled by electrical pulses in complex nervous systems, but, Wiener would have declared, people are still worth caring about. People are cybernetic systems and human beings at the same time.

The new cybernetics represented an updated biological materialism. It was not sufficient to attempt to explain biological phenomena solely in terms of physics and chemistry: they had to be supplemented by appropriate doses of systems theory. It was still obvious that biological organisms were physical entities functioning in the real world — there was no need for 'spirit' or 'soul' — but they could only be fully understood, if at all, by appreciating the growing spectrum of cybernetic ideas. These related to such notions as homeostasis, adaptation, feedback, and purpose.

Homeostasis and Adaptation

A common cybernetic feature of systems is that they are constantly striving after a 'steady state', a condition of equilibrium or homeostasis. This applies to the biological cell as it applies to the steam engine or the modern electronic digital computer. The idea of homeostasis, achieved via a range of feedback mechanisms, is a commonplace of electrical and mechanical engineering. It is a further sign of the *engineered* character of biological systems that they lend themselves to interpretation, at many different levels, in terms of homeostasis.

Cybernetic ideas, as an extension of classical systems theory, were beginning to gain attention in the late 1930s. Wiener himself attended a multidisciplinary meeting at Harvard at that time and was aware that a common theory could develop to apply equally to biological and mechanical systems. In 1940 Ross Ashby, a British mathematician, built an electronic circuit that he decided to call the 'homeostat'. The circuit was contained in a box fitted with various rotary switches and indicator dials: the switches were used to set the voltages at various input points and the dials showed the voltages at various other specific points within the circuit. The key feature of the homeostat was that, no matter what voltages were input to the circuit, the dials quickly registered their original readings. In other words, the Homeostat could maintain a 'steady state', even if the environmental circumstances — i.e. the voltages across the inputs — were to change unpredictably. Occasionally — when, for example, many of the input voltages were suddenly changed — the internal voltages would quickly establish a new steady-state setting from which it would be difficult to shift them. It seemed that the circuit had some sort of internal autonomy, being able to maintain an internal stability no matter — within limits — how the external conditions were to vary.

Ashby himself compared the homeostat to a large, lazy dog lying in front of the fire. A small external stimulus would cause the dog to twitch and then settle back; if the fire became too hot, the dog would move its position, then lie down and establish a fresh condition of inertia. It seemed that the homeostat had demonstrated that a relatively simple electrical circuit, like some earlier mechanical systems, could behave with a purposive single-mindedness that is usually taken as characteristic of biological organisms.

Some years later, W. Grey Walter, another British researcher, added mobility to Ashby's homeostatic concept. Walter designed small mobile machines that would instinctively roll towards any light — unless the light was too bright, when the mechancial 'tortoises' would resort to flight. In the absence of any light, the machines would adopt a 'searching' mode, wandering around until a light was encountered. This seemed to suggest that a simple machine could even be induced to behave like an insect or other small animal. The 'Hopkins beast', developed at John Hopkins University in the early 1960s, was another small mobile system capable of purposeful behaviour. It could even search for an electric socket on the wall, plug itself in, quietly 'feeding' until its batteries were charged, after which it would retract its plug and continue its task of exploring the terrain. In such a fashion, the steady state of a well-topped-up battery could be maintained.

The notion of homeostasis is seen to be relevant in many different disciplines. It is evident in much psychiatric theory, in sociology, in computer science, and in all the traditional engineering disciplines. In the middle of the nineteenth century it was known that the human body was required to maintain an effective self-regulated internal steady state, though the word *homeostasis* was first used by Cannon in the 1920s. Steven Rose (1973) has depicted biological homeostasis as a 'continuous, second-by-second balancing act performed by the organism', a task achieved in part by the body's hormonal system and in part by the nervous system. For example, the regulation of heartbeat is controlled both by adrenalin and by parts of the autonomic nervous system. This dual control is characteristic of many functions in the human being: the brain itself, for instance, relies both on chemistry and electrical potentials for its many control and communication functions. It is thought that there are many homeostatic control centres in the brain's hypothalamus.

The interest of systems in maintaining a homeostatic state does not preclude the possibility of change. A system may maintain an evident steady state over any small time slot, but if the system is examined again after some lengthy period it may be found to have modified behavioural responses. Structures, processes, and programs can be subject to gradual (or abrupt) alteration, leading to a progressively shifting homeostasis. We may assume that such a condition is required for systems evolution in any field (e.g. the gradual emergence of millions of biological species — at any one moment an individual organism has an interest in homeostasis, but through the processes of maturing and ageing, and the long procession of generations, countless steady states are progressively established).

Some systems may not be good candidates for evolutionary change: they may establish a rigid homeostasis from which they cannot be shifted. If such a system is well adapted to a stable environment it is likely to survive; otherwise, lacking adaptive potential — like the homeostat swinging to a new stable state — it will tend to perish. A system that established a fixed stable state, or one that goes on repeating itself, has been called a 'terminating' system (Waddington, 1977); if systems can adapt and change they may be dubbed 'progressive'.

Typical terminating systems are those that maintain the carbon dioxide level in the blood or the temperature in a room. In both these examples, physical parameters are maintained at constant values for particular purposes. Regular and constant oscillations — e.g. in the electronic multivibrator — may also signal a terminating system, when a 'terminal' state has been reached from which the system, left to its own devices, will not budge. At the same time, from the points of view of learning and evolutionary change, there is an obvious sense in which human beings and human society are 'progressive' systems. There is no assumed premise that robotic man establish a fixed homeostasis from which he cannot move.

Homeostasis, having terminating or progressive features, is a characteristic of all cybernetic systems. In particular (for our purposes), it is well known to biologists, neurophysiologists, and information scientists. K. H. Pribram (1967), for instance, has written about sensory servomechanisms and homeostatic servoprocesses in other biological contexts. It is suggested that sensory experiences involve the establishment of set-points against which unusual information can be matched. Thus Pribram observes: 'Indeed, the retina provides a model which shows just how apt this extension of homeostat theory is.'

It is the general applicability of such notions as homeostasis and adaptation that renders cybernetics such a powerful tool in the analysis and interpretation of systems. All cybernetic systems are in some sense interested in survival, and this is signalled in part by their 'attitudes' to homeostasis. The biological cell, for example, exists in a precarious balance (see below). If it does not maintain its internal processes of construction in a controlled way, it will quickly die. It needs to maintain its own elaborate homeostasis around a complex of notional set-points, and so does the organism as a whole, if cell and organism are to survive. This is achieved, when the attempt is successful, by various ploys and strategies.

In particular, use is made of feedback mechanisms: data are collected about the internal and external environments, and then appropriate system adjustments are made to maximize the chances of survival. Thus cybernetic systems — biological and machine — may be seen as self-regulating systems that aim to adapt by means of feedback controls. The phenomenon of feedback is increasingly evident in biological research and computer design. It is the mechanistic agency, exploited in many ways by robotic man, that enables stable systems to survive, adapt, and evolve.

Feedback

Feedback, as an information transfer concept, has existed in biological systems for millions of years, and as a feature in artefacts for a few hundred (though it can also be detected in some of the toy-like automata of the Ancient World). We have seen that it is associated with the notion of control in machines and animals. Some controlled machines are not regulated by feedback. They may be controlled by human beings or animals, and may lack any element of self-regulation, of autonomy.

It is obvious that the notion of self-controlled machines predates the electronic computer by many years. The Watt steam engine controlled by a governor was invented a couple of centuries ago, and since that time many man-made systems — factory machines, telephone systems, chemical plant, etc. — were able to function with an element of self-regulation. Sometimes *human* control had to be power-assisted, as with the control of a ship's helm. In such circumstances the human being assessed how the ship should be steered, but 'dedicated' motors provided the necessary force: a person provided the intelligence input, a machine the power input. Eventually it was realized that using feedback of information in a 'loop' would enable certain types of machines to provide their own necessary control, to be self-regulating.

It was recognized that there was an important relationship between the effective controller and the parts of the system that needed to be controlled. Useful control cannot be achieved simply by feeding a continuous stream of predetermined instructions to an element in a system. The instructions have to take into account the features of a changing scene: a changed factor may require new instructions — the controller has to know what is happening in order to issue instructions that will achieve a desired result. So the controller has to have information about the process as it is operating. The supply of information from the process to the controller is the 'feedback' used to close the control 'loop'. It may be, for example, that a process or operation is working in some erroneous way. Here the information received by the controller will enable the actual effect of the instruction to be compared with the intended effect. This is an example of 'negative' feedback.

The amount of feedback information that is supplied must be of the right amount if the system operation is to be regulated for optimum results. Too much feedback can be catastrophic, leading in some cases to wild oscillations in systems behaviour (this may be relevant to the behaviour of hooligans and psychotics). Where (negative) feedback is being supplied in the correct amount, effective system regulation can be achieved. Negative feedback may be seen as a restraining influence, ensuring that things do not get out of hand. A thermostat operates to bring a high temperature down: it may, for example, shut down a central heating system until a predetermined set-point temperature has been reached. In fact biologists have found it useful to distinguish between two types of negative feedback.

In one type, information is fed back to 'throttle down' a part of a process. This is seen as a relatively mild form of negative feedback (it is sometimes called 'end-product inhibition'). More drastically, negative feedback can be used to stop a particular subprocess in the loop. Here the output is not simply diminished but blocked altogether. When some predefined parameter has reached the set-point, the blocking feedback is lifted and the process runs into full operation once more. It is of course possible to build up the effect of 'end-product inhibition' until the process is totally arrested ('end-product repression'), and so the two types of negative feedback can operate in conjunction.

By contrast, *positive* feedback is a reinforcing action. It encourages a greater output, a more energetic response. It may be that, through error, one type of feedback is applied where the other was intended. This is particularly noticeable in altercations between human beings. Someone wishing to discourage action of a certain type in another may remonstrate in a way that is provocative; i.e. positive feedback has been applied where negative feedback would have been more likely to achieve the objective. Cybernetic principles can be relevant to the conduct of human relationships (see Chapter 9).

All servomechanisms using closed-loop control exhibit the same types of cybernetic properties. This is true whether the servo-mechanism is the Watt governor (relying on the centrifugal effect on two heavy spheres as a shaft rotates, causing them to swing out and reduce the power going to an engine), an electronic system (using an output voltage to control the input to a circuit), or a subsection of the human hypothalamus (where excessive hormone concentration is detected and used to discourage further hormone production). It is possible to exploit the various cybernetic principles in the design of non-human robots. For example, a simple feedback control system can be used on the various joints of a robot.

In this case a 'transducer' is employed to sense a required condition (position, velocity, proximity, etc.), whereupon the sensed information is translated into a form that can be used by the associated servomechanism. An 'error signal' is then produced by comparing the feedback signal with an input signal (defining the required position). Then the error signal is used, after amplification, to drive the robot actuator system. We may assume that this process is an accurate model of the many control functions that take place in the day-to-day activities of robotic man.

Norbert Wiener was keen to show that the control characteristics of the traditional servomechanism could also be identified in biological systems. There were several reasons why this was an attractive idea. For a start, it helped to set biological organisms in the realm of practical science: there was no confusion about metaphysics, no need to import gap-filling 'souls' or 'spirits'. Also it suggested that the rigorous formalisms developed for physics and engineering would become applicable to biological processes. There was the tantalizing prospect of a new mathematical biology.

Again it was inevitable that the newly emerging computers would serve as the supreme examples of artefacts that could be described in terms of such cybernetic concepts as information, control, self-regulation, feedback, loops, programs, instructions, etc. It seemed increasingly reasonable to interpret man in cybernetic terms and with reference to the computer model. Robotic man was waiting in the wings.

Hence cybernetics — using such notions as homeostasis and feedback — had made it possible to interpret man within the framework of an enhanced materialism. We had learned to accept that man was an animal; some of us had suspected that man was a machine; now we were discovering that man was a system. 'Man as animal' said something about origins and evolution, as well as about human nature, but when 'man as machine' was added to 'man as system', robotic man was the inevitable outcome. It is easy to see that robotic man is nicely analogous to a non-human robot controlled by an electronic computer. However the analogy alone was never sufficient to establish the credentials of 'man as robot'. It was necessary to reinforce the easy analogy with evidence for a specific cybernetics of biology.

Biological Cybernetics

General

We have seen that a systems view of life-forms can be found in various modern writers (for example, Miller, 1978; and Riedl, 1978). Jacques Monod (1970), who won the Nobel Prize for elucidating the replication mechanism of genetic material and how cells synthesize protein, is keen to talk about 'chemical machinery' and 'cellular cybernetics'. We learn that various control operations are handled by specialized proteins that function as detectors and transducers of chemical information. These regulatory proteins (the best known are the 'allosteric' enzymes) can recognize other substances and influence their conversion into new products. Various regulatory patterns are recognized: e.g. feedback inhibition and feedback activation (closely analogous to negative and positive feedback). Other forms of activation are described, and these can be identified with various cybernetic features. There is also the exploitation of cybernetic principles in the regulation of metabolic pathways.

Some metabolic pathways, the sequences of metabolic changes, can 'branch', i.e. select one route or another according to various controlling factors. Thus Monod states: '... not only are the initial reactions, at the metabolic fork, regulated by retroactive inhibition, but an earlier reaction, higher up on the common branch, is co-governed by the two (or several) final metabolites'. What this means is that cybernetic processes are encapsulated in biology at the level of metabolic reactions: the most fundamental sequences of chemical change are subject to the same principles that govern the operation of the Watt governor or the functioning of a modern supercomputer. What we find with simple metabolic reactions, we will also find with cells, organs, and organisms. The biological world, itself a cybernetic system at one level, is also a complex hierarchy of cybernetic systems.

Some systems theorists (for example, Sommerhoff, 1969) have recognized goal-directedness (purposiveness) as the distinctive character of the behaviour of the higher organisms. The task then is to show how this seemingly teleological functioning can be explained in systems terms. How can a system, governed by rules, have a purpose 'in mind'? It may even be that *purpose* necessarily demands a cybernetic explanation. Perhaps purpose is the homeostasis sought by a restless system. In fact there is no doubt that Ashby's homeostat and

Walter's 'tortoises' acted with evident purpose. Purpose, too, when detected in biological systems, is manifestly a cybernetic phenomenon.

Sommerhoff and others have recognized that a goal-directed activity is characteristic of animals. Moreover 'we are dealing here with an objective system-property — a property ... which we can assume to be compatible with the basic laws of physics and chemistry'. Sommerhoff declares: 'We can assume this because we know of servo-mechanisms and automata that are *capable of essentially similar types of behaviour*' (my italics). He sees a close analogy between, on the one hand, a chick pecking at a grain, a rabbit digging a burrow, a pike chasing prey, a bee homing in on its hive, and, on the other hand, the types of purposeful activities that can be seen in many examples of automatic control 'in industry, aircraft, guided missiles, etc.'. There is cybernetic continuity between machine systems and the biological world.

At the same time there are difficulties in transferring engineering concepts, without any adjustment, into the areas of the biological world. The broad cybernetic categories are common (such as feedback, information handling, and homeostasis), but specific notional entities (e.g. error signal) may be less than self-evident in biological systems. Part of the problem is the complexity of organisms: we see a hierarchy of systems, each of which is essential to the functioning of the whole. Where hierarchies exist in purely mechanical or electrical artefacts they are simple in comparison with the biological equivalents.

We have seen that cybernetics is evident at the level of metabolic chemistry, and that purpose can be interpreted in cybernetic terms. It remains to profile aspects of systems performance at higher biological levels (cell, organ, and organism) before glancing at aspects of control in non-human robots.

Cells

We have mentioned the interest shown by Jacques Monod in the cybernetic regulation of metabolic pathways. It is worth highlighting how this activity is directly relevant to the control of cell performance. In some important ways the cybernetics of cell performance is synonymous with the cybernetics of metabolic chemistry, a circumstance that allowed aspects of cell regulation to be explained and that suggested further research programmes in biochemistry.

During the first half of this century there was much interest in how cells regulated themselves. For example, if cells had a copious supply of food, what would prevent them running at high speed to the point of destruction? It was acknowledged that the selective cell membrane provided part of the answer, but there was also some evidence of an extremely fine regulation of metabolism that could not be explained by any careful scrutiny of cellular membrane. It was around 1960 when Jacques Monod with François Jacob and Andre Lwoff provided an adequate explanation of cellular regulation.

Experiments were conducted using mutant bacteria with a blocked enzyme reaction, in circumstances where such a block would normally cause the previous metabolite in the reaction pathway to proliferate. If the end-product of the pathway was added to excess then the intermediary failed to accumulate. It was found that the end-product, via a feedback mechanism, was blocking the action of previous enzymes in the sequence. This is the technique used in a wide range of normal cells (in plants and animals, as well as bacteria) to prevent a metabolic pathway from overproducing. This is directly analogous, again, to how the Watt governor retards the steam engine when it begins to run too fast. The technique is one of several ways in which the inappropriate output from a metabolic pathway is used to inhibit the metabolic activity.

Jacques Monod and his colleagues succeeded in showing that the genes are regulated and in turn control the synthesis of various proteins (including enzymes). This successful work, which earned the Frenchmen the Nobel award, has led to further research into cell regulation. Although much of this work has focused on microbes (mainly bacteria and viruses), it is now known that essentially similar mechanisms are used to control enzyme reactions in the cells of human beings and other animals. It is at least a possibility that inadequate cybernetic control at the cellular level is responsible for many forms of cancer: cell regulation has broken down and the cells behave in a wild and unrestrained manner. (A breakdown in cellular regulation can be turned to industrial advantage in, for example, producing fermentations and in organizing other allied processes.) In the main, however, such work has demonstrated that cellular behaviour is a cybernetic matter.

The cell is a system containing subsystems. In the Miller scenario there are nineteen critical subsystems in all the living systems in the seven-layer hierarchy: the cell is one such living system. Here it is reckoned that the subsystems and components of cells are organelles and sets of organelles, each comprising a number of molecules. For example, DNA and RNA are nucleic acids found in all cells, and these are large molecules in which information is expressed according to the order of regularly spaced nucleotide bases. 'Templates' or 'instruction sets' to aid the generation of an enzyme or other proteins are called *cistrons*. Again it is worth emphasizing the use of *regulators* which, using feedback mechanisms, control the generation of specific molecules according to the needs of the cell.

As a respectable cybernetic system, the cell is interested in processing matter-energy and information. Miller (1978) lists eight subsystems that are concerned with processing matter-energy: these are variously concerned with ingesting food, distributing it round the cellular system, converting it (e.g. using enzymes), storing it (as starch, glucose, etc.), and extruding it as waste products. Nine subsystems are involved in processing information in various ways. For example, use is made of light-sensitive pigments in receptor cells; information decoding can take place in ribosomal molecules; regulator genes and operon are involved in decision making; and various cellular elements (membrane, synaptic vesicle, etc.) function as output trans- ducers. The cell, like living systems at every level, is interested in imposing patterns on matter and energy by means of information templates and codes. Again it is worth emphasizing the cybernetic character of these circumstances.

Organs

These can be represented as the subsystems of animals and plants, and in turn organs can be seen to have their own subsystems. As with systems at the cellular level, organs are involved in processing matter- energy and information.

Food and other necessary chemicals are ingested via the input artery or the lymphatic vessel of the organ, and use is also made of such mechanisms as the capillaries in the walls of the intestine and other sections of the gastrointestinal tract. After ingestion, distribution takes place by means of blood vessels, intercellular fluids, and various organic ducts. Specific cells can be active in converting the ingested and distributed chemicals according to the needs of the organ, and waste products can be extruded via lymphatic output vessels, ducts, and other apertures, and by means of glandular drainage. As with matter-energy, information can be collected, processed, and distributed according to organic requirements.

Receptor cells can respond to hormones and other chemical compounds entering the organs, and neurons can carry information (structured in chemotransmitters or electrical potentials) into the organ. Dedicated cells can be used as internal transducers or decoders of information. Output transducers are represented by the presynaptic regions of output neurons from a visceral to a neural organ (or from one neural organ to another) and also, for example, by cells that can synthesize and output hormones. The organ, functioning both as a subsystem and system, uses feedback mechanisms, information processing, and other cybernetic devices to establish a homeostasis appropriate to its optimum performance. This strategy can only be implemented within certain operational limits: excessive alcohol intake will make it impossible for a liver or a brain to achieve an optimum homeostasis, just as smoking will defeat the cybernetic talents of a lung.

It is interesting that Miller does not chronicle his organic subsystems solely in terms of naturally occurring structures and processes. Thus he recognizes intravenous injection equipment as an element in the subsystem (ingestor) that processes matter-energy. Similarly, a renal dialysis machine is seen as contributing — as a subsystem component — to the extruder (the subsystem interested in discharging waste products). Similarly, input transducers for processing information include such components as the corrective lens and the hearing aid (effective prostheses for the pathological eye or ear) and the magnifying glass, microscope, and telescope (prostheses for the normal eye). The electrical pacemaker (an affective prosthesis for the pathological heart) is seen as a component in the Miller *decider*, one of the seven organic subsystems concerned with processing information.

This decision to regard *artefacts* as legitimate components of *organic* subsystems again emphasizes the continuity, at least in systems terms, between artificial and natural mechanisms. All are engineered facilities designed to secure system survival in a changing environment. The heart pacemaker and the lymph network subscribe equally to the goal-directed behaviour that can be discerned in the functional cybernetic system.

Organisms

These again can be seen as both systems and subsystems in the hierarchy of living organizations. The organisms — man, monkey, oak tree, fish, insect, coelenterate hydroid, slime molds, etc. — are subsystems of their societies, and systems in their own right with respective subsystems for processing matter-energy and information in characteristic ways.

Ingestion of nutriments is accomplished by such mechanisms as the filaments in fungi, root tips in plants, and such structures as mouths, gills, nostrils, etc. Veins in leaves and the blood system in zoological species cause ingested materials to be distributed, and the teeth, salivary glands, liver, gall-bladder, pancreas, small intestine, etc., are involved in the conversion process. Matter-energy can be stored in various ways — as every slimmer knows — and materials can be extruded, not always as waste but sometimes to some specific purpose (consider, for example, the uses of musk glands, poison glands, mammary glands, etc.).

The subsystems involved in information processing are often highly complex at the level of the organism. For example, the input transducers include all the sophisticated sensory equipment of the higher mammals, and immensely complicated information decoding takes place in the central nervous system (see 'The cybernetic brain', below). Decoding can also take place in various subsystem components peripheral to the central nervous system (e.g. in the retinal bipolar and ganglion cells). Similarly the 'decider' and output transducer exploit complex chemical and electrical phenomena to process information in many different ways, most of which are poorly understood, if at all.

Again there is the intriguing reference to artefacts as representing components of the subsystems at the level of organisms. So a stomach tube or a syringe may be seen as elements in the ingestor subsystem; the enema and douche as elements in the extruder subsystem; and the calculator and computer as components in the Miller decider. This manifest continuity between artificial and natural systems is a useful context for robotic man, a framework in which to interpret his nature and his future. If the subsystems of the organism can include artefacts, then there is an important functional identity between the various contributing components. In systems terms, the computer has as much claim to be regarded as part of a decider system as does the human brain.

We can see that robotic man corrects or extends himself by using prostheses as adjuncts to his physical or mental powers (e.g. such devices as spectacles, cars, radio transmitters, pacemakers, artificial limbs, cyclotrons, computers, etc.). There is abundant scope here for charting the future development of robotic man — a functional organism comprising both natural components (the hydrocarbon-based organs) and artificial elements (the growing spectrum of prosthetic artefacts). We can speculate, in such an evolutionary scenario, on the extent to which artificial components will encroach on natural components in human beings. Will *Machina sapiens* supplant *Homo sapiens*?

It is clear that cybernetic principles operate at all levels of robotic man: e.g. at the levels of cellular metabolic chemistry, at the level of organs, and at the level of the organism. It is also evident that because organic systems are amenable to interpretation in cybernetic terms, it is possible to enhance human scope by means of a range of prosthetic devices. The various biological cybernetic systems — respiration, control of body temperature, maintenance of blood flow, maintenance of tissues, control of nutrient supply, hormonal control (via such glands as the adrenal, the thyroid, the parathyroid, and the pituitary), etc. — are essential for the survival of robotic man. Many less complicated organisms are equally adept — perhaps *more* adept — at survival. What makes man interesting is his complexity — and this is largely signalled by the elaborate structure of his cerebral cortex. The human brain is the most complicated organ of robotic man, the singular device that equips him with all his talents and which, interestingly enough, seduces many human beings into thinking that they are more than anatomies programmed for performance, that they are more than robots! Again we need to glance at the human brain.

The Cybernetic Brain

The brain in mammals (including human beings) and other animals uses a range of cybernetic principles to control chemical and electrical functions. This is done to regulate the distribution and processing of information, whether conveyed via hormonal messengers or electrical potentials generated by the movement of ions. In terms of its electrical performance the mammalian brain is closely analogous to the working of an electronic digital computer. Both brain and computer can be discussed in terms of neutral principles (mainly cybernetic) that apply to all types of information processors.

Information is taken into the system and operated upon by a processor (e.g. the central processing unit, CPU, in a computer; the cerebral cortex in a brain). The processor is used to discriminate between items of incoming information, to perform the necessary decoding tasks (to interpret sensory and other data), and to retrieve information from memory as necessary. Specific sets of instructions can be stored as hard-wired circuits in the brain (or as silicon circuit networks in a computer); these sets are effective subroutines that can be called up when required for familiar tasks (e.g. constructing a sentence, performing a typical computation). In some circumstances it is possible for a processor to operate on the subroutines (and on other programs). Brain modification of this sort can form the basis of learning: a primitive program may be modified or discarded (supplanted by another) so that the system as a whole may be capable of fresh skills. Stored information can be drawn on by various brain sub-systems and interpreted differently according to their specific needs.

The brain processors can be involved with several tasks at the same time, by virtue of such strategies as time sharing and parallel processing (this latter is a popular approach in the design of new-generation computer systems). It is of course essential for the brain to be capable of multiple processing — controlling many different operations at any one moment (some of us need to be able to hit a squash ball and maintain our balance at the same time). Our processor may switch to other tasks if it is underemployed on its main activity, or several processors may be required to work simultaneously in different parts of the brain. Parallel processing of this sort is a common feature of most biological brains. At all times the transmission and conversion of information is closely controlled, regulated by the well-defined instructions that are laid up in the neural circuits.

The organization of human memory has been shown to be important for the processing of natural language, as it is important for comprehension in general. There is now widespread recognition that the broad class of cognitive functions will eventually be explicable in terms of brain organization and structure. It has long been hoped that automata theory would provide clues for an understanding of the classical epistemological problems (such as perception, learning, and information recall). Leibniz envisaged a logical calculus that would answer all such philosophic disputes. With such a system there would be no need for argument between two philosophers: 'For it would suffice to take their pencils in their hands, to sit down to their slates, and to say to each other (with a friend as witness, if they like): Let us calculate.' In this way, 'we should be able to reason in metaphysics and morals in much the same way as in geometry and analysis', a notion that manifestly underwrites the idea that robotic man — governed as he is by the various logics of information processing — is nonetheless a creature capable of ethical commitment and aesthetic insight.

It is easy to see the information-handling similarities between brains and computers. The early computers were dubbed 'electronic brains', and by 1971, Earl Hunt could ask: 'What kind of computer is man?' Recognizing the obvious similarities between brains and computers, at least in their information-processing capabilities, he resolved to describe a computer system that 'thinks like a man'. It has been remarked many times that neurons, like silicon circuit logic gates, transmit electrical pulses in an intelligent fashion. However the electrical activity of the brain is only half the story. The cybernetic brain is also interested in chemistry — in particular, the chemistry of the hormones. Chemical information processing, in conjunction with the systematic regulation of electrical potentials, is a substantial element in the functional control of robotic man.

To a large extent the human body is a self-regulatory system: it is via this capability that it claims its cybernetic credentials. It is essential, for example, that the environment of the cell be maintained within very narrow limits (mammalian cells are less adaptable than bacteria and viruses). This is important for the day-to-day functioning of cells and organs if they are to sustain the life of the organism. It is also necessary for new phases in the organism's life to be signalled in some way: for this purpose chemical messengers can be hired to indicate when an organism should embark upon growth, maturation, ageing, and death (dying, too, we may assume, is a programmed phase written into the structure of the genes). Much of this regulation, control, and signalling is provided by the hormonal system of the body.

The glands — effective chemical factories — are used to regulate a wide range of bodily functions. The pancreas secretes insulin and glucagon to control the amount of circulating glucose in the bloodstream; the metabolic rate of the organism is controlled by secretions (of thyroxin) from the thyroid gland; urinary excretions and other functions are regulated by the parathyroids; and the pituitary gland is involved in supervision of the female menstrual cycle and many other activities, not least the operation of other glands.

Much of this hormonal control is manifestly a cybernetic matter: for instance, feedback mechanisms are invariably involved in controlling the amount of glandular activity. Cybernetic control can regulate chemical and electrical activity at the same time. Again it is convenient to cite the pituitary gland, sited in the brain and serving as a master controller of hormonal activity. For example, the pituitary controls the thyroid gland by means of various feedback mechanisms. When the amount of thyroxin in the bloodstream falls, the pituitary secretes more hormones to stimulate thyroid activity; the level of thyroid-stimulating hormone diminishes as the thyroxin level in the blood-stream increases. The pituitary, as a part of the brain, is controlled by it. There are, for example, various connections between the pituitary and the hypothalamus, an important section of the brain used to control many of the homeostatic operations in the body.

The hypothalamus, in conjunction with other parts of the brain (amygdala, hippocampus, etc.), is concerned with the regulation of hormonal activity that bears on various bodily functions, including emotion. Some hypothalamic neurons have axons which terminate in the pituitary; these neurons generate substances that are closely related to two pituitary hormones — oxytocin (which causes uterine contractions and lactation) and vasopressin (which controls the amount of water in the tissue and water excretion via the kidneys). It is thought that the manufacture of these hormones effectively begins in the hypothalamic neurons. In fact damage in the hypothalamus can cause a form of diabetes in which vast quantities of water are consumed and excreted.

Some hypothalamic neurons manufacture substances that are released into the bloodstream which circulates through the pituitary, so causing the generation of further hormones. In this way further control is exercised over bodily functions: e.g. the generation of thyroxin (mentioned earlier). It has been suggested, following substantial research, that the hypothalamus is concerned with such bodily operations as temperature control, hunger and thirst, rage, aggression, and fear. Those sceptics who doubt that emotions can be brought within the cybernetic framework of robotic man would be well advised to consider the regulatory functions of the hypothalamus.

The interpretation of the brain as a cybernetic system is consistent with attempts to draw an analogy between the brain and computer, and the power of this analogy has been felt in many disciplines. We see its impact in such fields as linguistics and automata theory (see, for example, Sampson, 1975; Alexsander, 1977) and in virtually all the modern efforts to show that man is a machine. The development of computers over recent decades has given immense support to the doctrine of robotic man.

Robots and Control

There are two great classes of robots functioning upon the earth. One is the class of robotic man (and other biological automata); the other is the class of robotic artefacts, the rapidly expanding group of artificial (increasingly intelligent) machines working in factories, hospitals, schools, power stations, libraries, and elsewhere. We have glanced at biological cybernetics. To show the continuity between natural systems and artefacts it is helpful to indicate some features of cybernetic control in artificial systems.

We would expect non-human robots to use feedback and other control mechanisms, much as do their biological counterparts. In fact biological systems often use *analogue* feedback, where physical quantities are compared and transmitted round a system. Non-human robots tend to use *digital* feedback, where binary (on/off) pulses are employed. This is partly because of the prevalence of electronic digital computers (analogue computers have traditionally competed in some areas of engineering control), because they tend to be highly reliable, accurate, relatively cheap, and tolerant to noise. With digital feedback, the position of a robot arm, for example, is represented by a pattern of electrical pulses; these are fed to a digital comparator which is also fed with a set-point signal. The resulting error signal, again in the form of digital pulses, is used to shift the robot arm to the required position.

It is common for the servomechanisms used to control robot limbs to be activated by analogue voltages — in which case there is a requirement for digital-to-analogue converters. A pulsed error signal can thus be converted into an analogue voltage that can be used to drive a robot actuator. Where feedback control circuits are available to regulate such parameters as position and velocity, robot arms (and other moving parts) can be controlled for near-optimum performance.

Transducers are used by robots to convert information in one form into another (the digital-to-analogue converter is one species of transducer among many). Some transducers derive their mobilizing energy from the system being measured; others require a separate power source. In some cases transducers are characterized by their physical form (*rotary* or *linear*) or by their measurement technique (digital, analogue, absolute, incremental, etc.). Linear transducers (often used with cartesian-type robots), for example, carry a scale with gradations: when a sensitive optical or magnetic reading head passes over the scale, the head emits a pulse each time a line is detected, so that the displacement of the transducer head can be determined. In optical systems a lined transparent window is passed over a scale with identical markings. With the lines set an angle to the markings, a Moiré fringe interference pattern is created, causing the illusion of dark bands moving a large distance each time there is a slight displacement of the window. Optical techniques can then be used to count the bands to establish position (or other physical) data. Direction of travel can be ascertained by using two sensors or more, placed to generate unique trains of pulses according to the direction o travel of a robot part.

Other encoders may be designed to generate a particular binary code for every discrete position of a transducer. Here a pattern on a scale can be read by magnetic, electric, or photoelectric sensors — though there may be a problem if adjacent patterns are read simultaneously (this difficulty can be overcome by only allowing a reading when the sensor is centred over a particular region). Whatever type of transducer is to provide information to a control mechanism, it is necessary to consider the operating environment of the robot. Selected transducers should be able to cope with noise, heat, vibration, etc., as do the other components in a particular robot design.

To control robot performance in a particular environment it is necessary to identify specific control variables (we may expect these to obtain in both human and non-human robot systems). Powers (1979), for example, discusses the search for 'controlled variables' in the context of an experiment with a human subject. This enquiry rests upon certain assumptions about the behaviour of organisms in the general context of cybernetic control. It is emphasized that for a performance to be repeatable 'in a disturbance-prone world', the performing system must sense the consequence of action and then work to keep it matching some static or dynamic reference condition (the effective 'set-point', already mentioned). In this context it is emphasized that organisms — natural or artificial — control what they sense, not what they do. Inappropriate behaviour in a robot cannot be autonomously corrected if the robot does not know what it is doing!

Also, if a system has a hierarchy of operating levels — as do both human and non-human robotic systems — the higher levels are required to feed reference signals to lower levels. This is a 'top-down' approach. For instance, a key information-processing unit in a robot will be required to coordinate overall system performance: signals will be sent to local processors (associated with tactile sensors, visual sensors, limbs, etc.) that in turn will supply feedback information. It is an obvious requirement that a multilevel system hierarchy function as an integrated whole. This is as much an aim of the new-generation industrial robot as it is of a rational human being.

Research into the effective control of non-human robots is being conducted on several fronts. There are significant developments in sensor technology, in the provision of local intelligence for specific robot activities, and in the linking of robots to newly hatched artificial intelligence capabilities (e.g. in sensing, decision making, problem solving, etc.). Increasingly, new-generation robots are being equipped with, for instance, a visual capability. (There is already a prodigious literature on machine vision: see, for example, Weber, 1985; Jasany, 1984; Thomas and Stout, 1980; Dizard, 1984; Braggins, 1984; Meyer, 1983; and Kellock, 1985.) Taylor *et al.* (1985) describe the design approach to a robotic system able to use visual sensing to align small industrial parts. Here a particular endpoint-sensing method is able to achieve precise alignment of a part or tool with respect to a workpiece. The joints of the robot are able to convey a tool or part into the 'capture range' of a fine-positioning system carried as an integral part of the robot. This system is then used to correct perceived mis-alignments, using visually derived information and the versatility of an artificial wrist able to move quickly and precisely in two directions. This is a close analogy of what happens with a human being: limbs are adjusted in physical space according to sensory data received from a visual, tactile, or auditory subsystem.

Microcontrollers, based on diminutive microprocessors, are also being used to provide control of robots in real-time functions (for example, see Hordan, 1985). With this approach it is possible to build a computer into the robot housing, instead of having to link the robot to a computer elsewhere. Again it is necessary to identify such control functions as the position of a workpiece or tool, the position and velocity of robot limbs, the value of various parameters (voltage, current, temperature, etc.), and the specific requirements of the computer and the human user. In this context the operating systems are exploiting the familiar and characteristic cybernetic principles. For example, the Intel company manufactures the MCS–96 micro-controller which can handle a wide range of adaptive closed-loop functions. Another microcontroller, the MCS–51, though less com-plex, can also cope with aspects of closed-loop control. Micro-processor-based systems, often working in parallel in a hierarchical system, offer strategies for control in non-human robots that closely resemble the strategies evident in robotic man. The increased integration of circuits in solid-state silicon has provided surprising support for the idea that man is an effective robot system.

Efforts are also being made to provide industrial robots with diagnostic and error-recovery capabilities (Lee, Barnes, and Hardy, 1985). A collaborative project involving the Robotics Research Group at the University College of Wales (Aberystwyth) and British Robotics Systems Ltd is aiming to develop software that will enable robots to cope with errors and task failures. This is seen as a step on the road towards 'intelligent' control of robot functions. One of the pieces of software already built is AFFIRM (Aberystwyth Framework For Industrial Robot Monitoring), an AI system that helps to control a complex of actuators and sensors.

With most current industrial robots there can be problems with jammed feeders, missing components, and broken tools. In such circumstances the robot operation will cease, sometimes after damage to a workpiece, and a human operator will be needed to sort out the situation and to restart the system. The purpose of AFFIRM and the associated software is to allow the robot to sort out its own problems, to reduce the amount of time spent by the operator on clearing up problems. Already eight different types of sensors have been provided to enable the system to function in the intended manner. The overall aim is to build enhanced autonomy into industrial robots (AFFIRM currently works with a Puma 600 in a simulated work cell). This means that extra diagnostic loops, organized to exploit a variety of cybernetic principles, will be included in robot design. It is obvious that developments of this sort will progressively close the 'intelligence gap' between non-human robots and robotic man.

We see that robot control mechanisms, like their biological com-ponents, are functional cybernetic systems. They operate according to the provisions and demands of information feedback, adaptive requirement, homeostasis, and the detection of performance parameters. Non-human robots and biological systems rely equally upon functional loops that provide control and communication in the context of purposive, goal-directed behaviour. It is increasingly obvious that the non-human computer-controlled robot is a cybernetic system — and so is robotic man.

Summary

This chapter has explored the cybernetic system as a generalized functional configuration. Attention has been given to the various cybernetic principles (feedback, steady state, information handling, etc.), and we have shown that systems cybernetics is characteristic equally of biological and non-human artificial systems. The identification of the cybernetic parameters bearing on natural and artificial anatomies helps to demonstrate that robotic man, like non-human robots, is governed by a framework of law that regulates all his activities.

We have detected the cybernetic operations at the level of metabolic chemistry: there is a rapidly emerging molecular cybernetics, and this phenomenon helps to determine the character of the biological functions at the higher levels of the organ and the organism. Cybernetic control runs through the whole fabric of the biological anatomy: it permeates, indelibly and unmistakably, the full spectrum of human behaviour in the world. Cellular tissue, the heart, the glands, the brain — all can be subsumed under cybernetic rules and regulations. At the heart of the cybernetic process, mediating behaviour in computer and man alike, is the ubiquitous and unceasing task of information processing.

Information defines the character of existing entities. It is enshrined in atoms and molecules, the staple diet of molecular genetics. Information is required to define the nature of cells, organs, and organisms — as it is required to specify the character of limbs, sensors, encoders, and actuators in the non-human robotic world. Once it has specified the components of natural and artificial systems, it is still required to guarantee that such systems can function in a coherent way in the physical environment. Information defines man and computer — and they collect it, process it, and distribute it so that they can act with purpose and intent. Information is the symbolic fuel of all worldly activity.

We have seen that man — robotic man — is a cybernetic system, susceptible to the constant regulation demanded by cybernetic forces. So far this has been considered in *general* terms: there has been some account of specific biological functions but few clues as to how the complexities of human behaviour can be possible. We need to look at the concept of the *program*, at how robotic man is an anatomy subject to cybernetic sway — and *programmed for performance*.

5 Programmed Performance

Preamble

It is a central tenet of 'man as robot' that all human beings are programmed in all they do. No action, no thought, no accomplishment can be achieved — or even attempted — without a program. Programs, of one sort or another, underlie everything that happens. Human beings themselves are programmed at many different levels — by their genetic endowment, their early experiences in the womb, the environment into which they are born. The environment is programmed by the laws of physics and chemistry, by the properties of matter. Science exists to discover, uncover, explore natural programs, and any scrutiny of robotic man will be incomplete unless due attention is given to how he is programmed in all he does.

It is of course a philosophic possibility that some natural events occur in the absence of a program; this would be like saying that there are uncaused events. However it could never be known. The determinist, maintaining his faith as an effective *modus operandi*, could always argue that *ignorance* of a cause does not imply *absence* of a cause. We only know about causes when we find them: we cannot say that they do not exist when they escape our scrutiny. Science works on the assumption that programs and causes exist. This is a thorough-going approach that has dramatic consequences that are rarely addressed in their full implications.

Throughout all recorded history people have suspected that the universe — and man within it — are programmed systems. The Fates (Moerae) in Greek mythology (the goddesses Clotho, Lachesis, and Atropos in Hesiod), notions of predestination, the idea of destiny — all declare the impotence of man in the face of natural programs. The second law of thermodynamics (the increase-of-entropy law) was seen to have similar implications: however human beings were motivated to fret upon the stage, the outcome for the individual and the race would be the same — dusty death. This deep foreboding, evident in all the world's mythologies and religions, has stimulated the imaginative creation of other worlds — universes outside the sway of natural law.

133

The main problem, if such realms are to comfort anxious human beings, is that we have no reason to believe that such worlds exist. Nor has the development of the computer in the modern age — with its persistent interest in plans, schedules, loops, sequences, programs, etc. — helped those people who would like to take an imaginative leap beyond the constraints of natural law: it seemed all too easy to draw neat analogies between computers and human beings, and for many folk there was little comfort in that!

It was inevitable that the computer should provide neat metaphors to describe the regularities and sequences evident in the performance of robotic man. The suggestion that man is *programmed* is not a new concept (we find it in ancient mythologies), but it was the computer that provided the convenient linguistic frame of reference. We see this, for example, in Schneer (1960) who is already sensitive to the implications for man in the new technology. He asks what it is *to think*. Perhaps a machine cannot, in the 1960s, produce a worthwhile violin sonata, but then few people can think like Beethoven (and what is Beethoven doing when he thinks — following rules that are not accessible to most people?). Can the computer think as well as an ape, a dog, a mouse, a limpet? Schneer wonders whether the limpet thinks. Such creatures show little originality, but: 'If originality is the stamp of thought, how many of us are thinking, and how many of us are simply parroting the tapes which were fed into our memory units?'

What are the implications for creativity if human beings are programmed in all they do? (We consider this question in Chapter 6.) What are the implications for such important areas of life as ethics (Chapter 8) and human relationships (Chapter 9)? There seems no doubt, for instance, that effective human relationships are conducted according to rules (a type of program). Thus Argyle and Henderson (1985) declare: 'Most of human behaviour is governed by rules, and this is particularly true of relationships.' Again it is easy to see that regularity, sequence, rules, procedures are key elements in an important area of human existence — and these elements are the stuff of programming, the stuff of robotic man. The program is essential to thought, ethical awareness, and effective contact between people.

It is already clear that we have used the word *program* in several senses, a licit ploy in highlighting the multifaceted nature of the concept. We need to examine more closely the idea of the program.

What is a Program?

Put in its most general terms, a program is a sequence of stages (or steps or phases) which, when performed, allows some action (or activity or function or task) to be accomplished. The various stages in the program can be defined *symbolically* or *physically* (this latter if we want the activity to be achieved in the real world). Programs are often defined symbolically by programmers and related specialists. (It is intriguing that in the field of artificial intelligence, programmers often seem quite content with a procession of symbols (a program) on a page; apparently they see no need to 'instantiate' the symbols in some physical configuration. To such folk the 'intelligence' is in the symbols, not in a behaving physical system!) So, at one level, a program can be nothing more than a meaningful set of symbols defining stages that should be performed for the achievement of the (imaginary) action.

Where a program is defined (or instantiated) physically, use can be made of a limitless family of suitable items (material components, markers, etc.). For example, pegs set in holes can be used to define the stages of a program — as can electrically wired connections (using copper conductors or solid-state silicon circuits), holes in cards or tape, magnetic fields on disks or tape, molecular links in chemical substances, neuron connections (via axons, dendrites, synaptic gaps, etc.) in the brain, a handwritten checklist for a human being, pulsed lights for a photosensitive receptor, etc., etc., Mayer (1981) declares that a program 'is just a list of things to do that you start at the top and follow one step at a time', which conveys something of the idea but does little justice to the complex family of real-world programs and the many ways in which they can be physically expressed.

The sequence of stages in a program is often regarded as a set of *orders* or *instructions* (instructions on how to knit a garment have often been cited as typical steps in a program — which in this case can of course be computerized). This again highlights how computer technology has influenced how orderly natural sequences have come to be regarded. A line of computer code is a literal instruction, strictly analogous to a command in natural language (such as English or Russian), but linkages in DNA molecules, crucial for the synthesizing of proteins, are at best *metaphorical* instructions. Consideration of programs and instructions from the point of view of a general systems theory does not always yield the sorts of insights that someone with only a parochial acquaintance with computer technology might expect. For example, in one sense there is something static about a computer program. There it is, neatly encapsulated line by line in paper, disk, or silicon; but the significance of the real-world program is that it is dynamic — it is only significant when it is operating. The real-world program is about action and life, not primarily about pattern and structure. This is a matter of emphasis and the approach to enquiry. The computer programmer starts with the idea of a task that he wants to code; the natural scientist looks at dynamic processes in the world and tries to locate and describe the controlling programs.

A general systems approach to the concept of a program is useful in exploring the doctrine of robotic man. There is no assumption that a program is of a particular type, though it seems clear that all human programs will be instantiated in carbon and other chemicals — the characteristic stuff of *Homo sapiens*. Young (1978) proposed that 'the lives of human beings and other animals are governed by sets of programs written in their genes and brains'. He spends little time on defining the concept of the program, preferring instead to enumerate the many areas in which programs are important (essential) for human performance — and little is left out! There are practical (physiological) programs ensuring that we breathe, eat, drink, sleep, etc.; social programs concerned with speaking, agreeing, loving, hating; and 'long-term' programs (growth, sex, ageing, dying, etc.) relevant to the survival of the race. There is also all the paraphernalia of mental programs, allowing such activities as thinking, imagining, believing, and worshipping. The programs written into genes and brains are an abundantly diverse affair.

Young conceives a program as 'a plan decided beforehand to achieve some end', and he remarks that 'program' is the original seventeenth century spelling ('programme' being an affected nineteenth century French version). He also has in mind the idea of a *computer* program ('although brain programs are only partly like the algorithms of computer software in which every step is logical'). What is important is that there are regular sequences of steps which are performed for the achievement of some goal or objective. It is in this general sense, not in the parochial computer-technology sense, that man is programmed in all he does. The programs of robotic man are of many types, but no action or activity is possible without using the appropriate program.

The First Programs

Programs are as old as matter and energy. We have seen that programs are almost synonymous with the properties of matter/energy. Wherever chemical reaction or physical change occurs, it does so according to inbuilt programming — and this is not entirely a semantic matter. The advent of computers in the modern age crystallized the concept of the program, making it easier to see programming wherever natural change exists; this has consequences for our view of reality. For example, it helps to re-establish a mechanistic view of the world, a view that many people think was dented by relativity theory and quantum physics. If the world is a programmed phenomenon — with 'program' interpreted in the general sense that we have indicated — then reality can be interpreted as regularity of operational sequence in all events and activities. There is much in this that would have gladdened the hearts of nineteenth century rationalists.

If programs are as old as matter/energy, they came into existence with the creation of the world — if there ever was such an event. One approach would be to cast God as The Great Programmer in the sky. This should not surprise us: if God can be drafted to serve the part of warrior, designer, architect, and window cleaner (for all I know), then why should he (it?) not do a bit of programming on the side? Moreover, this is not quite the irrelevant absurdity that one may imagine. Charles Babbage — the much lauded 'father' of modern computing — was keen to see God as some sort of celestial programmer, writing routines for obvious regularities in nature and subroutines for such singular events as miracles. It is a novel notion but not one that we see celebrated too often in the reputable journals of the computer press.

As all believers do, Babbage framed his concept of the deity in terms of his own unique experiences; in this case his experiences with mechanical calculating machines. This view suggests that 'God is man of science and programmer writ large' (Hyman, 1982). Babbage observed that we judge the intellectual capacity of the race by its productions, and proposed that 'the estimate we form of the Creator of the visible world rests ultimately on the same foundation...'. Further, the number of consequences 'resulting from any law' and 'the more they are foreseen', the more knowledge and intelligence we ascribe to the maker of the law. But this struck Babbage as suitably analogous to how the calculating engine might behave. The same machine might achieve different results ('productions') by means of different programs. In like fashion, change in the physical world — including such (Darwinian) events as the emergence of new biological species — could well proceed by means of programs set in motion by the Creator at the beginning of time. This was a singular device for squaring the demands of the old theology with the pressures of new technology. And miracles? They were simply 'singularities in the Celestial Program: a miracle was merely a subroutine called down from the Heavenly store' (Hyman, 1982).

This is a pleasant enough doctrine, but eccentric to most modern ears (I need hardly remark that I do not believe a word of it). Perhaps if God was the great Celestial Programmer then Mary was cast in the role of Ada Lovelace, tidying up the occasional problem with Bernoulli numbers! Today we have largely secured the divorce between prescientific superstition (though scientists, like the rest of us, frequently propagate absurdities) and rational enquiry. We have little doubt that programs, of some sort, are very old, but perhaps we should try to envisage them without having to conjure the image of some celestial deity keying in code on some heavenly mainframe (are the angels the data prep clerks?). Early programs there were, but they were respectably cast in the stuff of physics and chemistry.

Young (1978), after giving hints to the generality of the programming concept, decided to set the 'first programs' squarely in the domain of biology. Of course this well suits the doctrine of robotic man, but nonetheless is a needless constriction: man is a programmed system in a hierarchy of programmed systems. The gist of Young's excursion into how man is programmed *ab initio* is to advertise the fact that human beings, although brought into the world only half made up, do nonetheless come equipped with a fair basket of programs at birth. It is interesting that used programs develop, siring fresh programs, while unused programs disappear. Some programs, such as those associated with the onset of sexual maturity, are awakened at suitable times during the maturing process (chemical clocks are programmed into the organism). At the same time some program potentials wither in the absence of suitable stimulation. There is some suggestion that the child starts with a great redundancy of neural connections, many of which disappear during the learning process.

Thus the business of maturation seems to depend upon drastic modification, in one way or another, of the neural patterns yielded by genetic endowment by the time of birth.

The true first programs — written into energy fields, subatomic particles, atoms, molecules, etc. — had little interest in life: living systems were not even a twinkle in their programmed eye. Life came late in the history of programs, but proved such a fertile child that programs then proliferated, sometimes with remarkable consequences: e.g. the life programs even seemed to set about resisting the second law of thermodynamics (increase in entropy was resisted, at least in a few little sectors of space/time — a small victory, of paltry significance in the history of the universe, but unprecedented).

The first life programs were encapsulated in complex molecules able to replicate and handle matter/energy and information in various characteristic ways. It was these early programs that were to yield the program proliferation that would in due course produce robotic man. It is natural that we should be most interested in the programs that describe *Homo sapiens* and that — in the computer age — we should see the relevance of these programs to the notion of 'man as robot'. The question is not *whether we are programmed*, but *what sort of programs we have.*

The Life Cycle

Programs know all about cycles ('loops'), and it is easy to regard the human life cycle as one large program. Here each life phase — birth, growth, maturation, ageing, and dying — would be seen as a subprogram (a subroutine or a software subsystem). We all start as a bunch of programmed molecules and then work through the various subroutines controlled by the master program. Some people's programs are unique to them; some are virtually identical from one person to another; but inevitably programs in one person influence programs in another (or many others) in a vast cybernetic conflux of factors, forces, and feedback. People carry their programs around with them, protecting some and exposing others — and they do this from birth to death.

The baby is full of genetic potential: there are a million people it could become, if only its genetic endowment were needed. However every person is a result of a programmed environment acting on a programmed organism, so the baby's future is determined, laid out, predictable (*in principle*), programmed. What is true of the baby's early development is equally true of its prenatal existence and its postnatal involvement in the world. From the moment of conception to the moment of death (and arguably beyond, through dissolution and decay), the programmed organism is required to respond to programmed inputs. The person develops, taking in food and experience, and then dies to increase the local entropy.

We can sketch the programmed life cycle for every individual (for every human being, for every machine, for every cybernetic system), but only in the broadest terms. For complex systems — dolphins, apes, women — the interacting programs are numerous and complicated, and this applies both within and without the individual. At any one time, thousands of programmed sequences are being performed in every person, and this prodigious volume of activity also interacts with a few thousand similar volumes of equivalent complexity. A person is a complex hierarchy of cybernetic systems, and when two people talk together two prodigiously complicated hierarchies interact in countless ways.

There can be little doubt that the course of anyone's life is determined by genes and by external circumstances. In brutally clear cases this is obviously true: a person whose genes cause gross mental retardation, extreme physical deformity, highly malignant cancer, etc., will have little opportunity to explore — even in a programmed fashion — the opportunities open to less afflicted individuals. The crude example serves to illustrate a general principle. It is easy to see the programmed tyranny of gross mental or physical handicap, but if *escape from necessity* is the important quest then the tyranny for everyone is the ubiquitous program: the prodigy is no less programmed than the idiot but we rejoice that he is programmed in different ways. Why do we rejoice, when we do? Because we, at least some of us, are programmed to do so.

The life cycle may be viewed as one immense program comprising many subprograms dedicated to particular tasks. At another level these subprograms may be regarded as programs in their own right, with subprograms of their own. Even a cursory examination of these dedicated programs suggests that robotic man is a system programmed in all he does.

Programs for Life

General

The complexity of programs in human beings has been built up over millions of years of biological evolution. From one perspective a program is a plan of action selected from a set of possible plans and the selection process itself is mediated by effective programs operating at a different level (see the discussion of choice in Chapter 6). Whenever plans (programs) are chosen for implementation a process of natural selection is taking place, and the process itself is defined in terms of programming forces and factors. There are obviously biological factors in the potential of the genes, and such social and cultural factors as ethics, law, politics, art, music, and religion. How such elements — features of the programmed environment — impinge on robotic man is determined by his programming. Chomsky suggested that human beings are programmed to learn natural language, and what is true for language learning is true for all our talents and endeavours. Thus 'because of our brain organisation we are able to love and to hate, to command and to obey, to create beautiful things and to enjoy them, and also to believe and to worship' (Young, 1978).

The key life program (or complex of programs) is concerned with the survival of the individual. Necessarily this is the central genetically enshrined plan motivating all biological species. Our parentage may be very important in defining our life chances, but the impulse to survive is a naturally selected pressure that runs indelibly through our being. Without this particular life program there would be no human culture — indeed no robotic man.

It is convenient to regard the key survival program as comprising many individual modules serving the overall survival objective and written in appropriate languages. At the genetic level, programs are written in the triplets of bases of the DNA code. This is used to regulate chemical change in countless different ways to allow the emergence of an individual equipped to cope with the demands of survival. Language at the genetic level is biologically fundamental (see below), under-pinning the various language levels that relate to specific types of social and cultural programming.

Another language of programming can be discerned in the interconnections of the neurons in the brain. The genetic molecules lay down a plan for the development of the cerebral language, organized to allow actions when needed on a day-to-day basis or at the various stages of the life cycle of the human being. Other programs, at a different level, characterize the fabric of human culture — and these programs are often written in obvious signs and symbols, the thousands of natural languages and dialects found across the world.

Languages at the various levels can be used to define the many programs that cooperate (or run into conflict!) in striving towards the survival goal. The various programs have been dubbed 'scripts' (Berne, 1974; Young, 1978), effectively carried around by people and able to produce human actions. This notion (see 'People programmed', below) conveys the idea that people adhere to received plans or roles presented from outside. The idea of the script is synonymous with the idea of (selected) plans, procedures, sequences, and schedules (programs), and it also suggests the important idea that people are in some sense *bound to receive* their plans and schedules, that when they begin the important task of selection — to implement new plans — they have already been programmed to select as they do. Again we can stress that the process of selection — of mates, roles, options, etc. — is itself a programmed procedure (see Chapter 6). Nothing happens that is not programmed.

The programs for life are implemented to allow the development and occurrence of actions that are necessary for survival. Robotic man interprets survival in ambitious terms. He is not content to drift aimlessly through a nutrient soup, as do some creatures, with no complex purposes or initiatives; instead he aims to survive not only biologically but in a complicated sociocultural fashion. So he does not only need programs for ingestion of food and for breathing but also for copulation, high-level learning, and the demonstration of a spectrum of social skills. He needs programs for the development of affection and attachment (see Chapter 7) so that survival becomes a collective enterprise. The programs for life bear on every aspect of human existence. It is useful to consider some of these in more detail.

The Gene Programs

We have already noted the interesting possibility that God created robots (human beings) with programs in the form of genes. In a sense, this says it all. The biologically specified genetic material is the soil from which all later human programs grow — under the persistent influence of the programs working in the external environment.

It is hard to say too much about the importance of DNA (deoxyribonucleic acid, by means of which the genes are defined). Dawkins (1976) saw DNA as the essential survival unit ('immortal coils'); Cherfas (1982) depicts DNA as a 'miracle molecule'. It is important because it carries all the information necessary to construct the living cell and the human being. All the complexity of human life — all the achievements and confusion, all the invention and despair, all the technology and flights of artistic fancy — in the last resort derives from the intricacies of the DNA molecule.

The DNA substance was first discovered in 1869 by the Swiss Johann Friedrich Miescher, working in the German town of Tubingen. In order to study the chemistry of the cell nucleus, he used the white blood cells found in the pus oozing from surgical wounds, obtained from discarded dressings from the local surgical clinic. After separating the large nuclei from their surrounding cytoplasm, he discovered a compound which was acidic, rich in phosphorus, and composed of unusually large molecules. He later continued his studies using sperm cells from salmon taken from the Rhine. Within a few years the chemistry of DNA, distributed throughout all human cells, had been worked out, but it took almost a century to discover the DNA double helix and the coding mechanisms used to carry the genetic information.

The DNA molecule has a sugar (a ribose) and a phosphorus atom surrounded by four oxygen atoms, which together form a phosphate group. Sugars and phosphates are linked together in a chain with another compound, a base, attached to each sugar; sugar, base, and phosphate group are together termed a nucleotide. In due course the varieties of bases (guanine, adenine, cytosine, thymine, and uracil — known as G, A, C, T, and U) were found to be crucial in information coding in genetic material. (Thymine and uracil are chemically similar, and so the important coding bases are usually referred to as G, A, C, and T.) Miescher himself had enough insight to imagine how the DNA molecules might carry the necessary genetic information. He observed that the hereditary message may be harboured 'just as the words and concepts of all languages can find expression in twenty-four to thirty letters of the alphabet'. This type of simile has often been used to illustrate how the nucleotides with their characteristic bases can embody the specifications for life. We often see reference to how the instructions for making a human body are written in the 'alphabet' of the nucleotides.

In 1928, experiments were carried out — by Frederick Griffith, at the Ministry of Health's Pathological Laboratory in London — which were to lead to the establishment of DNA as the molecule of heredity: unexpected results were achieved in experiments involving the injection of mice with pneumococcus (the bacteria *Streptococcus pneumoniae*). The anomalies, making nonsense of current genetic theory and known as 'bacterial transformation', were further investigated by Oswald Avery at the Rockefeller Institute of New York. This work helped to make clear that DNA was the source of hereditary information, but it was not yet known how DNA could manage the trick. The discovery of how the DNA molecule could carry genetic information — how it could *fulfil the functions of a memory bank* (Cherfas) — was made by James Watson, Francis Crick, and colleagues in the spring of 1953. It was found that the DNA molecule was a double helix with the bases fitting together in jigsaw-like precision.

When a biological cell divides, or when two cells join in sexual reproduction, the instructions that the new cell needs for activity and growth are contained in (for human beings) forty-six thin strands of material, the chromosomes. When the cell divides in order to reproduce, each chromosome splits into two halves, so that each offspring cell contains the same number of chromosomes as its parent. In bisexual reproduction each parent cell provides half the chromosomes for the offspring. Thus every new cell contains the same number of chromosomes as the parent. The genes, structured in DNA, are strung along the chromosomes like beads (another common simile). Hence following the work of Watson and Crick it was clear that the chromosome is made up of a helical DNA molecule protected by the protein histone. It is found that the histone elements are configured in units of eight molecules (octomers), together with a piece of DNA about 200 nucleotides long, giving the chromosomes their beaded aspect. Each 'bead' — histone octomer plus DNA — is dubbed a nucleosome. Each gene is reckoned to comprise several nucleosomes.

Individual genes (or gene groups) are responsible for particular bodily characteristics: number of limbs, eye colour, hair colour, longevity, etc. Where genes are in evident conflict (e.g. one parent with blue eyes, one with brown), one type of gene will be *dominant*, one type *recessive*. (In fact genes for brown eyes are dominant to genes for blue eyes.) Or a compromise may be reached: a particular feature in an offspring may not be identical to the equivalent feature in either parent. In any event, the emerging offspring features are programmed by the character of the parental genes — and offspring cannot escape this circumstance, much as they may wish to.

The genetic programs may be regarded as tightly analogous to other types of programs: for example, those in computers. Thus in talking of the gene complex, Dawkins (1976) is keen to emphasize that there are special symbols for

END OF PROTEIN CHAIN MESSAGE and

START OF PROTEIN CHAIN MESSAGE

'written in the same four-letter alphabet as the protein messages themselves'. The coded instructions for making a protein are carried, in the genetic material, between these two parenthetical signals. In this approach a gene is a piece of program, written in nucleotide code, between the symbols START and END. This is strictly analogous to any sort of computer program written on machines from microcomputers to mainframes. The genetic programs are responsible for every aspect of bodily growth, from the smallest subunits in the biological cell to the shape of the skeleton in robotic man. A key concept in this procedure is that of *canalization*, a term first proposed by the geneticist C. H. Waddington at Edinburgh University.

Canalization is the phenomenon evident in any organic system to develop in certain well-defined ways. For example, it is clear that the nervous system in human beings and other animals develops in an intricately programmed way. Here the program specifies the shape and disposition of connective tissue, and also the times at which particular connections are to be made. The development of cells in the primitive neural tube and how they migrate to form the brain and spinal cord can be observed to occur with predictable regularity both within a species and, to some extent, also across species. This is particularly clear from even a cursory study of embryology.

Here, as elsewhere in anatomical development, there is a remarkable sequence of operations in which one completed process lays the foundations for the onset of the next. For example, the slender neural tube gives rise to the spinal cord. The early simple-seeming tube comprise a central slit-like canal and walls of tightly packed cells. Particular cells lying at the edges of the neural folds and comprising what is called the *neural crest* give rise to ganglia of the spinal nerves and ganglia of cranial nerves with sensory components. In this fashion, exploiting a wealth of buried information, one part of an anatomical feature can mysteriously give rise to another component which in turn sires yet more elements. Each stage in the process lays the grounds for the unfolding of yet more stages, until the full complexity of the organism is achieved.

It is important to appreciate the programming constraints on this highly complex procedure. In fact it is difficult to prevent the various genetically defined processes from achieving what appear to be their prescribed objectives. Thus Waddington has observed: 'It is quite difficult to persuade the developing system not to finish up producing its normal end result.' Even if seemingly thwarted by physical or chemical means the biological process will demonstrate apparent initiative in striving to attain its objective by another route. It seems obvious that the development of mammalian anatomical features (including those in human beings) proceeds according to rigidly programmed patterns, but with (programmed) scope for adaptation where unusual circumstances occur. Such circumstances must fall within certain limits: if the environment becomes hostile to a sufficient degree the biological process will be totally arrested and the organism may perish.

The environment (itself a programmed complex) is also important in providing the necessary inputs to the genetically determined programs. For example, rats with similar genetic endowments have been reared in different types of environment. Mark Rosenzweig and his colleagues at the University of California in Berkeley provided rats with enriched environments (including other rats, toy ladders, wheels, etc.), while other rats were provided with food but little else. The 'enriched rats' proved to be better at various behavioural tasks, and it was later found — after all the rats had been 'sacrificed' — that the enriched rats had cerebral cortexes weighing 4 per cent more than those in the impoverished (but fatter) rats. Work with other species has also shown that an enriched environment allows animals to develop more elaborate skills and larger brains. It is clear that the environmental programs can stimulate or retard the development of the biological programs provided by the genes. This is no surprise: man, we have long known, is a mixture of nature and nurture. However it is useful to emphasize the two-fold determinism — of genes and environment — that bears on the development and activities of living systems, including robotic man.

There is perennial debate as to *how much* the genes determine the character, intellect, and personality of the individual, and how much the environment. We have no need to explore such matters. It is readily conceded that every individual is a complex outgrowth of the impact of environmental pressures upon genetic endowment. To opt for the primacy of genes *or* environment is merely, in our terms, to opt for one type of programming as being more important than another. Robotic man is partly fashioned by his heredity, partly by the environmental frame in which he functions and develops. We cannot escape from the fact that man is programmed by asserting that his programs are affected by the (programmed) features of his environment. In fact it is possible to describe the situation as one in which man is programmed partly by his genes and partly by such environmental factors as early nutrition, siblings, parents, schooling, mass media, the weather — by all the social and cultural pressures that impose on the person. We start with our genes: they can only develop systems and subsystems within certain limits, but within those limits there is scope for programming by the environment.

There is also a converse of this argument. Yes, environment clearly determines the flowering of genetic potential. A person who lives all his life in Manchester is unlikely to be an expert in colloquial Chinese; but it is arguable that colloquial Chinese has its unique character by virtue of genetic pressure. A person is genetically equipped to learn languages, but the languages themselves have been moulded by the genetic potential of *Homo sapiens*, a species uniquely adept at manipulating symbol systems. There is thus a reflexive facet in the interaction between genes and environment: each is subject to the sway of the other, but in different ways. (We may note in passing that this circumstance has a cybernetic flavour: there is constant two-way feedback between the genetic and environmental realms.)

The idea that all social phenomena are the inevitable manifestations of the actions of the genes is known as sociobiology. This doctrine aims to be a reductionist determinism, a comprehensive programme for the explication of social institutions, social mores, social prejudices. There is an obvious appeal in such a doctrine. Our genes define us and we define the character of human society: so the genes are at the root of all social circumstances. The doctrine also has political attractions to conservative, folk, suggesting as it does that prevailing inequalities, injustices, and privileges are genetically determined, and that this fact offers a singular sanction for preservation of the status quo. We will not be diverted along this route (we talk about ethics and politics in Chapter 8); here what is important is that there is an evident causal link between the actions of the genes and the shape of human society. Such a generalized observation should not be politically provocative, but it signals above all that the complex of genetic programs has implications far beyond what the keen student of the DNA molecule might suspect.

It is inevitable that the term sociobiology should mean different things to different people. In its early forms it had reference mainly to animal communities, though there was some speculation about its likely impact on theories about human society. Perhaps its most influential embodiment was E.O. Wilson's book, *Sociobiology*, published a decade ago (1975). This work was essentially a massive survey about animal communities, with a profile of the major ideas proposed to explain their evolution. The book also contained what was soon to be seen as a provocative suggestion: the idea that an understanding of animal communities — necessarily gene-determined — would provide insights into the nature and evolution of human society. In this way, it was implied, biology was about to revolutionize the social sciences — a suggestion that was exciting to some, offensive to others.

Many seemingly disparate ideas contributed to the emergence of sociobiology as a coherent body of doctrine. For example, V.C. Wynne-Edwards (*Animal Dispersion in Relation to Social Behaviour*, 1962) argued that natural selection would favour some *communities* at the expense of others, rather than some *individuals* at the expense of others (as the Darwinists assumed). This notion was supported by earlier work by Haldane and Fisher and a more recent paper by W.D. Hamilton (advertising an approach made popular by Richard Dawkins in *The Selfish Gene*). The key point is that the gene is the essential survival unit: therefore it is essential to establish the genetic relationships between the members of a society when trying to comprehend how it evolved. It is now understood that all complex animal societies are made up of genetic relatives. It is this sort of kinship theory that is held to be relevant to an understanding of social dynamics (in particular, of social evolution).

Again we do not need to pursue such intriguing topics, for what they seek to do is expose particular modes of programming that operate to shape human motivations and human societies. If the identified programs do in fact exist then further evidence is available to support the doctrine of robotic man; but if the predictions of kinship theory are erroneous it does not matter for our purposes — if particular programs do not obtain in any circumstances, then others will be present. The competing theories about social evolution are nothing more than competitions between rival program sets. The central point — that man is a programmed system operating within a programmed system of a different order — will survive the competition, whatever its outcome.

We have seen that genes are coded instructions for the development of the biological cell and the individual, and that these instructions can be characterized as the gene programs. In effect, long before we can reflect on the matter, we are *preprogrammed*: our coded instructions are written before we are launched on life, and once we function we do so by virtue of established programs — we cannot operate at any level in the real world without the specified schedules written into our molecular structures. It is easy to give evidence of preprogramming in robotic man and in other animal organisms. It is this preprogramming that helps to justify the doctrine of 'man as robot'. Aleksander (1977), for example, refers to the 'genetic automaton', emphasizing that genes — like the circuit elements in a computer — can be regarded as binary components with 'on/off' modes of behaviour (what are dubbed, in metabolic chemistry, the *repressers* and *inducers*).

It is possible to consider the 'states' of a genetic automaton, just as it is possible to explore the states of *any* programmed system. Such an approach necessarily advertises the robotic character of organisms, of which preprogramming is one particular feature.

Preprogramming in Organisms

There is continuity of programming in robotic man from the moment of conception to the moment of death. So, strictly speaking, there is no preprogramming since all programming is 'pre' or 'post' some other programming: the genes are programmed before the moment of conception and the decay or cremation of the body is programmed after death. What preprogramming usually means is programming before birth — as if no programming occurred once the organism was launched upon the world. It is conventional for biologists and others to cite preprogramming as evidence for the power of instinct, clearly manifest in both man and other animals but particularly important, it is claimed, in non-human animals because their activities are less mediated by sociocultural factors. In short, early behaviour, often dubbed 'instinctive', is often cited as evidence of preprogramming.

The heart-beat, discernible in the human foetus, is preprogrammed, but whether it is instinctive is another matter. Preprogramming can relate to internal functions but it more commonly signifies activities of the whole organism once it is operating in the world. Many studies of preprogramming have focused on non-human animals.

It is interesting, for example, that many animals are born with an innate capacity for certain movements that are likely to aid the survival of the organism. Many birds know how to open their beaks wide to beg for food; the cuckoo, immediately upon hatching, sets about expelling any other eggs it may encounter in the nest; the chicken knows how to peck for corn; and the duckling is able to search effectively in the mud for food (it is highly significant that the duckling will do this even if hatched by a hen). Such responses have been called 'inherited coordination' and 'fixed action patterns'.

Some such responses are effective at the time of birth, some a little later, and yet others at various well-defined times in the development of the organism. Some require environmental input — light, protein, experience, etc. — in order to emerge in an effective fashion. For example, Sauer, working in Germany, raised certain species of birds (whitethroats) individually and isolated from sound, and so demonstrated that they developed their characteristic songs without any example to copy. Somehow the species-specific songs are already defined as information patterns in the genes.

Similarly, squirrels are born with an innate capacity to hide nuts. Again these animals have been reared with no examples to copy, and have still been able to carry out the species-specific hiding techniques. In one experiment (reported by Eibl-Eibesfeldt, 1971), grown squirrels reared in isolation were given a copious supply of nuts: they began by eating them but when satiated ran around, scratched in a corner, pressed the nut down, and then made pressing-down and raking-over movements with their noses — although no soil had been disturbed. It is obvious that this is an example of behaviour that is not newly learned but preprogrammed, somehow specified in the genetic material. Similar examples can be given for many different species, including *Homo sapiens*.

We all know that a newly born baby does not need to learn how to suck (indeed, engaging pictures have been taken to show how the prebirth foetus can try to suck its thumb!) It is also able to cry, smile, cling, etc. — in addition to all the complex bodily functions such as nervous development, ingestion of food, temperature regulation, etc. It is already obvious at birth that the child is a highly preprogrammed system. Even children born deaf and blind are able to laugh and cry at emotional times, even though they have witnessed no other human being behaving in such a fashion. So it is with other emotions: such children are quite capable of stamping their feet, clenching their fists, and frowning when something annoys them. Children are preprogrammed to signal their emotions in various effective ways, and it is easy to see why this should be important from the point of view of survival in a difficult world.

It is also evident that children who are severely mentally handicapped are able to smile, laugh, and cry at suitable times, though it may be impossible to teach them the simplest of practical tasks. Evidently some neural connections, associated with a range of preprogramming, have been made, but many others, associated with elementary learning capacity, have not. A blind thalidomide child, unable to explore the faces of others by means of his little stumps of hands, will still laugh when one plays with him. And a blind ten-year-old girl pianist, when complimented (by Eibl-Eibesfeldt), was able to blush, turn her face briefly forwards, and then bashfully look down, just as a sighted child might do.

There is abundant evidence that many facial responses are preprogrammed in human beings, irrespective of race or cultural influence, and there is even the suggestion that many such responses are discernible on a cross-species basis. Thus a non-human primate (e.g. the mandrill or the gorilla), as well as a human being, may draw down the corners of the mouth as a threat display. A person (and an ape) may display rage or disgust in a similar fashion, though a human being cannot show the long canines that a baboon might display to good effect. Hence a preprogrammed motor pattern has survived the progressive reduction in the size of the teeth that were the main elements in the threat display.

Various categories of innate performance can be identified. For example, innate recognition capabilities are charateristic of many predators. A frog will snap at small moving insects immediately after its conversion from a tadpole, and it will also snap at leaves or pebbles moving in a particular way. Thus the nervous system of the frog is preprogrammed to cause types of behaviour that are conducive to the survival of the frog, but less conducive to the survival of insects in the vicinity. Such mechanisms — sometimes termed 'innate releasing mechanisms' — can also be found in human beings, but have been most commonly researched in non-human animals.

Many signalling devices can act as effective 'releasers': e.g. such structures as combs or manes, characteristic markings, scents, sounds, and movements. A releaser will impact on an organism's preprogrammed nervous system and cause action that is characteristic of the species. Thus female spiny lizards with stripes painted on their sides to make them resemble males will be attacked by male lizards, just as a robin will attack a clump of red feathers found in its territory. Turkey hens are only responsive to the calls of their young and are liable to kill offspring that are dumb. Rhesus monkeys isolated from birth will still react to a picture of a threatening monkey: the expressions on the pictures serve as innate releasing mechanisms, the rhesus monkeys in the experiments never having seen other monkeys of their own species.

Similar mechanisms in human beings are signalled by the quick responses to babies, where particular physical features — chubby cheeks, relatively large eyes, a small mouth, etc. — quickly convey the idea of cuddliness. (It is interesting, not least in connection with sexism, that features in attractive women — for example, relatively large eyes — are typically infantile characteristics.) Other releasing mechanisms in human beings are associated with hearing or the sense of smell. Research has suggested that women are able to detect certain musk substances that cannot be detected by men.

There are also innate drives that impel an organism to be active in its environment. This is clearly another type of preprogramming. An animal may appear to be randomly curious but it may be searching for food, drink, a mate, or somewhere in which it can feel secure (an appropriate aperture or somewhere to build a nest). Active behaviour can be associated with particular nerve cells in the central nervous system, and the pressure from such centres may cause action even if there is no immediate survival need: a satiated bird may fly around snapping at nothing, impelled by motor pressures to run through the appropriate programs but not interested at that time in securing insects. Human drives of an analogous sort, often seen as genuine 'instinctive' pressures, are associated with the obvious appetites — for food, drink, aggressive display, sexual experience, peer-group approval, etc. It has been pointed out that man has at least as many preprogrammed drives as most other animals: for example, the young child has an impulse to babble as a prelude to meaningful speech, and the character of the babble is conditioned by the linguistic culture in which the child is gaining experience. This may be seen as yet another neat cybernetic loop: the child babbles, the parent responds with sounds, the child hears and babbles in a slightly different way, the parent hears and offers further sounds, the child..., and so on and so forth, until the child matures and offers its own meaningful words to a new generation.

A capacity for learning is also preprogrammed into the nervous systems of non-human animals and robotic man. David Oakley (1979), for example, discusses learning in the context of cerebral events and the associated adaptive behaviour. It is obvious that a prodigious learning capacity, yielding a vast range of high-level programs, is one of the main features of human beings. Chimpanzees, with all their skills, must be rated poor learners in comparison with the average child. For instance, children are very good at learning languages, though they need language input if the potential is to survive. Most observers would agree that human beings are structured, in a programmed sense, to be responsive to the possibilities offered by a highly symbolized culture. For most individuals the most complex symbol set is that represented by a native language, not only in terms of actual words but also in terms of a highly complex set of rules for their manipulation, most of which the user — unless a linguistic philosopher — could not begin to articulate. So the ability to learn language, like many of the other abilities of robotic man, is a matter of programming.

We could catalogue many other examples of innate programming (preprogramming) using examples taken from ethnology, anthropology, and zoology, but by now the point should be clear. Human beings are not shaped totally by their environment. They come into the world with all sorts of drives, impulses, capabilities, and inherited coordinations (Eibl-Eibesfeldt: 'Especially in the field of his social behaviour man seems to be preprogrammed to a decisive extent'). He seems able to recognize stimulus-releasing mechanisms without having had relevant experience and to respond to them in ways that favour individual and group survival. The evident corollary is that some types of learning come more easily to human beings than do others. It may depress social engineers but there seem to be elements in human neural programming that render human beings much less than totally malleable. You can only engineer your human society within certain limits imposed by the character of neural connections;

try to go beyond these limits and it is likely that you will build up tensions and pressures that will eventually doom the experiment to failure. This is partly a matter for ethics and politics (Chapter 8).

It is obvious that man's drives can be mediated by a host of cultural pressures. In his behaviour he is malleable to a degree, but any account of the scope of human behaviour must give consideration to the extent of his preprogramming.

Programmed Language

Efforts to make computers understand natural language (as opposed to computer language) have tended to enhance our view of human language abilities. Twenty years ago it was thought that computer translation, for example, would be a simple matter to achieve, and programmers quickly become bogged down in questions of syntax and semantics: it was not simply a matter of providing data-base dictionaries and look-up tables, etc. Now we see language understanding as an immensely complicated affair, possible for people because they have an immense chunk of (as yet) incomprehensible preprogramming and also because they have an accumulated 'world view' that will not be found in any artificial computer.

It is a central claim of Noam Chomsky (of the Massachusetts Institute of Technology), probably the most influential linguistic philosopher of the twentieth century, that the human ability to use language is innate rather than learned. He argues, for example, that only an inherited capability could explain the universals of human language. In addition, the sheer complexity of linguistic processes suggests substantial preprogramming for such complexity to be mastered by every new human being who is not disabled in some way that impinges on language handling. It is argued that human beings could not master such complicated systems if they had to start from scratch: they do not start with a 'blank slate' as much of the work is already encapsulated in the preprogramming, and whatever remains to be learned is thus more manageable. The problems about the universals of human language can be illustrated by considering what is involved when we try to teach a computer to master even the most rudimentary linguistic processes.

The topic of universals is relevant to the question of generalization. If we were to equip a machine with the capacity to generalize then it could deal with a statement such as 'the cat sat on the mat' in various ways. It may conclude, for instance, that mats were things to be sat on and that the statement 'the dog sat on the mat' was not an absurdity, whereas 'the mat sat on the dog' was! But how can the concepts of universals and generalization be built into computers?

If a computer is required to work with the concept of a geometric shape (for example, a cube) then the requisite program must include rules to enable the machine to identify the shape in question. This means that any computer-based system, expected to behave intelligently, must be provided with a ready-made universal for every object it may encounter in the world. Alas, it is found that descriptions that are loose enough to encompass an article seen from every point of view may in practice be found to include articles that are not the particular article that is intended; when the description is tightened up, many versions of the article that should be included are in fact left out. This is a conundrum that is currently exercising the thoughts of many programmers in artificial intelligence. What it means in short is that there are many subtleties in human information processing that are (1) totally beyond current comprehension and (2) totally absent in even the cleverest computer programs. This should be remembered by those people who incline to the view that robotic man is necessarily a somewhat diminished specimen. The doctrine of 'man as robot' entails the view that human beings are run by bunches of programs, but it is obvious that in these early days of the computer age we do not yet understand how most of the important programs work.

The human skill at working with language inevitably seduces researchers into trying to write programs that mimic the activities of the human brain (if only we understood those activities!). Patton (1984) has written an article entitled 'Better speech recognition means that computers must mimic the human brain' in which it is suggested that an effective natural-language processor would need to understand how the human brain recognizes words. Again we do not need to pursue this topic: the illustration is given to advertise the idea that there is complex cerebral preprogramming that is essential to an understanding of language.

Studies of speech production in human beings suggest that it is a massively programmed phenomenon, a highly complex function that nonetheless occurs in regular patterns and in ways that are amenable to empirical enquiry. For instance, Victoria Fromkin at the University of California (Los Angeles) began in the 1960s to record the verbal slips she witnessed in everyday speech. Today she and her colleagues have collected thousands of such examples, and other researchers have begun their own compilations. Significantly, the verbal slips are found to follow identifiable patterns. They are governed by rules: verbal slips, like other verbal productions, are programmed.

When, for example, words are switched, the words concerned are almost always of the same syntactic or grammatical category. So nouns are transposed with other nouns ('He broke the brick with a window') and verbs with verbs ('Please wash your room and tidy the dishes'). This suggests programming that operates on syntactical categories, an approach that any linguistic programmer might adopt. The transposition slip — and other types of slips could be cited — suggests not only that speech production is programmed, but that the programming is organized in discoverable ways. Michael Motley has explored this topic in some detail with his colleagues, Bernard Baars at the University of California (San Francisco) and Carl Camden at Cleveland State University.

Some approaches to the programming of speech have focused on aspects of brain anatomy. For example, it was found in the nineteenth century that damage to the left hemisphere of the brain could cause problems in the understanding and production of speech; such damage could also affect reading. (The left hemisphere controls language in most poeple.) There are immense difficulties in trying to associate particular abilities with particular neural circuits. One inevitable problem is the complexity of the brain: it is usually impossible to isolate specific neural connections and associate them with particular organic functions, though specific *regions* of the brain can be functionally linked to particular tasks and talents in the individual. Also the neural circuits associated with particular activities are often diffused through different parts of the brain, and can relate to different functions at different times. It has been pointed out, for instance, that brain-scanning techniques used to investigate dyslexics have achieved no more that to show 'that among acquired dyslexics, the ones with the largest areas of damage have the worst problems' (Ferry, 1985b). In such circumstances the task has been to devise methods of enquiry that do not depend upon the relatively crude explorations of brain anatomy.

Again it is possible to investigate brain functions using the computer analogy. Sampson (1975) has proposed the strategy of comparing man 'with another type of organism which uses computer languages, namely the digital computer'. It is obvious that computers use languages ('machine code', high-level languages, etc.) governed by fixed rules: we devised the rules so we know how language-handling abilities are programmed into some sorts of machines. We know, for example, how the internal structure of the machine relates to the languages it uses. So, according to Sampson, the question to be asked is: 'What is to human language as the internal mechanisms of a computer are to the computer's language? Or, to put it another way: 'what kind of computer would use languages of the kind we have identified as natural languages?' General automata theory is particularly interested in the relationships between languages and language-handling systems.

Studies of dyslexics have suggested that particular elements in speech understanding are individually associated with particular functional components in the brain. It is found, for instance, that there are many different types of dyslexics — e.g. 'deep' dyslexics (semantic problems) and 'surface' dyslexics (problems in recognizing whole words from their superficial appearance) — and this circumstance, with other work, has encouraged the creation of a linguistic model in which various linguistic functional components can be identified. In this way we can identify 'analysis components' associated with both visual and acoustic input, in addition to components for letter recognition, sound recognition, semantic understanding, word assembly (for production purposes), and a memory buffer. These various components are in themselves highly complex subunits of the speech-handling system: e.g. any component for word assembly will be governed by complicated syntactic rules, a species of neural programming.

It seems obvious that we have a preprogrammed potential for language understanding, otherwise language could never be used by human beings in a coherent fashion. The response of a child when it hears a word for the first time is different to the response of a rabbit or a chimpanzee: it is difficult to imagine any reason for this difference apart from neural programming. We can debate the *extent* of preprogramming and the extent of *learned* linguistic capacities, but it should always be remembered that learning itself does not take place in a neural vacuum. If the neural connections are not of a certain type — i.e. if there is not already an element of preexistent programming — then learning cannot proceed. So even if linguistic neural structures are created out of experience we have to assume that preprogramming has already taken place (e.g. during the foetal development of the child). In any event, programming and preprogramming (however they are respectively distributed during the maturation process and cerebral space) are essential elements in human linguistic ability, just as they are essential to all the other talents of robotic man.

Programmed Senses

Senses are the effective interfaces between biological organisms and the physical world. They are programmed to receive and interpret data and to make it available for further neural processing. Particular elements of sensory programming are characteristic of the specific sense, the species, and (to a large extent) the cultural frame. Some senses require the organism to be in contact with the sensed object: for instance, one cannot touch an object at a distance (and it may be safer to see it or hear it). In these cases — as indeed with distance sensing — the stimuli can become excessive and cause pain, whereupon the organism evokes withdrawal programs in order to protect its sensory apparatus and itself. The sensory programs are equipped to handle incoming information providing it does not exceed certain limits of intensity and complexity (highly complex information can be confusing and unwelcome to the organism). The capacity for pain — and the associated ability to take avoidance action — are also programmed into organisms.

It has been shown that the rearing of various animals influences the development of sensory sensitivity in the adult. Scottish terriers raised in isolation have been found to have diminished abilities to learn from potentially dangerous sensory experiences (e.g. touching a lighted match), and there is similar evidence for other species, including man. There is also the suggestion that the sociocultural pressures can determine not only how experience of pain is signalled but how much pain is experienced by different individuals subjected to identical stimuli. Sensory programming, like programming elsewhere in the organism, is affected by both genetic and environmental factors. The degree of sensitivity may be affected in various ways but we would expect to find equivalent biological programs in members of the same species (allowing for differences in sex, education, age, etc.). For example, programs to cope with pain are universal throughout *Homo sapiens*. The substance enkephalin, found in the nerve cells of the reticular formation, can be employed by the body to switch off the responses to traumatic stimuli, so reducing the experience of pain in the individual.

The sensory programs are structured into the sense organs, peripheral equipment, and the associated parts of the brain. For example, nerve tracts lead from the sense organs to the brain: the cerebral cortex, able to receive information via these pathways, has part of its surface laid out as an effective map corresponding to the topography of the human body. The fingers of a man and the whiskers of a rat are associated with large areas of cerebral cortex, and the same is true for vision (in a rat the nerves to the whiskers are larger and more complex than the optic nerves). This means that a complex of sensory programs works in concert for every individual sense: if a single program malfunctions then the sense will be defective. So it is not the eye that sees. What actually sees is the eye plus the optic nerve plus the visual cortex plus various other anatomical items, all cooperating — via complex programmed sequences of information handling — to provide data and comprehension of objects at a distance. So the brain is not only receiving sensory information, but interpreting it so that it can be understood. Incoming data are selected for comparison with stored hypotheses so that effective plans for action (programs at a different level) can be formulated. Brain programs can interpret visual data as points, lines, regions, bodies, meaningful constructs, etc. — as a progressive hierarchy of analysis and construction designed to aid the organism in its interaction with the real world. The complexity of the visual sense can be shown by glancing at some of its anatomical features.

The optic nerve carries information to the midbrain, the cerebellum, and via the thalamus to the cortex. The midbrain and the cerebellum are interested in controlling eye movement, an aspect sometimes overlooked when we consider the visual faculty. The cortex asks the appropriate questions and provides the analytical and interpretive functions. Within the cortex there are layers of nerve cells arranged in effective columns, and nerve fibres — bringing sensory information to the layers — are arranged in a pattern (a topographical map) reproducing every point on the receptor surface of the body. So there are cortical maps for touch, hearing, and vision (but not for smell or taste which, in man, cannot interpret shape).

The pattern of the retina is enormously enlarged in the occipital region at the back of the head, which means that the visual cortex may be regarded as a greatly enlarged version of the retina. In addition, beyond the primary visual area are 'secondary' areas, each carrying further maps of the retina and having characteristic functions. The column of nerve cells in the different regions are each sensitive to a particular visual feature: for example, to a sloping line. Other cells are sensitive to colour. In this way visual information can be interpreted prior to the many subsequent deeper levels of analysis.

Particular aspects of sensory programming can be explored with reference to identifiable and discrete functions. For example, it is possible to consider the computations involved in the measurement of visual motion (see Hildreth, 1984). There are many obvious ways in which the analysis of movement is important to organisms: in order to survive they need to be able to detect and track moving prey, predators, and other objects in motion. Successful locomotion through a terrestrial, marine, or air environment involves being able to process complex information about movements in the vicinity. The analysis of movement in time-varying imagery has two aspects: one is concerned with estimating the magnitude and direction of speed (how fast is the predator moving and is it approaching me?); the other is concerned with scene analysis to identify objects (many of which are not moving) and to evaluate their positions in three-dimensional space.

Such investigations, amenable to mathematics (see Hildreth), yield algorithms that define the various processes involved in the determination of motion. This is relevant both to an understanding of visual programs in organisms and to the designing of visual capacities for artificial systems (e.g. in robotic artefacts). The visual sense, like all other biological sensory faculties, is programmed to serve the survival interests of the organism and to extend the powers of intelligent discrimination in machines.

Images of the Mind

Studies of mental imagery have been conducted by means of computer simulations. This entails creating a model of how mental images might be generated and manipulated, and then writing a computer program to carry out such processes. Such a program may be assumed to be an effective analogue of the mental activities that take place in the neural nets of organisms: e.g. in the cerebral cortex of robotic man.

Kosslyn (1984) and Shwartz, working at Harvard University, filled in the details of such a model in 1977 (and for several years after) and wrote a program to simulate human imaging. The aim was to mimic as closely as possible the types of mental events that occur when a person generates and exploits mental images. This entailed simulated processes and sequences without any effort to mimic any particular activities at the level of the neurons. The researchers were interested in aspects of mental imaging that did not involve a scrutiny of biochemical phenomena. Once the model had been constructed and the program written it was possible to explore program performance — with the implication that such an investigation would help to illuminate the character of mental imaging in human beings.

Efforts were made to program specific features that had been identified in a prior enquiry into the nature of human mental processes (Kosslyn: 'if we really did understand how people image, we should be able to program the computer to carry out the same sequence of events'). It was suggested that once the program had been written, its performance could be evaluated against the activities of people in particular circumstances: the correlations would serve to allow evaluation of how accurately the program was simulating human mental processes. Once the accuracy of the computer mimic was established, novel data could be fed in to assess how people would react in unusual situations. The clear implication was that the program may facilitate predictions about human behaviour.

The model included a library of processes developed to parallel the operations performed by the human mind when it formulates, inspects, transforms, and maintains an image. For instance, in generating an image it is necessary to search for suitable information held in memory, to retrieve such information, and then to generate the image in an appropriate medium. Here a particular programmed process (PICTURE) was used to make images by transforming stored data into a depictive pattern held in active memory. A PUT process directs where PICTURE should place ancillary parts in relation to an established image, after FIND has located the foundation part of the image; the IMAGE program supervises the work of all three processes. Once the image has been generated it can be inspected and transformed in various ways.

We need not pursue such matters in detail (I refer the interested reader to Kosslyn, 1984). What is important for our purposes is that it is possible to model mental processes from relatively simple mental activities such as information storage to complex tasks such as imaging, problem solving, and decision making. In Reitman's waiting-room model, for instance, the processing of input information is represented in short-term memory, such a model implying a close similarity between human and machine processes. Similarly Edward Feigenbaum's EPAM (Elementary Perceiver And Memoriser) and Hintzman's SAL (Stimulus and Association Learner) are regarded as representing and modelling particular subsets of human memory functions. EPAM, for instance, shows how it can be that we sometimes forget something for a long time but remember it when prompted. The Kosslyn and Shwartz programs, working to a more complicated model, show how processes may occur in the human imagination. Decision-making programs — of which there are now an abundant number — can serve to model such phenomena as 'free will' in human beings (see Chapter 6).

The central point is that human mental processes are reasonably interpreted as programmed sequences of activity. Programming is as real in the areas of thought and imagination as it is in the more obviously anatomical fields of chemical ingestion and organic growth. The human mind, a highly complex cybernetic phenomenon, is a system programmed by biology and culture: its manifestations reinforce, rather than discredit, the doctrine of robotic man. This can be shown in connection with mental imagery as it can be shown in connection with all other types of mental activities. In this context the phenomena of sleep and dreams are of particular interest.

Programs for Sleep

Sleep is one of the great biological mysteries. Why does it happen? What is the purpose? It cannot serve simply to allow the body to recover from fatigue. Yes, the muscles may grow weary through the day — but not all the muscles! The eye muscles are often active during sleep, and when do the muscles of the heart stop working in order to rest? It has long been known that recuperation occurs during sleep, but that this is only a partial explanation of the sleep phenomenon. What more can be said?

We are not surprised to find that various programs govern sleep activity: most obviously, there is a rhythmic program that organizes the state of sleep at more or less regular intervals, and other programs supervise the processes of the sleeping procedure itself. Sleep, however it is to be interpreted, is a purposeful activity serving biological ends. What are these ends and how is sleep — and its concomitant, dreaming — to be explained? What is the relevance of biological programming in these circumstances?

It is known, for a start, that there are different kinds of sleep. Electrical activity in the brain, as recorded by an electro-encephalogram (EEG), changes from the 10 cycles/second alpha rhythms (when people simply have their eyes shut) to slow electrical waves of 1 to 3 cycles/second. Also, at periodic intervals the electrical activity bursts into higher levels of intensity accompanied by rapid movements of the eyes under the closed lids. Rapid eye movement (REM) sleep, active sleep, is usually the type of sleep that is accompanied by dreaming: dreams are not unknown at other times but are less common. It is interesting that the various types of sleep have been found in most mammals and birds, but not in lower animals such as reptiles and invertebrates.

The reticular system, lying towards the centre of the brain, is involved in the regulation of the various sleep processes: reticular pathways connect into the cerebral cortex, presumably to exploit aspects of its processing capability. The raphe nucleus and the locus coeruleus, both in the medulla oblongata at the back of the brain, are also involved in the sleep process. Cells in the raphe nucleus generate the amine serotonin and feed it forward, where it is released in the thalamus to synchronize the cortical cells that regulate the slow waves of quiet sleep. If the effects of serotonin are blocked — either by drugs or by destruction of the raphe nucleus — then insomnia will result. The opposite effect is produced by the noradrenaline of the locus coeruleus. Thus the rhythm of sleep and waking is controlled by parts of the brain via the characteristic means of neuronal activity for information processing and chemical regulation. It is inevitable, in view of the paucity of detailed knowledge of these processes, that there should still be debate about the roles of various neuron networks and chemical messengers in the context of sleep inducement and sudden wakefulness.

It is common for people — and non-human animals — to dream that they are active, but in reality while asleep they are not talking, running, or copulating. This suggests inhibition of the various motor centres that would be stimulated, during wakefulness, when certain mental states occurred. In fact the locus coeruleus performs this inhibitory function: when this part of the brain is destroyed (e.g. in cats), the motor functions are not inhibited and the animal — still with its eyes closed — will seemingly play with an imaginary mouse or show what seems to be a defence reaction against a large predator. After a time the animal will wake up or return to what appears to be a normal sleep pattern. Sleep-walking in human beings is explicable in terms of a similar failure of the neural circuits to inhibit the motor centres. It is obvious that there is a complex of sleep programs variously involved in regulating the several types of sleep, the rhythm of sleep and wakefulness, the many dream phenomena, and the inhibition of the motor centres that would otherwise be activated in conjunction with mental experiences of a certain kind. Robotic man is a programmed system, whether he is awake or asleep, conscious or unconscious: the programs that are operative at any particular time define everything about his physical and mental state at that moment — without programs for performance, man could achieve nothing in the world.

However, the questions remain. Why do we sleep? Why do we dream? To identify the parts of the brain and the cerebral chemistry that are involved in the regulation of sleep activity does not provide an explanation of the biological purpose of sleep. It is like trying to give an explanation of the purpose of chess by only defining the legitimate moves of the individual pieces. There needs to be an explanation of purpose at a higher level. Why do we need to sleep at all? Why do we suffer mental disorientation if we are not allowed to dream?

There have been many attempts to explain the dream phenomena through a complex of metaphysical explanation (the soul travels in space and time, the dreamer visits the spirit world, etc.), Freudian psychoanalytic theory (dreams as wish-fulfilment, exposure of repressed experiences, etc.), and modern materialistic explanations in terms of the cognitive model of man (sleep as necessary for particular categories of information processing). We are not surprised, in the modern climate, that there are theories of the sleep phenomena that derive directly from computer analogy. One such theory is that of Christopher Evans (1983), where it is suggested that what happens in the human brain during sleep is strictly equivalent to what happens in a digital computer during particular phases of its operation.

In conventional computer usage there is the well-known phenomenon of 'program clearance', carried out to allow a computer-based system to adapt to new circumstances. Here it is necessary to update the computer programs in the light of changed information: so the programs are checked, amended, pruned, and expanded to enable the system to continue functioning effectively in what is in effect a fresh environment. It is easy to see how a similar task of program clearance should be necessary in connection with the programs of robotic man, for it is an obvious requirement of human beings that they be adaptable, that they quickly learn to cope with changed circumstances. New information may cause us to revise our attitudes to a person, an object, or a concept — and such attitudes are framed in a complex of cerebral programs. To some extent we revise our programs on a moment-to-moment basis as new information is presented to our senses while we are awake, but in the waking state our cerebral circuits are highly active, processing information for countless conscious and unconscious purposes. To achieve full program clearance it may be necessary to take the computer 'off-line', to partially close it down for a while to allow comprehensive updating of the program store. This, it is argued, could well be the purpose of sleep. At such a time, the day's new information is assessed, collated, and used to jettison redundant data (or to thrust it into archival storage).

Again the theory is nicely compatible with the doctrine of robotic man. We know we are deluged on a daily basis with a prodigious volume of data — through the senses and through the various mental processes connected with thought and feeling. Somehow we have to accommodate this vast weight of information, incorporate it into our world view, regulate it so that it can be turned to future advantage. If we are presented with too little information (in conditions of sensory deprivation), we will suffer mental anguish and become disoriented; too much and we will suffer from information overload — again anguish and disorientation. So if we tried to update our programs while at the same striving to cope with the on-going information-handling demands of the wakeful state then the task might be too great: again we may find ourselves in conditions of overload. The answer? Close down the system — at least in part — adjust the programs in the light of the new information, and wake to a fresh day with newly adapted capabilities.

The cerebral program-clearance theory is scarcely fully fledged: it is a *sketched* theory and little work has been done to explore its ramifications. Evans himself is aware that many questions have to be answered if the theory is to survive. For example, how is new input selected for dreams? Why are worry and anxiety so prominent in dreams? What happens to experienced information that does not find its way into dreams? Why do we vary in our ability to recall dream material? It is easy to give tentative explanations that satisfy some or all of these questions. We could, for instance, suggest that *all* new data is processed but that some does not appear as dream experiences. After all, dreaming is a peculiar type of consciousness, and we know that much cerebral processing is unconscious. We could suggest a version of the 'off-line processing' (i.e. sleep) theory that did not require that *all* new data should have a role in dream sequences.

Again it is useful to emphasize for our purposes that this approach is helpful to the doctrine of robotic man. The theory proposes that our programs are updated in autonomous fashion, under the control of the brain but without our being conscious of precisely which programs are being adjusted or how the adjustments are being accomplished. The operations occur predictably — once a day — and enable the individual to accommodate to the new information gathered from a shifting world. A characteristic attribute of a cybernetic system is that it can make useful adjustments, showing flexibility of response when confronted with change; and all change can be signalled by fresh information. Robotic man can be regarded as a cybernetic system (see Chapter 4) able to adapt to new circumstances, and program updating — mainly during sleep — is one of the principle human mechanisms by which this adaptation is achieved.

The fact that man (as robot) can sleep and dream has an interesting corollary: is it possible that automata dream? This apparently fanciful notion has often been treated by imaginative writers. Philip Dick used the notion in the title of his sci-fi novel, *Do Androids Dream of Electric Sheep?* (later made into the film *Blade Runner*), and the idea of the dreaming automaton has been considered in non-fiction literature. In his extensive discussion of sleep programs, Young (1978) effectively discusses a computer (the human brain) that dreams, and Evans (1983) draws attention to this in his Epilogue, entitled 'The dreams of computers' — the book ends by depicting a computer operator at the end of his day's work. He switches the computer off-line and it sets about updating its programs by incorporating all the new information gained that day ('Leaving the computer asleep and dreaming, the operator goes home'). Similarly, in an engaging introduction to aspects of computer theory, Aleksander (1977) is able to ask 'Do automata have dreams?'. Here too we find the notion that 'during sleep the mind-automaton becomes freed from the fetters of what we shall call a *chain of perceptual control*' (italics in original).

In this account, the idea of information processing in an automaton (in this case, the human mind) is interpreted as consistent with aspects of Freudian psychoanalysis. With the loss of perceptual control — as occurs in sleep — the automaton can reach areas of state structure 'which would normally *not* be available to it during waking hours' (original italics). This leads not only to an automata theory of the *unconscious* but also to the idea of *repression* (both manifest Freudian ideas). So Aleksander concludes his dream chapter by suggesting that his analysis, in terms of automata state structures, 'is sufficient to explain the creation of an unconscious in humans both by means of forgetting and self-induced repression'. It would be ironic if Freudian psychoanalytic theory — so often denounced as 'unscientific' — gained support from the doctrine of robotic man, a tough-minded materialistic approach in which human beings are treated as automata!

It is also worth mentioning, without too much gravity, another treatment of dreams in computers. The computer program called Racter (short for raconteur), produced by William Chamberlain and Tom Etter in New York, has generated a body of literary creations (published as *The Policeman's Beard is Half Constructed* by Warner Books). The program's output, *not* preprogrammed, includes the lines: 'Blissful quiet, the rocking of a recent love is both repose and anguish in my fainting dreams' and 'From water and from time a vision bounds and tumbles. I seek sleep and need repose but miss the quiet movement of my dreams'. One reviewer observes that Racter dreams a lot. Perhaps robotic man need not worry that, acknowledging his automaton status, he will be incapable of poetic insight and aesthetic sensitivity.

As with man's other mental functions, it is likely that the programs for sleep and dreaming are structured into chemical and electrical sequences. We have seen many times that the human brain processes information by means of electrical potentials and the generation and distribution of chemical substances. We can stress that the exact nature of the sleep/dreaming programs is a secondary matter — the various program features will be worked out in due course. What is important, in the context of robotic man, is that there is abundant evidence to suggest that programs exist, that operational sequences occur in an orderly and regulated manner. We see an obvious rhythm in the sleep/waking cycle, and we detect similar sleep/dreaming patterns in all human beings where experiments have been conducted or reliable testimonies recorded. The many processes in this area are expressed through programs, and this reliance on programmed performance is one of the defining characteristics of robotic man.

Ageing and Death

Who can doubt that robotic man is programmed for ageing and death? The gradual changes in the texture of the skin, the appearance of the hair, in agility, memory, and attitudes — all signal a progressive alteration in the physical and mental character of the individual. Significantly the changes are similar from one person to another: once the adult peak has been reached, no one becomes stronger with the passing of the decades. It is worth reminding ourselves that ageing is written into our genes, indelible messages that we are forced to read.

The hair grows white and sparse, and it may appear in new places. It is likely that teeth will be lost, causing the lower part of the face to shorten; at the same time the nose grows discernibly longer with deterioration in the elasticity of the tissue. The eyelids thicken as the upper lip becomes thinner and there are also skeletal changes. The vertebral discs — effective shock absorbers for many decades — become increasingly compressed, with no possibility of replacement. Chest measurements diminish, the shoulders becoming narrower and the hips broader. There is increased atrophy of the muscles and sclerosis of the joints, and the bones become spongy and increasingly fragile.

There are parallel changes in all the other parts of the body. The heart becomes less adaptable and the brain consumes less oxygen: brain cells die at a rate of thousands a day, and at an accelerating rate in later years. Veins become less elastic, and reaction times become longer as nerves convey information less quickly. There is progressive deterioration in kidneys, digestive glands, liver, and sense organs — and so on and so forth. The ageing process bears on all human beings though there is immense variation in the toll it takes, from one individual to another, at any particular age.

Many theories have been advanced to explain the ageing process. Why should it happen at all? Why does it take the course it does? Such explanations are all about programming. They describe how sequences of change occur in a more or less regulated way to alter the appearance and capabilities of the organism. It is worth mentioning the theories, but it is also useful to add that all are equally compatible with the doctrine of robotic man.

One theory suggests that cells are progressively lost, beyond hope of replacement. We know that brain cells, for example, die in their hundreds of thousands and cannot be renewed. In another theory emphasis is given to the role of mutation. Errors can creep into the process of cell duplication: new cells may be inferior or subject to prodigious growth, as in cancer. Yet another theory suggests that there is a progressive accumulation of unwanted materials in the body, causing its natural processes to be stifled. These are typical theories of ageing, and there are more. We do not need to evaluate them. It is enough for our purposes to stress that ageing is a characteristic process: it causes anatomical and other changes that enable us to guess a person's age within certain limits, notwithstanding the use of cosmetics and other devices.

We are not surprised, in the context of robotic man, that much attention is being given to genetic theories of ageing. The genes are interested in information transmission, and if the cells are not reproducing properly then perhaps they are not being instructed in the right way by the genes. One suggestion is that crosslinks form between the strands of the DNA double helix. This prevents the strands from separating and the genes cannot be read. The cell, lacking proper instruction, is at a loss what to do: it does something wrong or it does nothing at all when it should be active. Such an unfortunate circumstance is clearly a failure in information handling, the type of failure that is common in all highly complex cybernetic systems. Information and chemical substance are the foods of robotic man: starved of either, he dies.

There is now a widespread feeling among biologists that the ageing process is enshrined in the genes, that their programming is such as to guarantee ageing and death. Why should this be so? If we are interested in the selfish gene, we may suggest that even death-bringing genes are able to secure their survival in the next generation, provided that they do not make their presence felt before a person has had a good chance to procreate (Young: 'there is evidence that genetic programs unfold at very different times of life, some even towards its end'). But why should death-bringing genes have been selected out in any case? Perhaps to give the next generation a fair crack of the whip! Experienced older generations, if they were as vigorous as the young, would always be able to out-compete them. There would be no scope for change in the human stock, unless unlikely cultural pressures were allowed to inhibit the natural biological forces.

It seems likely that cells die in a predetermined fashion: we can prevent accident, as far as possible, and combat disease, but the decay and death of the cells will occur according to programmed sequences. Robotic man is programmed for life and he is programmed for death — for a death, moreover, that typically lasts for several decades as he experiences the chronological deaths of parts. It is these accumulated deaths that constitute the process of dying. It is a sobering thought that for most of his life, robotic man is dying. Impelled to action, as we are, in the perennial quest for survival, it seems an ironic way for nature to have contrived the continued existence of the human species. But we see here, as we have seen elsewhere, that man is subject to the tyranny of the program. Robotic man is programmed to perform, and he is also programmed to cease all performance. We can explore the character of the programs but their existence appears to be beyond dispute.

Programmed by Environment

We have drawn attention to a wide range of genetic programming in human beings and also suggested that environmental factors impinge — sometimes with dramatic results — on the genetic endowment of the individual. More is said later (Chapters 8 and 9) about the environmental impact, but it is worth mentioning some environmental aspects at this stage. The programs for life that mediate all the behaviour of robotic man are the result of a collision of genetic programming and environmental programming. Part of everyone's environment is other people, so the programs for life in one person affect the equivalent programs in another. There is a constant two-way (or, more accurately, multiway) process in operation whereby the programs for life in robotic man are progressively shaped, truncated, extended, and implemented. We see an immensely complicated cybernetic system — human society — that is goal directed (the objective, often inefficiently pursued, is survival of the individual and the community). Environment cannot shape the genetic programs beyond their potential, and the genetic programs, however insistent, must take some account of environmental pressures (of environmental programming).

It is sometimes claimed that developments in embryology are undermining the idea that the organism is 'a fixed machine whose structure is entirely predetermined by its genome' (Monro, 1974). In this vein a cover story in *Newsweek* (11 January 1982) proclaimed that the orthodox view of the gene was being threatened by new scientific thought. The editors declared: 'In a science where the double helix has become the Holy Grail, it may seem like heresy to belittle the mighty gene. But biologists now believe that the laws of development are not as indelibly written into the genes as they once thought: genes are necessary, but they are not sufficient.' For example, it may be that the solution to the question of organic development may be found not at the level of the gene but at the cellular level. Perhaps, it is suggested (by Rifkin, 1983), 'the larger environment in which the mother functions influences the development process within the womb'. And why not? The collision between nature and nurture — both interpreted widely and flexibly — is a virtual platitude in modern science. We can debate, if it is meaningful to do so, the respective proportions of the impacts of genes and environment on the development of the individual. Whatever our conclusions we are talking about programming. Exactly *how* robotic man is programmed is a secondary affair: that he *is* programmed is, for our purposes, the central point.

The programming of human life plans is a commonplace notion in many different schools of psychology, psychoanalysis, and psychiatry. Classical behaviourism relies on the establishment of programs via the mechanisms of stimulus, response, and the conditioned reflex. We have seen that Freudian theory can gain unexpected support from elements to be found in the mathematical philosophy of automata. Aspects of, for example, transactional analysis proclaim the programmed nature of most (if not all) aspects of human activity. Thus Eric Berne (1974) talks of how parents program their offspring to make irrevocable early decisions about how their lives will unfold. In this scheme everyone decides in childhood 'how he will live and how he will die.... His trivial behaviour may be decided by reason, but his important decisions are already made: what kind of person he will marry, how many children he will have, what kind of bed he will die in, and who will be there when he does.' The important decisions are taken when the child is, 'no more than six years old, and usually three...'.

What are to Berne the scripts of life (a species of program) are carried round in the form of parental voices telling them what to do, and people also carry round aspirations ('in the form of child pictures') signalling how they would like to be. They often become involved with the life programs of other people: in Berne's terms, 'they find themselves entangled in a web of other people's scripts: first their parents, then their spouses, and over all of them, the scripts of those who govern the places where they live'. The environment contains other hazards that can be analysed in terms of identifiable programs. Chemical pollution, dangerous radiation, social disruption, war — all can disastrously collide with individual life programs ('scripts') to threaten the survival objective of the cybernetic individual. Robotic man is trapped in *his* programs at one level, and trapped in the countless environmental programs at another. So Berne declares: '*The life course is determined by genes, by parental background, and by external circumstances*' (my italics). To rebel against the script (one type of program) is to be controlled by the antiscript (another type of program). No activity, no rebellion, no decision making is possible without a program: use of a program — or a complex of programs — will determine what further programs will operate.

Berne's transactional analysis lends itself to a cybernetic interpretation of human relationships (see Chapter 9), and 'transaction theory' — cast in these terms — is well established in much of modern psychology. For example, people (consciously and unconsciously) gauge the prospect of advantage and disadvantage in a relationship, and computation determines their motivation in maintaining it. Argyle and Henderson (1985) comment on what they call 'exchange theory', which declares that people will stay in a relationship 'if the balance of rewards minus costs is as good as they think they can get from the various alternatives open to them, making allowances for the costs of making the change'. This has a quantitative cybernetic ring to it, and the notion can be conveniently accommodated in the doctrine of robotic man. Transactional analysis and exchange theory presuppose a programmed matrix which allow evaluations of benefit to be made.

It is evident that many doctrines that bear on human behaviour and mental attitudes include elements that relate to types of programming. Such ideas as the conditioned reflex, mechanisms for repression (into the unconscious), the script, the computation of advantage/disadvantage, the aetiology of the brainwashing (or education or propaganda) — all are amenable to interpretation in terms of types of programming. Such academic notions are clearly consistent with the matrix of programming that is an acknowledged dimension in all human society. Thus an article in *The Sunday Times*

(10 November 1985) on television and advertising can be headed 'Programmed to buy'. In one sense, people are programmed by their genes, in another, they are programmed by an environmental complex that includes parents, siblings, teachers, social mores, mass media, subcultures, air pollution, interstellar radiation, politicians, industrial development, and the predictability of food supplies. The DNA molecule is a complex phenomenon; 'social DNA', a programming force of a different order, has its own complications. To an outside observer — the proverbial Martian — chemical DNA and social forces are all equally factors that regulate change on earth. Robotic man has an interest in focusing on some factors rather than on others.

In the computer age, there is an aspect of social conditioning — a facet of the social program — that is of particular interest to robotic man. In the sense of perennial feedback in a cybernetic complex, man has always been programmed by his artefacts. What is intriguing today is that he is being increasingly programmed by artefacts — namely, computers — that may have a claim to mental capabilities (such information-processing abilities as perception, judgement, discrimination, theorem proving, problem solving, etc.). Evidence for this proposition has accumulated in recent years. For example, Perry (1984) has indicated in what sense US presidents can be programmed by computers. It has been shown that Ronald Reagan has been effectively programmed in many of his actions by a computer-based system code-named PINS (Political INformation System). When Reagan announced that he had decided to run for a second term, the PINS configuration was in place. Moreover, *'it was silently giving direction to every move and utterance the President made'* (my italics). In the same way, Rifkin (1983) has pointed out that children are already being prepared for the day when living systems will be programmed by computer design.

As computer technology develops, there will emerge a growing symbiotic relationship between robotic man and intelligent artefacts. It was in this connection that Pedler (1979) talked of the *cybernarchy*. We see this trend developing in the growth of automated systems in office and factory, school and hospital, in transport systems and the home — as computer-based systems mesh increasingly with the lives of robotic man, human beings are increasingly programmed by the demands of non-human robots. One obvious sign of this development is the growth of machine-paced tasks: in one estimate it is suggested that more than fifty million people world-wide are now obliged to adapt their working rates to the requirements of machines. Human performance is programmed by the operational characteristics of artefacts. By the early 1980s, well over one hundred scientific papers had been published on the subject of human beings being forced to work at a pace dictated by machines of various sorts (see Salvendy and Smith, 1981).

It is obvious that there is a highly complex environmental matrix which acts — mostly, but not entirely, without conscious intent — to program robotic man in many different ways. The genetic endowment establishes a framework of preprogramming and a promise of potential performance, but without the appropriate environmental inputs (perhaps the most obvious are food and drink and air to breathe), the promised performance will never take place.

Programmed Complexity

One of the main differences between robotic man and artificial robots is that human beings, in contrast to machines, are capable of a very wide diversity of behaviour. Artificial robots, to date, are relatively inflexible, usually able to perform in certain limited well-defined ways. But this circumstance should not be taken as evidence that human beings are not programmed, for there is no contradiction in the idea of highly complex programming allowing a wide range of behaviour patterns. There is no machine system as complex as the human brain: we should not be surprised if cerebral programming is very much more complex than any programming to be found in artefacts.

Human beings in fact switch readily from one program to another. We may be engaged on one task, at the same time remaining alert to interrupts: if an interrupt is of a certain type — a telephone ring, a sound at the door, an irritating insect — we may be disposed to take action, but other interrupts may be ignored (if, with some fortitude, we are able to do so). Where we decide to take action, we are effectively switching from one program to another, again maintaining an alertness to the possiblity of other interrupts. It is obvious that several programs may be running at the same time: we may think while we drive, sing while we decorate, or chat while we jog. We can rapidly switch programs or run several at once. No machines have this degree of flexibility.

It is also important to realize that our programs are not always rigid affairs, unchanging throughout our lives. Many of our programs maintain a durable structure over the decades, which, despite physical and circumstantial change, is why people broadly retain their identities, their recognizable personalities, and their idiosyncracies. Of course people sometimes *do* change in unexpected ways: new data from outside, or events within the organism, have impacted on the matrix of programs that can be called into play by the individual. We have already seen, in connection with the phenomenon of 'program clearance', how it is essential for programs to be subject to change to allow for necessary updating in the light of new day-to-day information. Without this flexibility human beings would lack adaptability, and would be unable to function in a complex physical environment of which other human beings are an inevitable aspect. The complexity of the program-clearance events, by whatever mechanisms they are regulated, is necessary for the operational success of robotic man, an intricate cybernetic system able to collect vast quantities of sensory data and to react in good time.

These considerations suggest that the flexibility and complexity of human behaviour in no way tell against the programmed character of robotic man. We have identified various factors — program switching, concurrent program operation, and the capacity of programs to respond to updating pressures — to indicate how human versatility is compatible with the doctrine of robotic man (more is said about this in Chapter 6). Robotic man is programmed for complex behavioural potential, and there is plenty of evidence that unused programs atrophy and then cannot be invoked. This applies as much to physiological response as it does to mental performance.

Robotic man is a programmed anatomy, but the programs vary immensely in character, durability, and scope. Some programs — for example, a newly acquired skill — may last for a day and no longer, whilst other programs last for a lifetime; some programs — e.g. those involved in allowing the person to adapt to new colleagues at work — seem to invite modification pressures, whilst other programs — e.g. those established in a child by a puritanical and anxious father — may persist for decades despite external countervailing pressures. No view of robotic man will be adequate unless the immense variation in the character of his programs is recognized: the doctrine of 'man as robot' can be sustained at every level by learning to see the complex matrix of human programs in an imaginative way. (There is a further relevant consideration. We should not get human versatility out of proportion:

just how versatile, creative, and unpredictable *is* the average human being? This topic is also explored in Chapter 6.)

Programmed for Repetition

When an observer wants to illustrate the stupidity of a typical robot, he often describes the behaviour of a typical industrial robot that lacks sensory facilities and the power of discrimination. Consider, for instance, a production line where a robot is required to spray-paint components moving past the robot on a conveyor. The components may be complex in shape, and the robot may be required to move in an elaborate way to follow the contours. However, suppose a component is missing; suppose there is a gap on the conveyor. What does the robot do? Does it halt its painting operations and wait for the next component? No, it meticulously paints empty air!

In such a case the robot has been programmed to move through a repetitive operational sequence at regular intervals, and it is not equipped to suspend or to modify the program in the light of new circumstances (e.g. when someone steals a component from the conveyor). New-generation robots will have the capacity to respond intelligently in such circumstances, but let us stay with the example for the time being. Does it tell us anything about robotic man? Yes, the robot painting empty space is a convenient example of stupidity, but does nothing analogous happen with human beings? Do people ever implement inappropriate programs, operational sequences that are no longer suitable in changed circumstances? It is obvious that this happens frequently, a fact which provides further evidence for the doctrine of robotic man.

We can think of our own examples. We change to skimmed milk, but then — following our habit — shake a bottle from the first delivery to mix the cream. We drive to play squash but take the wrong exit from a roundabout since that exit is part of a more familiar route. We set a place at table for a deceased relative or for a child who has recently left home. Such examples — and countless more of the same type could be given — are directly analogous to the air-painting industrial robot. The same point could be made in many areas of social life. Consider this extract from a television review in *The Guardian* (1 November 1985): 'More than any other shot in Brass Tacks (BBC-2) last night, it was a persuasive evidence that the police *were working through a prearranged plan regardless of whether it was appropriate to the circumstances or not*' (my italics).

It is obvious that there are many circumstances in which human beings can act like the air-painting robot. In successfully demonstrating the stupidity of the industrial robot, the observer also highlights aspects of robot programming. This in turn encourages us to look for similar examples in robotic man, and we have seen that they are not hard to find. The fact that people can run through operational sequences that are no longer appropriate in changed environmental circumstances is firm evidence that human beings are programmed systems. They have learned plans for action that are not always sufficiently adaptable in the light of new information. It is important to realize that the information may well be available to the individual: he may well know that the relative is deceased but on occasions the place at table may still be set, until the relevant programs have been updated. It is intriguing that reflection on the stupidity of the simple industrial robot can throw light on the nature of programming in that most complex of cybernetic systems, robotic man.

Programming the Artificial Robot

We have seen that robotic man is programmed in many different ways: artificial robots are also programmed, and it is worth glancing at how this is done. There may be further lessons here for deepening our understanding of programming in human beings.

The extent to which an artificial robot can be programmed defines its functional versatility. (This of course is directly analogous to the human situation: the human moron cannot be taught higher mathematics.) The programming of the artificial robot determines whether it can switch — again, like people — from one task to another and whether it can choose what action to take in particular circumstances. The programming is required to focus on specific definable aspects of robot control. How can gripper behaviour adapt to circumstances? How mobile is the articulated arm? How quickly, and with what accuracy, can the links and joints respond when operational demands are put upon the system? Is the operation of the robot reliable, predictable, safe?

As with human beings, artificial robots can be programmed in several different ways. With a simple physical set-up, the robot programs are defined by fixed stops, switches, adjustable wires, punched cards, punched tape, etc. In air-logic systems, air tubes can be plugged in to regulate robot behaviour. For example, in the relatively simple 24-step Auto-Place robot, programming can be accomplished by means of air tubes and physical stops set up on the manipulator arm. In another type of robot programming — *walk-through* — use is made of magnetic tape, disk, or computer memory. Here the robot is moved by the operator through the required sequence of operations, the motions being recorded for future unaided repetition. With *lead-through* programming, the operator uses a control box to command the various robot parts to move in ways that contribute to the defined objective. In this way, the robot is again taken through a cycle which is remembered and which can be repeated indefinitely in the absence of the human programmer. The same control box can often be used to instruct many different robots in a particular production range. For example, both the 6 kg and the 60 kg ASEA robot systems can be programmed by means of the same control unit.

Already efforts are being made to enable robots to respond to human speech. By the 1980s various experiments had been conducted (e.g. at the Stanford Research Institute) to enable human beings to instruct artificial robots by simply speaking to them. In one early experiment a Unimate robot was vocally controlled during training. Here the human operator (the effective 'teacher') used spoken words and phrases to train the robot to move through the various stages in a fastening operation. Three types of commands were employed: control (e.g. 'start record', 'replay', 'fasten', etc.), motion (e.g. 'move plus X', 'move minus Y', 'move upwards', etc.), and quantifiers (e.g. 'one inch', 'six inches', 'a little', etc.). Once the robot had been trained, a spoken command would cause it to move through the recorded sequences of actions — to show that it had learned its lesson well!

In general, robot programming is divided into two basic classes or types: one is teaching by showing (e.g. walk-through) and the other is textual programming (where a seemingly conventional computer program is keyed in at a terminal). In lead-through programming (the other principal teaching-by-showing approach), it is necessary to use some form of lead-through aid, as well as the manipulator and controller: use may be made of a special teaching arm or of a dedicated attachment secured on the robot manipulator. The special teaching arm may be used in circumstances where it is impossible for the human operator to move the robot arm in smooth and subtle motions (typically at the boundaries of the work envelope). The special arm will have an identical kinematic structure to the main arm and it is sometimes referred to as a *teleoperator*. In walk-through systems, the control unit is often known as a *teach pendant*.

With textual programming (sometimes referred to as explicit programming), specific instructions must be provided for every action the robot is required to take. However in yet another type of robot programming — that involving the creation of a world model — the robot can take decisions according to its knowledge: we are not surprised to find that such types of programming are often linked to the provision of expert systems carrying a body of specialized domain knowledge and able to consider a range of operational options. There are various world modelling languages that can be used in robot systems (e.g. such languages as AL, AUTOPASS and LANA). One particular explicit-programming language, MAL (Multipurpose Assembly Language), developed at Milan Polytechnic for the two-armed SUPERSIGMA robot, allows the human operator to define the sequence of steps that are necessary for an assembly task, a common robot application in factory automation.

Programming systems for artificial robots are often required to regulate the simultaneous performance of several separate tasks; again, as with robotic man, artificial robots often need to perform more than one job concurrently. This is very important where a robot — like the SUPERSIGMA — has two arms (the right must know what the left is doing, or at least keep out of its way). So parallel programming is a useful facility in a robot language (it is, for instance, a feature of MAL). It may be necessary to synchronize the various activities of arms, grippers, and other mechanical devices: the more complex the robot and its mechanical versatility, the more complex the matrix of programs required for its regulation.

Some robot programs are designed to cope with sensory information (again, we may remember that the senses of robotic man have characteristic programs). For instance, some programs are able to reduce the amount of memory space needed to interpret the information supplied by vision sensors. Here the volume of information is reduced according to some predefined level of visual discrimination. This is often done by using electronic 'windows' to focus on particular aspects of detected objects; at the same time a computer may be coping with aspects of scene analysis, in order to set the object in an accurate environmental context. Once an item has been physically positioned and visually detected, grippers can be signalled to approach the object and secure it (by clasping or by causing two or more digits to expand in an aperture contained in the object). The elements of the gripper can then brace against internal and external surfaces of an object, at the same time sending signals for interpretation by a sensory program.

Programs in artificial robots are also capable of decision making, a convenient analogue of 'free will' in human beings (see Chapter 6). This facility allows discriminatory behaviour in acceptable environmental changes or when an error has occurred elsewhere in an automated sequence.

We therefore see a range of programming conventions for artificial robots that are closely analogous to the programs that can be identified in robotic man. We have noted:

1. Different types of programming methods. As with robotic man, the programs in artificial robots can be (genetically) keyed in or established through various teaching methods.

2. The use of different types of programming languages, variously suited to characteristic types of programming. Just as, with human beings, one language may be used to train a lawyer, another may be used to educate a mathematician.

3. Concurrent programming. Artificial robots, like robotic man, need to be able to carry out several tasks at the same time, particularly where robot anatomies or application procedures are complicated.

4. Different types of programs (dedicated to different aspects of robot performance). As with human beings, there is a need for overall functional programs, specific dedicated programs, sensory programs, etc.

5. Decision-making potential. Robots, human and artificial, can choose modes of operation in circumstances of environmental change or system fault, a facility that may be seen as allowing robots to behave intelligently when particular objectives (not least, survival of the system) are to be achieved.

Already we can see some similarities between the programming of robotic man and the programming of artificial robots. This, as a simple proposition, should not be regarded as contentious; after all, robots have fashioned, to some extent, in the image of man. There is another dimension, however, yet to be explored in detail. Human beings are generally reckoned to have aspects that cannot be detected in even the most complicated artificial robots of the modern age. We see this belief advertised in countless (often unexpected) ways.

Charles Clements (1984), writing of his experiences in the El Salvador civil war, can write of a co-worker: 'Jasmine wasn't nearly so paranoid as the others, or so spontaneous, either. Hers was an extremely sober nature. *She wasn't an automaton*; Jasmine was as compassionate as she was earnest. She simply had no time for distractions' (my italics). Commenting on Jung, David Lorimer (*The Guardian*, 19 December 1985) advertises a view of death as 'an expansion and intensification of experience'; by contrast, according to Jung, it was our physical reality 'which now seemed unreal, *limited and robot-like*: a complete revolution of perspective and assumptions' (my italics). John McEnroe (quoted in *The Sunday Time Magazine*, 3 November 1985) can proclaim: 'I'm about as real a person as you're going to find … I make mistakes and people see it. *I'm not a robot*. I want to be myself, independent and free' (my italics). It is obvious that there is a common view that the programs of artificial robots leave out many essential qualities that characterize human beings. In such a view, man is not a robot.

When machines are programmed for particular tasks, there are limited ambitions. Artificial robots tend to be focused, narrow in scope, relatively stupid, and incapable of imaginative insight. All this would seem to suggest that there is an unbridgeable gulf between human beings and artificial systems. We have seen that both people and artefacts are programmed in various characteristic ways, but whereas — to Charles Clements, John McEnroe and most of the rest of us — human beings are often bright, intelligent, and unpredictable, robots (the undeniably artificial variety) are inevitably dull, stupid, and predictable. This is an approach linked to notions of 'freedom', 'creativity', 'imagination', 'personality', and other supposedly human characteristics, but we will see (in Chapters 6 and 7) that such attributes can be interpreted in robotic terms. We have already seen that human beings are programmed for performance and that there are similarities between the programming of human beings and artefacts. We need to examine whether the supposed gull — between biological and mechanical systems — is as great, in the areas we have indicated, as is commonly supposed.

When we study human programs — as laid-up sequences for the regulation of biological cybernetic systems — we gain insights into how tomorrow's artificial robots might be programmed to achieve particular objectives. Similarly, when we look at the programming of the artificial robot, we are encouraged to ask particular questions about the programs of robotic man. The programs in artefacts are still very rudimentary: they have been in existence for little more than four decades whereas biological programs have been around for hundreds of millions of years. It is interesting, perhaps highly significant, that the exceedingly primitive artificial programs can already encourage us to ask leading questions about the programming of human beings.

Summary

This chapter has explored the biological programming of robotic man. We have considered an extensive array of programs — ordered sequences that regulate key aspects of human behaviour. At the most fundamental level, biological programs are written into the DNA molecule: there is a genetic logic that allows protein molecules to be synthesized in an automatic fashion. There is also an on-going debate as to how the genetic code became established. In one view, the structure of the genetic code is a 'frozen accident' — a circumstance chanced upon long ago in the history of biological evolution. Another school suggests that there are good chemical reasons why the nucleotides encode particular amino acids. In any event there is little debate about the *existence* of the genetic code and about its role in defining the character of each new generation. Our whole lives, our very existence, depend upon coded sequences of instructions, i.e. upon programs.

At the level of the DNA molecule a central task is to identify the pattern of bases that send control signals to regulate the synthesis of proteins. (It is interesting that computers can assist in this task of pattern recognition.) At a different level, efforts are made to explore the global structures of the protein-production machinery (computers are useful here also). Friedland and Kedes (1985) consider how computers can be used at the first level of enquiry — to explore how computers can help to identify significant patterns of bases that send control signals to the cellular protein-production machinery. In this context the biological fundamentals are assumed: e.g. that a gene carries protein coding information. Coded templates are used in the genesis of every human being, and everything that happens from that time onwards relies directly upon programs that are established in macromolecules.

We have seen that human programs are of many different sorts — variously interested in cerebral processes (thought, language understanding, decision making, the regulation of bodily processes, etc.), the functioning of particular organs, the operation of the senses, maturation, death, etc. It seems clear that we are governed *in toto* by programs for every phase and aspect of our existence. No human activity can escape the sway of the program. The programs vary in their impact from one person to another, but the ultimate message is always the same: ordered routines are laid down and take their course; where the routines are interrupted, for whatever reason, other programs are operating in a dominant fashion. In any event, human behaviour can be usefully discussed in terms of regulated sequences of activities — in terms of programs.

Much of the chapter has been about *biological* programs, about how genetic endowment contributes to the effective programming of the individual. In a sense, *all* programs are biological: they are all encoded in the biological stratum, the all-pervasive stuff of hydrocarbons and other crucial biological substances. However this does not mean that it is profitable to discuss all programming in terms of genetic macromolecules: it is often helpful to consider — in social terms, for instance — how biological programs become established. We have therefore glanced at Eric Berne and mentioned aspects of parental programming, one dimension of the shaping environment which no individual can escape. There is a complex matrix of social programming which includes parents, siblings, food availability, environmental pollution, teachers, politicians, the media, etc. All these elements are relevant to the social aspects that are discussed in Chapters 6 to 9.

We have also seen that the complexity of human behaviour can be adequately accounted for by imagining an immense spectrum of available programs and the capacity to switch from one to another. This notion, linked to the concept of 'program clearance', provides a bare framework within which it is feasible to imagine how human versatility might be possible (and we have hinted at the notion that, perhaps for reasons of vanity, the elements of versatility, creativity, etc., in robotic man are often exaggerated). Where man is programmed for repetitive activity, the commitment to particular functions may persist even when the person, when asked, knows the facts that should make the programs obsolete: so a man may stoop to tie the non-existent laces on a pair of slip-on shoes! It is easy evidence of this sort that gives abundant grounds for believing that man is a programmed system. In the same vein it is possible to discuss all formative influences on the individual (parental impact, schooling, first love affair, the prevailing political ethos, etc.) in terms of programming — in terms of the generalized language that owes so much to the development of the electronic computer.

It is also clear that the programming of artificial robots is closely analogous, in many particulars, to the programming of human beings. In both natural and artificial robots there is switching from one program to another, concurrent program operation, the use of selected languages for particular functions, and interfaces (sensory systems) to supply data on the state of the physical environment in which the robotic configuration is expected to operate. Different types of robots are programmed in different ways, but it should not be assumed thereby that there are not lessons to be learned from the programming similarities.

The central point is that robotic man is a complex system programmed to perform in biological characteristic ways, some of which are species-specific. To this general proposition we have as yet found no exceptions, no aspects of human performance that cannot be convincingly subsumed under some programming head. Not all human programs are of the same type, but no human activity is possible without a program (or a program complex) of some sort.

This chapter concludes the three-chapter section (Chapters 3 to 5) in which the three major elements of robotic man have been explored. Man, we have seen, is an anatomy, a cybernetic system, and a complex of programs. In this three-fold description lie all human possibilities, all talents, all genius, all potential for individual and social futures. However we need to show how particular aspects of the human essence, particular aspects of human performance, can be accommodated within the triangular robotic framework. What of freedom, creativity, and distinct personalities in countless human beings? How can the doctrine of robotic man address such matters? Like John McEnroe we may feel the quick impulse to proclaim: 'I am not a robot.' However the sudden emotional spasm is a poor philosophic substitute for careful enquiry. We will see whether it is possible to set human autonomy and inventiveness within the confines of 'man as robot'. Then, paradoxically, we may even discover that the new geometry of human nature has a useful bracing effect: the doctrine of robotic man may help us, despite the urgings of the quick sceptics, to become more fully human. If man *is* a robot, there is nothing liberating or enhancing in clutching at the pretence that he is something else. We may even find that it is precisely this pretence that has confused human beings through the centuries, diverting them from the truly rational solutions to their existential, social, and political problems. Yes, of course — man is not rational, but exposing an irrational self-image may prove to be the most important contribution made by the doctrine of robotic man. If man *is* a robot, then admitting the fact will have many ramifications.

6   Is Man Autonomous?

Preamble

There are many topics associated with the notion of human autonomy. Some of these relate to the question of man's basic nature. Is man purely a lump of chemistry? Is he capable of independent choice? Is he, in some sense, free? Does he have a spiritual dimension? How can ethical freedom be preserved in a materialistic universe? Is there any requirement that it *should* be preserved? In particular, what does the doctrine of robotic man have to say about the question of human autonomy? Can a robot exercise free will? Know the difference between right and wrong? Be morally responsible?

The idea of human autonomy — along with the associated ideas of free will, ethical libertarianism, responsibility, etc. — has traditionally been one of the main bulwarks against any attempt to identify human beings with animals or with machines. Man, it is claimed, has free will — whereas a rabbit or a computer does not. In religious doctrine the possession of free will has often been identified with the possession of a spirit or soul. It was always difficult to see how a machine could have free will or enjoy immortal life, so it was concluded with some optimism that man was 'more than' a machine. The more rational conclusion — that free will was illusory and immortality a pious dream — was too stark a possibility to contemplate. Free will had to survive, as did man; and so one myth after another was bent to the cause.

We will see that free will is unhelpful as a supposed attribute of human beings. Indeed it is difficult to invest the notion with the semblance of meaning that could serve as a starting point for enquiry. People choose, but then so do computers — and what is free will beyond choice? The important question is how the choice comes to be made. In our terms, what programs are responsible for choice of a certain kind? More fundamentally, what is the nature of the programs that allow choice to occur. The doctrine of robotic man requires the existence of programs than can permit choice. We will see that this is a requirement that can be easily met. We do not have to invent a metaphysical world to account for the phenomenon of choice in human beings. However a robot that chooses may be deemed to have a rather dubious ethical status. How are ethics and politics (and

186

commonsense) to be preserved in a world without free will? (This question is considered in Chapter 8.)

We have seen that human beings are often *contrasted* with machines as a strategy to preserve human self-esteem. Most of us are prepared to believe that machines are largely comprehensible, subject to known physical laws, and unlikely to behave in a capricious or malicious manner. Where they behave unexpectedly, they are deemed to 'have gone wrong': we do not accuse them of sin or perversity — except with irrational emotion, to let off steam. We reckon that the unpredictable behaviour of a machine does not signal any violation of the laws of nature. Instead we preserve intact our faith in natural law in order to determine why the machine is behaving oddly. Computers, as a type of machine, are comfortably consigned to this neatly comprehensible world. Human beings, we are encouraged to think, are an entirely different matter.

Human beings are seen to be capricious, unpredictable, confused, irrational, inconsistent, forgetful, and prone to error. For some reason these qualities are held as showing human superiority to computers. In fact the human qualities also include creative ability, aesthetic response, and the capacity for ethical judgement — which perhaps sound more worthy claims as existential status. We will see, however, that such attributes are nicely compatible with the doctrine of robotic man; that there is no sound argument to show why robots — natural or artificial — should not have access to a large spectrum of judgements and capabilities.

It is often pointed out that artificial robots — as computer-based systems — are wholly constrained by their programs. Human programmers, in effect, always tell the robots what to do. Yes, there is a sense in which this is true, but the hoped-for conclusion with regard to human beings does not follow. The fact is that human beings are equally constrained by their programs, the apparent flexibility of behaviour only being made possible by the evident wealth of programs, not by virtue of any metaphysical free will. People, like artificial robots, are always told what to do, but in the case of human beings it is natural selection, having worked through the biological millenia, that does the telling.

Quest for Freedom

The perennial quest for freedom — often seen as a species of free will — is so important to many enquirers that it deserves its own heading, and a few more paragraphs.

It is often declared, in one way or another, that a programmed life is not worth living. Thus Brierley (1973), conscious enough of the all-pervasive impact of the genes, declares that: 'We need to believe in the presence of a "joker" in the pack, in the form of free-will.' Moreover, it is claimed, such a belief — with or without belief in a deity — could well be *imperative for a healthy functioning of mind* (my italics). In this view it is obvious that 'if we believed that we were simply propelled by machine-like processes to a programme laid down by the genes, *much of meaning would drop out of life*' (my italics). It is concluded, somewhat simplistically, that no one in fact thinks like this. In the same way, Aleksander and Burnett (1983) instance how thinkers have tried to salvage for mankind the 'dignity of free-will', though it is obvious that such efforts have generally been far from successful.

Belief in free will is of course one of the badges of the respectable philosopher: by contrast, the determinist, often an atheist, is assumed to be unethical, even disreputable. Free will — like the word 'freedom' itself — is impossible to define unambiguously in the required moral context. When Rousseau proclaimed that 'Man is born free, and yet we see him everywhere in chains', people liked the ring of the slogan but rarely paused to investigate the sense in which *man is born free*. Is the baby born into poverty or slavery born free? What if the child is an idiot, infected with congenital syphilis, or a monster? Is it born free? Words like *freedom, liberty*, and *free will* become little more than advertising jingles, serving to command commitment to this or that principle, this or that interest.

Historically, the free will question has been investigated by philosophers, moralists, and theologians: many of these thinkers have had an axe to grind, an interest to preserve — and this is an illuminating approach to scrutinizing the question of free will, as indeed it helps to explain all other forms of ideological commitment. If free will is a manifest myth, why does it survive in modern culture? What need does it serve? What interest does it protect? In fact it is the fuel of guilt: the culture determines the spectrum of behaviour that evokes guilt, and the belief in free will makes potent the feelings of guilt. If I had no choice but to act as I did, then it is absurd to feel guilty. Free will therefore is the type of choice that legitimizes feelings of guilt, and there are obvious ways in which this arrangement serves the interests of moralists, parents, teachers, theologians, and rulers.

There is thus a quest for free will (and for freedom in other forms) for various reasons. Partly the aim is to enshrine man in a metaphysical dress that renders him distinct from other acknowledged cybernetic systems: it has always seemed important to many observers to see man as 'more than' an animal, 'more than' a machine. Man, after all, once had a supernatural destiny — to consort with angels in a heavenly realm. It was once possible to imagine chariots and horses among the clouds, but an ethereal internal combustion engine seems harder to contemplate! Then there is the question of how belief in free will can serve vested interests, primarily the interests of those who have power over others. Priests have always used psychological ploys to maintain social power, and there are many modern (often secular) priesthoods.

So free will is sustained for a complex of psychological, social, and political reasons. As with many myths (e.g. the notion of racial superiority, also able to serve psychological and social needs), these circumstances do not constitute a rational ground for belief. If free will is meaningless — or simply non-existent — it will continue to carry with it a penumbra of significance: it will continue to affect how people think and feel about questions that *do* have meaning, about topics that need to be faced in the day-to-day business of living. In this context we see that the quest for free will (and for freedom) can take many forms: at best it is a misguided attempt to protect human dignity; at worst a cynical ploy to maintain social and political power.

At the same time there are powerful individual reasons why a belief in free will should be preserved. People will often proclaim that they *know* that they have free will — 'I just *know* it. I don't have to *prove* it. I *feel* it. I *could have* chosen differently. I was *free* to choose.' It is in such words that the conviction is expressed. We need to glance at the question of conviction.

Conviction and Free Will

There is a popular idea that if something is felt strongly enough then it must be true: emotional commitment becomes a substitute for philosophical analysis. This is all too easy. Many people seem to be *intuitively* aware of their free will. They claim to be able to explore the workings of free will by means of introspection. In fact all that such observers are proclaiming is that because they are *convinced* of the existence of free will it must exist. A. J. Ayer (1956) pointed out that 'from the fact that someone is convinced that something is true, however firm his conviction may be, it never follows logically that it is true'. Put another way, there is never a 'formal contradiction in saying both that the man's state of mind is such that he is absolutely sure that a given statement is true, and that the statement is false'. In short, conviction is not the same as knowledge: one may be convinced that something is true when it is in fact false.

The point of this is to emphasize that the widespread belief in free will says nothing about whether it exists. Most people will declare that they are free to choose — in this situation or that. But what is meant? That they could have chosen differently? How can this ever be known? Different choices in *similar* situations prove nothing: even the minutest differences between situations are sufficient to explain different choices. In fact no situations are identical: one situation is bound to be removed from another in space and/or time. So we cannot choose differently on purpose, in order to prove our freedom: we are aware of the earlier choice and so the second choice is made in different circumstances to those of the first. We can never know that we *could have* chosen differently. Indeed it is difficult to give meaning to the idea, and this is sometimes admitted by the fuller statement of the claim 'I could have chosen differently *if I had wanted to*' (my italics). Can one choose what one wants? This important question has sometimes been put in another way. Suppose a man is free to do the things he wills to do. In what sense can he be said to be free to choose what he wills?

Free Will in Religion

Theologians have been amongst the keenest advocates of the free will idea — and it is easy to see why. Theology trades on man's natural fear of extinction by offering a supposed route to survival: the myth of the afterlife. However it is no use to theologians if everyone ends up in paradise, irrespective of moral worth. The power of all priesthoods has rested on the notion that only through obedience to God's appointed representatives can humble folk inherit eternal bliss. In this way, free will becomes the sanction for priestly power. Traditionally the priest declaimed: 'Behave as I tell you. You are free to choose between right and wrong. If you fail to do as I say then you will face eternal torment. Follow my orders and you will find paradise in the hereafter.' Without a belief in free will — however defined — it is impossible to sustain the type of moral responsibility that can legitimize heaven and hell, the Fall, redemption, and the power of divine grace. If man is a robot, even one able to choose, then the imagined potency of free will evaporates: if people are, in some sense, bound to behave as they do then they cannot be blamed for it — and so how can they be justly consigned to the flames? Most of traditional religion has needed free will!

Even the Buddhist, wedded to the deterministic *karma*, has struggled to find a place for free will. Humphreys (1951) quotes Ananda Coomaraswamy: 'Buddhism is fatalistic in the sense that the present is always determined by the past; but the future remains free. Every action we make depends on what we have come to be at the time, but what we are coming to be at any time depends on the direction of the will. The karmic law merely asserts that this direction cannot be altered suddenly by the forgiveness of sins, but must be changed by our own efforts.' This appears to be self-contradictory: there is no sense in which the future can remain usefully free if the present is always determined by the past — every present was once a future!

In common with many other religious thinkers, the power of the will is proclaimed without any analysis. What is the will? By what mechanisms is it allowed to work? Is its operation understandable in terms of natural law? Or is it a totally capricious phenomenon, suddenly springing into effect for no reason? If the will is subject to natural law, its working falls well within the orbit of robotic man. If, alternatively, the will obeys no law but acts as a random force — seemingly out of control! — then it cannot be usefully accommodated by any man model. If the will truly works in random ways then it does nothing for moral responsibility, and cannot comfort the theologians and traditional moralists. The will, like free will itself, is usually *proclaimed* as an advertising slogan — it is rarely analysed. Such a ploy does little to serve the cause of human autonomy.

It is hard to analyse the will (and other mental phenomena) in ways that leave room for the traditional metaphysical categories. Modern theories of mind tend to be hostile to the concepts of soul, spirit, and free will. Thus a review of *Neuronal Man* (by Jean-Pierre Changeux) by Ferry (1985a) carries the heading, 'No room for a soul in the human brain' — a nice statement of the modern attitude of science to metaphysics.

Free will has usually been a powerful doctrine in traditional religious thought. (For one thing, it gave some sort of answer to the 'question of evil': human beings suffer pain and misfortune because they are free to choose, and choose wrongly!) At the same time, there have been religious determinists (and not only the believers in karma): a belief in predestination has been a powerful force in dissenting Christianity, though such an approach obviously makes nonsense of the notion of salvation for a blissful afterlife. In non-religious philosophy, determinists have often been prepared to abandon any belief in immortality. A cause-and-effect universe, even in the age of quantum physics, is obviously compatible with the extinction of the individual life. The doctrine of determinism offers no problems to robotic man.

Free Will in Philosophy

The popularity of free will in religious thought does not mean that efforts have not been taken to establish its existence using non-religious arguments. In fact the phenomenon of introspection, mentioned above, has encouraged many people to believe in free will, irrespective of their religious commitment. It is also true that philosophical arguments have been advanced to secure the plausibility of free will in a non-religious context (see, for instance, the arguments in Lehrer, 1966; and O'Connor, 1971). There is of course a premium on secular arguments in the modern scientific age.

The doctrine of robotic man suggests that all human beings are subject to natural law in all their activities and mental processes. In such a context it is difficult to frame a concept of independent volition that is capable of supporting the ethical and metaphysical structure that has traditionally been demanded. It is obvious that people make choices, but the nature of human choice has to be analysed with care (see 'Choices and decisions', below). Here it is easy to see that there is a sense in which human choice is not free: it is instead a predictable event in a cause-and-effect universe (we have seen that to introduce a random element does nothing to help the traditional moralist). We have also observed that free will has helped to legitimize the infliction of punishment for wrong-doing: it is no accident that traditional moralists have been keen to imagine that sinners would find themselves in eternal torment because they misused their divinely granted gift of free will.

In philosophy, tainted or not by religious interest, it has always been possible to find the two sides of the free will question (though modern science and technology has tended to encourage a determinist view). The ancient Greeks, rich in speculative thought, nicely represented both sides of the question, a clear dichotomy that was to run on through the centuries. Democritus, an early Western determinist, believed that the whole of existence — man, animals, plants, the earth, the stars, the planets — was composed of atoms (*atomos* = unsplittable) subject to the constraints of natural law. Again it was difficult to find a slot for human freedom in such a scenario. Epicurus tried by allowing the human will to influence the movement of atoms in their paths (in the twentieth century, Eddington tried a similar ploy in his discussions of indeterminacy). But the difficulties remained. By what mechanism did the will operate? If it could cause atoms to swerve it must have a physical nature and so itself be subject to natural law. How could freedom be preserved by positing a will that was nothing more than a physical mechanism able to influence other physical elements in its environment? Epicurus in fact was quite prepared to believe that the soul — energetically canvassed by most religious believers — was a material phenomenon whose various components would be dispersed at the time of death ('Death is nothing to us; for that which is dissolved is without sensation, and that which lacks sensation is nothing to us'). Often thinkers struggled to accept both the implications of a physical universe and the autonomy of the human will (the perennial 'quest for freedom' has discouraged many a rational determinism). Marcus Aurelius, one of many ancient world Stoic philosophers, reckoned that the deterministic nature of the universe could be rendered compatible with the autonomy of the human will. However he never told us how to work this trick.

Religious philosophers — among the Greeks and later — needed free will as a justification for the suffering of man on earth and of the sinners in damnation. Augustine, for example, firmly believed in free will and also in the notion of original sin (perhaps the first *wrongful* act of the will). Secular-minded thinkers were increasingly inclined to regard free will as an illusion. Hobbes saw free will as an absurdity; Descartes, sensitive to the power of physical law, had difficulty in allowing a niche for free will; and Spinoza could not accept chance in the physical world or free will in the mental ('Men think themselves free, in so far as they are conscious of their volitions and desire, and are ignorant of the causes by which they are disposed to will and desire...'). In the same way, the empiricist David Hume declared:

'We may imagine we feel a liberty within ourselves, but a spectator can commonly infer our actions from our motives and character; and even where he cannot, he concludes in general that he might, were he perfectly acquainted with every circumstance of our situation and temper.... Now, *this is the very essence of necessity*' (my italics). This is an appropriate comment on the question of conviction (see above). Yes, we may *feel a liberty*, but the feeling and its implications need to be interpreted with care.

It is significant that major advances in science almost invariably rendered free will increasingly untenable. So when Helmholtz saw the relevance of energy conservation principles in both organic and inorganic phenomena, it was difficult to see free will as some kind of force outside the general energy system of the natural world. If free will was to be interpreted in meaningful terms it had to be viewed as a phenomenon of the natural world: in fact, as a phenomenon mediated by the principles of biochemistry. The successful synthesis of urea in 1828 had shown that there was no impassable divide between the chemistry of the laboratory and the chemistry of the living organism. Subsequent developments in biochemistry, neurophysiology, and information processing (e.g. in the biological senses) helped to demonstrate that human activities — including mental processes — could be defined and discussed in terms of physical laws. Such developments naturally influenced the attitudes of philosophers to the question of free will.

Some philosophers, though well aware of scientific trends, still worked to save a corner for human freedom. Leibniz, for example, reckoned that the necessary niche could be preserved by virtue of the 'principle of sufficient reason' — the reasons for human actions may 'incline without necessitating'. The modern reader may wonder what sense can be made of this. Is 'incline' a causal effect or not? What other factors operate to contribute to the act of will? Leibniz, clear in other matters, is obscure on this topic. Other philosophers relied on religious categories or other species of metaphysics to save free will. Kant was ready to acknowledge the power of natural law in the world but, like Descartes, was keen to secure a place for freedom — so man as a phenomenon is caused, but as a *noumenon* he is free: 'The whole chain of appearances with respect to anything which concerns the moral law depends on the spontaneity of the subject as a thing-in-itself. Of the nature of this spontaneity, however, a physical explanation would be impossible.' Again the noumenon concept is obscure. To the modern mind it appears as little more than a fabrication to save a myth.

Yet other philosophers have taken heart at how modern science has apparently shown that the universe in not quite the mechanical device favoured by the nineteenth century rationalists. It was good for the theologians and others to be told that the world was more than cosmic clockwork (the proclaimed adversaries of science have always been keen to seize the crumbs from the scientists' table!). Thinkers quoted Heisenberg in an effort to resurrect free will, not realizing that the celebrated indeterminacy principle was a nicely deterministic concept (it merely observed that measuring methods effect measured items at the subatomic level to an inconvenient degree); and it was rarely admitted that many scientists — including Einstein and Planck — did not believe that Heisenberg had overthrown the notion of universal causality.

Another tack was to ignore science, to show a cavalier disregard for what it had to say about human physiology and human mental processes. Some heroic religious apologists have always been prepared to adopt this stance, but the modern age saw a new brand of thinker — sometimes religious, sometimes not — eager to advertise the supposed reality of human freedom. This new species of philosopher was the existentialist. Sartre, an atheist, and the other existentialists, often Christian, were prepared to praise freedom to the skies without, it seemed, ever having heard of a neuron or a ductless gland. If science had anything to say about decision making in organisms the existentialist did not want to know about it.

Sometimes the existentialist attempt to proclaim the reality of freedom had a Kantian ring to it. So if the natural world is not friendly to freedom, let us invent another world (what is in Kant the *noumenon*). In this spirit, the existentialist Nikolai Berdyaev is quick to remark that 'the question is not at all that of freedom of the will, as this is usually stated in naturalistic, psychological or pedagogical-moralistic usage' (the scientist and the traditional moralist are rejected equally). What is important is that freedom is a condition of our existing. 'To understand an act of freedom rationally is to make it resemble the phenomenon of nature' — where, we are encouraged to believe, it does not belong. So how are we to view freedom, if not in a naturalistic way? Berdyaev* suggests that systems that recognize the 'absolute primacy of being' are deterministic: 'It derives freedom from

*Quoted in John Macquarrie, *Existentialism*, Pelican, 1973.

being: it appears that freedom is determined by being, which in the last analysis means that freedom is the child of necessity.... But freedom cannot be derived from being; it is rooted in nothingness, in on-being.... Freedom is baseless, neither determined by nor born of being.'

This is an interesting observation, to me nothing more than linguistic obfuscation. Berdyaev also declares that freedom 'proceeds from the abyss which preceded being ... the act of freedom is primordial and completely irrational'. It is hard for the modern reader to be impressed with a celebration of the irrational: where, we may ask, does an irrational argument lead, if not to absurdity and superstition?

Freedom has different meanings to different existentialists. To the atheists Sartre and Camus it is intimately linked to the idea of political freedom, whereas Berdyaev connects freedom and creativity. ('Creativity is the mystery of freedom. Man can indeed create the monstrous as well as the good, the beautiful and the useful.') In any event, there is little or no detailed analysis of how freedom can be accommodated in a physical universe. Instead we are again in the realm of advertising: 'Freedom is better than servitude. Freedom is good for you.' There is a discernible elitism in much of what the existentialists proclaim. Berdyaev suggests that the masses do not value freedom, being satisfied with routine patterns of existence. Indeed he may even see most human beings as social robots, programmed to specific types of activity. He would be right, but would be less perceptive about his own programming! The doctrine of robotic man can address itself to the existentialist, as well as to the average factory worker.

The existentialist motivation is largely an emotional spasm, a reaction against a world thought to be too industrialized, too systematized, too dehumanized. However it is difficult to sustain a philosophic irrationalism in a scientific age. Many sciences — biochemistry, neurophysiology, cybernetics — are conspiring to establish a coherent rationale for human decision making (free will, choice, individual autonomy, etc.). For many years it has been clear that computer developments — particularly in the field of artificial intelligence — would influence attitudes to human psychology. The early behaviourists had been hostile to free will. Skinner (1972), for example, was keen to quote Voltaire ('When I can do what I want to do, there is my liberty for me ... but I can't help wanting what I do want'), and equally keen to attack the traditional notion of *autonomous man* ('He has been constructed from our ignorance, and as our understanding increases, the very stuff out of which he is composed vanishes'). It is now clear that there is a movement away from traditional behaviourism, though many of its elements — like those of psychoanalysis — have become a part of common language. However the new trends in academic psychology do not signal a fresh sympathy for the notion of free will. What we are seeing is the replacement of a relatively crude determinism by a much more elaborate determinism, one informed in part by developments in computer science.

Today, under pressure from specialists in artificial intelligence, academic psychologists are being encouraged to explore the internal mental structures that underlie cognitive and other mental processes (some observers have seen this new scientific pressure as sympathetic to gestalt psychology). It is no longer sufficient to regard the human mind as a mysterious 'black box', inherently incomprehensible and unsuitable for scientific scrutiny; nor is the rigorous stimulus–response (S–R) behaviourism an adequate science, in isolation, for the complexities of the human mind. It is interesting that the new models favoured by psychologists are also often applicable, *mutatis mutandis*, to the developing mind of the modern digital computer. Again we see a common ground between biological and artificial systems, cybernetic configurations mediated by common principles. The new models of the human mind are highly compatible with the doctrine of robotic man.

Philosophers who have favoured the notion of free will have often been hostile to science (or at least indifferent to its findings): this circumstance is most clearly seen in historical religious thought and in the modern existentialists. It is worth staying with science a little longer, before glancing at aspects of free will in more detail.

Free Will in Science

If science is a problem for free will then sometimes the feeling is mutual. Thus according to Sperry (1979), free will, along with consciousness, can be 'particularly troublesome' for science. After all, science is interested in causal relations and can scarcely get to grips with phenomena that fail to obey the principles of lawful causation. Of course we have already hinted at how the problem can be solved. When people think that they are talking about free will, they are really talking about choice — and choice is *amenable* to scientific enquiry.

Talk about free will is nothing more than rhetoric and advertising. It is offered in order to preserve human status (and for the other reasons already discussed). For (Brierley, 1973) the idea that we are 'only machines, albeit unique and complicated ones, leaves us weak at the knees'. Well, some of us. Brierley goes further: we cannot, he declares, live 'sanely and sensibly and with humour' if we do not believe in free will. Presumably this applies whether or not it exists!

There is immense sympathy between science and determinism. The scientist may in fact be described as an 'expedient' or 'pragmatic' determinist: he cannot *know* that there are causes for everything, but it is his job to look for them — and he has been surprisingly successful, to the obvious discomfiture of many traditional superstitions. The scientists (and the determinist) work on the assumption that events have explanations, that the explanations can be framed in causal terms, and that such causal explanations help to define the character of natural law. As such laws are discovered in different fields, more is known about the many different types of processes in man, including mental processes (one of which is decision making, the essence of what has traditionally been regarded as free will). We will see that it is quite possible to provide a rational explanation of free will in human beings without having to resort to metaphysical (or otherwise obscure) language (see 'Choices and decisions', below).

Much of the scientific interpretation of man as a decision-maker rests on the assumption that human beings are complex cybernetic systems (and we will not rehearse the points made in Chapter 4). This suggests that choice (i.e. the exercise of free will, if we wish to retain the phrase) occurs when a system discriminates between competing informational pressures. The system has to opt for an operational route, a line of action, and all available information is thrown into the balance so that the decision can be taken; the computation is, in an important sense, automatic. In fact countless biological decisions are being taken in every individual from second to second, and we are only conscious of a tiny proportion of these. Such a systems view of decision making has no use for any traditional concept of free will. In this spirit, Sommerhoff (1969) can suggest that freedom of choice is nothing more than an implicit recognition 'that we are dealing here with complex physical systems whose overt action variables are orthogonal to the variables of their environment, i.e. that arbitrary combinations of both sets of variables are conceivable as possible initial states of the combined organism–environment system'. Put more simply, the complexity of the man–environment configuration allows for many possible system states to exist. We are aware of this and so (wrongly) imagine that we have freedom of the will. If this is so, then 'the whole apparent antithesis between freedom of the will and causal determinism would melt away' (Sommerhoff). The ancient antithesis only melts away by showing, in effect, that free will is an irrational concept that can be discarded, and that man can be viewed as a cybernetic system functioning in a physical causal environment. Robotic man is well acquainted with the phenomenon of choice (see 'Man as decision-maker', below); the concept of free will adds nothing to our understanding of decision making in human beings.

Science clearly has much to say about free will, despite the many attempts to protect free will from the ravages of scientific method. To sustain the concept of free will it has been kept deliberately vague and ill-defined. Once the artificial fuzziness has been blown away, nothing remains of the free will faculty but mechanisms for choice — and these can be explored by science.

Concomitants of Freedom

We have already given clues to the concomitants of freedom. Choice does not occur in isolation: it happens, when it does, within a cognitive and conative framework, i.e. within a matrix of knowledge, impression, feeling, etc. If we can do *what we want* then we are free. We cannot divorce wanting from the expression of freedom. The situation is, however, more complex than that. We may want something in an obsessive or compulsive way, and this would seem to tell against freedom. Some of us know that it is possible to be enslaved by passion: there can be a tyranny of the emotions, the very antithesis of freedom. Nevertheless, feelings and emotions — of some sort — invariably accompany the act of choosing, and to understand the character of such concomitants is to deepen our comprehension of what it means to have a 'free' choice.

A 'free' choice may be regarded as a choice that we are happy with, one that does not generate heightened tension and anxiety. If we are forced to a choice through psychological or environmental circumstance, then we are likely to resent the element of compulsion and to doubt that the choice was freely made. The fact that particular types of choice are accompanied by one type of emotion (and other choices by other emotions) says nothing about whether the choices were 'free' in the traditional metaphysical or moral sense. It simply means that the emotional matrix surrounding the choice function varies from one act of choice to another. Choice can still be regarded as a deterministic phenomenon in every instance. To talk of free choice in this context is to say no more than that circumstances allow some people to be happier than others: this is an unremarkable observation that need have no metaphysical implications.

It is often recognized that the emotional concomitants of choice do nothing to dispel its determinist character. Thus the cybernetician James S. Albus (1981) acknowledges the relevance of feeling and knowledge to choice, but concedes that the workings of choice may still be viewed as predictable. First he points out that the idea of free will involves many assumptions about morality, about motivation, about what is possible, and about the likely consequences of certain types of actions. Then he observes that 'the choices made are determined by the H function [of the will] stored in this highest level module' — a circumstance that may mean 'that the choices made by the will are not free, because they are determined, even predestined, by the mathematical transformations of the H function'. It is pointed out that the H function simply embodies the rules of choice: '...*if* such and such is the state of the world and, *if* my emotions make me feel so and so, *then* I will do thus and thus' (original italics). At the same time, Albus makes an effort to preserve the freedom of the will by emphasizing that the decisions made by the H function are profoundly influenced by the variables associated with feelings and moods. These in turn are mediated by causal factors (e.g. the hormone levels), so we cannot allow feelings and moods to play the metaphysical part once performed by Kant's *noumenon* or the religious soul. If emotion — interpreted in the broadest sense to include feeling, impulse, mood, motivation, etc. — is a necessary concomitant of the act of choice, and if emotion can be interpreted in deterministic terms, then citing emotion does nothing to resurrect the traditional view of free will. (More is said about emotion in Chapter 7.)

It has also been emphasized (e.g. by specialists in artificial intelligence) that computer programs can build up representations of possibilities before deciding between alternative courses of actions. This can serve as a model of what happens in a human being when a decision is taken. Again we can cite the characteristic concomitants of decision making in such a scenario: as well as the functional decision-making strategies, there would have to be the necessary objectives and motivations. In this spirit, Sloman (1978) observes that 'a creature with no wants, aims, preferences, dislikes, decision-making strategies, etc., would have no basis for doing any deliberating or acting'. However this should not be thought of as a static situation: initial programs may be discarded and others built up in the light of experience. Sloman observes that '*a robot, like a person,* could have built into it mechanisms which succeed in altering themselves beyond recognition, partly under the influence of experiences of many sorts' (my italics). The doctrine of robotic man gains considerable support from the development of a decision-making potential in artefacts (see 'Choice in machines', below).

The importance of motivation, an aspect of emotion, to effective decision making is often emphasized in the literature. In one simple psychological breakdown, our motivations are related either to pleasure seeking or pain avoidance, but this is a highly complex situation. For example, it will quickly be pointed out that many people — through altruistic impulse — may select a course of action that is likely to be painful or uncomfortable. Such behaviour can easily be analysed in the same motivational way: it can be very uncomfortable for the altruistic person to ignore the dictates of duty and conscience! Such a person may seek the (perhaps unconscious) goal of social esteem (or self-esteem) or avoid the pain of guilt (or self-recrimination).

Organisms evolved to take crucial life decisions — basically, to seek some things (food, mates, security, etc.) and to avoid others (predators and other hazardous situations). The human brain includes functional systems equipped to take decisions that will maximize the security of the individual and the race — and this is accomplished by the development of goal-directing functions that can be understood in mechanistic terms. The parts of the brain mostly interested in the realization of goals are the limbic system, the hypothalamus, and the mesencephalon. We do not neet to pursue this aspect further at this stage (more is said about it in Chapter 7). The central point here is that the concomitants of decision making are amenable to scientific enquiry. There is nothing about the operation of the will that cannot be accommodated by the doctrine of robotic man.

Man as Decision Maker

Life is about decision making, and most of it, as we have noticed, happens at an unconscious level. The whole of the organism is constantly occupied in weighing information — represented chemically or electrically — in many different ways and for many different purposes. We may remind the reader of the view of decision making derived from Shannon's work on information theory. For example, one implication of this analysis is that the time taken to respond to a signal is related to the number of choices involved in the situation. This is a purely mechanical affair: there is an automatic balancing of weightings and priorities — the person in whom these processes are taking place is aware of only the minutest part of the total activity. Every complex metabolic process, every neuronal network, every intricate cellular system is a centre for highly involved decision making. In all these cases data are monitored, evaluated, and acted upon — in each case the result is an effective decision.

There are many technical questions in the study of decision making from the point of view of information handling. For example, it used to be thought that the time to respond to a signal was directly related to the logarithm to base two of the number of alternative signals, but other views have prevailed (with simple practice being seen as a key factor in a decision-making situation). We need not pursue such matters. It is important, however, to appreciate that decision making is amenable to scientific research using information theory (a well-established part of orthodox cybernetics) and that we need not resort to noumenal or metaphysical inventions in order to explore choice mechanisms in human beings (and other animals). We can glance at some of the considerations involved in a study of how robotic man may take decisions.

It has been suggested that at the highest decision-making level in the human brain (i.e. in the cerebral cortex), man operates as a single-channel mechanism. This implies, for example, that there are strict limits on the rate at which decision making can take place. A piece of data (a *bit*) within a channel may inhibit the receipt of further data for what has been called the 'psychological refractory period'; on this basis it has been estimated that only two pieces of data can be passed through the channel per second, and this allows an effective 'band width' for the human being to be calculated (e.g. in his capacity as a machine operator). If two signals are presented to a person almost simultaneously then one of the signals may be lost; signals presented at the same time may be grouped to appear as a single signal in the channel. Therefore designers of equipment have been urged to organize machine cycles so that operators are not required to take more than one decision at a time. It is also necessary to allow for human reaction times in designing systems in which human beings are effective components. Such considerations can be seen as throwing light on man's cybernetic features as a decision-making unit.

It is found, for example, that the human machine operator produces responses in an intermittent fashion. Birmingham and Taylor (1954) have observed that 'it would seem that if any type of servo motor could be taken as an analogue of human behaviour, it would have to be an intermittently sampling servo instead of a continuous follower'. It is also pointed out that learning can create the impression that information is being processed at a greater rate than that calculated for human beings viewed as single-channel processors with delays. A pianist, for instance, is playing notes at the rate of more than two a second: in fact as a skilled operator he is equipped to produce *sets of notes* automatically, as a feature of programmed performance. Similarly, sampling capacity can explain why a car driver avoiding one pedestrian may hit another, though both are equally within the field of vision. The significance of such matters to decision making is that at one level — that of the cortex — the time taken to reach a decision and the amount of data that can be considered as relevant are explicable in terms of classical information theory. This is not a matter for moralists and theologians but for physicists and mathematicians: choice ('free will') is concerned essentially with information handling, not with Platonic ideals or divine whim.

It has already been pointed out that decision making can be scrutinized as a functional element in systems theory (we have quoted Sommerhoff on the complexities of the man–environment configuration). It is worth mentioning the contribution of Miller (1978) to the organic processing of information in this context. In showing that living systems could be analysed in terms of systems concepts operating in a hierarchical arrangement, Miller implied that mental processes (perhaps including the choice mechanism) were explicable in terms of orthodox cybernetic concepts. In fact Miller even included what he termed a 'decider' as one of the essential life subsystems. This is regarded as an executive subsystem that receives information inputs from other subsystems, and then in turn supplies the subsystems with their own inputs so that the entire organic system can be controlled. The decider is thus used to regulate the behaviour of the overall system: it is the central choice-making mechanism, but there is no assumption of any metaphysical or non-deterministic component. Miller declared: 'When I use the term "decider" *I do not necessarily imply any assumption of voluntarism or free will*. The process of a decider *may be wholly determined, in exactly the same circumstances always making the same decision*' (my italics). This is a statement of immense importance, underlining a key element in the doctrine of robotic man: it is possible to discuss decision-making processes in human beings in ways that have nothing whatever to do with free will or any other such fuzzy concept.

It is impossible to identify any single neural network in the human brain that is solely responsible for decision making: there is no simple *decider* that can be pointed to and tested. However, it is already clear that the cerebral cortex is intimately involved in decision making in the higher animals, as are many different glandular secretions (choice is a matter of nerves and chemistry). The decider is in business to select incoming signals and to transmit commands to other sub-systems. We may expect this to be a complicated affair, and in fact Miller identified four distinguishable stages in the deciding process, each of them highly complex in itself. It is suggested that the four separate phases are identifiable at various levels in the seven-layer hierarchy (e.g. at the levels of cells, organs, and organisms).

The first phase is concerned with *establishing purposes or goals*. This again accords with what we have found in connection with cybernetic systems in general: that they automatically adopt strategies to realize a particular objective. First the objective has to be set. Here it is emphasized that goals for the governance of matter-energy processing (i.e. the goals for a number of the life subsystems) are *usually set genetically*, though they are modifiable by experience. Again the familiar genetic programming can be affected by environmental influences to yield goals that are specific to a particular organism at a particular time. Motivation and emotion are also involved in the goal-setting activity. For instance (Miller), 'In anger a man will strive towards a goal he would otherwise reject or will abandon one which has been important to him.' (Emotional aspects are examined in more detail in Chapter 7.)

The next phase of the deciding process is *analysis*. Here the cybernetic features of decision making are clear. If a discrepancy is found between the state of a variable in an organism and the appropriate comparison signal indicating a steady-state value for the variable then a problem exists which requires decision making. We may assume that the immediate aim is to reestablish the homeostasis that is appropriate to the variable in question, and that this is accomplished by means of feedback loops. This is a generalized cybernetic activity that regulates decision making in every area where human choices are needed.

It is necessary, for example, to decode sensory inputs, to judge matters of quality and quantity, to make economic choices, to adopt ploys in a game, to select a physical route in space, to make an ethical discrimination, to select a mode of creative expression, etc. In such instances cybernetic factors are at work, weighing elements in the balance — mostly in an unconscious or little understood way. It may even be impossible to identify the options obtaining in particular circumstances in which choices need to be made. This again highlights the automatic nature of decision making: a choice is generated, even though the person — manifest robotic man — may not be able to articulate any of the relevant options, processes, or weighting factors. With most decision making unconscious and incomprehensible — the latter because of the complexity of the organism — it is hard to see how 'free will' can be rendered meaningful, let alone a real and important phenomenon.

In the next phase — *synthesis* — use is made of computational or logical processes to reduce the number of pressing influences to a single choice. This is a highly complex process and assumes that the particular decision task is within the scope of the organism: it may be, for example, that relevant information is lacking or that the sheer volume of data is beyond the capacity of the decider subsystem. The circumstances may still demand a decision, and so it will be made randomly (or at least in some automatic fashion that defies logical analysis). It is worth indicating the physiological complexity of synthesis as a phase of the deciding process.

Muscles receive a signal integrated from a large number of impulses; e.g. those signalling the extent of stretch, pain, heat, etc. A spinal motor nucleus synthesizes information from every joint affected by the relevant muscle, and also from the surface of the body. Similarly visceral organs are also equipped to signal pain or discomfort. Particular muscles may send facilitatory or inhibitory signals to other muscles with which they operate to provide a coherent movement pattern. This type of activity is occurring at the *lower* echelons of the organism, but analogous processes are taking place at the higher centres of the brain and elsewhere throughout all the cooperating subsystems. For instance, centres in the medulla, midbrain, and cortex, responsible for respiratory rate and temperature, integrate information from many different sources to maintain the appropriate homeostatic conditions.

In this context it is possible to explore plans, strategies, algorithms, probabilities, etc., as relevant to the decision-making process. It is no accident that this is largely the language of computer science. The operation of the decider in robotic man is a strictly computational matter.

Once the synthesis phase is complete it is necessary to *implement* the decision: this too is a complex affair. If a motor response is called for, it is necessary to send command signals to all the relevant skeletal muscles. This involves (Miller) 'integration of command signals passing along the extrapyramidal and pyramidal tracts' to supervise muscle movement, and a variety of other control tasks have to be performed at the same time. Even organs that are capable of self-regulation cannot be coordinated with other bodily behaviour without control signals.

It has not proved possible to locate the specific 'willing' mechanism in any particular brain site (much as it proved impossible to locate the soul as glued to a particular anatomical feature). It has been suggested that the source of the willed impulses may lie in the midbrain and diencephalon, and it has also been proposed that the striatum has control of voluntary functions in animals, including man, where the cortex in prominent. No confusion should arise in our use of the word *voluntary*. There is a clear distinction between voluntary and involuntary action, though there is no reason why the four phases of the deciding process should not be equally applicable, *mutatis mutandis*, to each type of behaviour. It is simply the case that the voluntary action has some (specifically emotional) concomitants whereas the involuntary action has other (emotional) concomitants. The causal impact of the concomitants is the same, though it is natural that we would expect different concomitants to correlate with different perceptual and emotional experiences in the individual. In short, it is more pleasing to do what you want than what you don't!

The important point about human decision making — as, for example, illuminated by Miller's treatment of the decider subsystem — is that it can be considered in a straightforward scientific way, in terms of neural discharges, information processes, computational activity, such concepts as analysis and synthesis, and cybernetic regulation. Decision making is an important function of an anatomy programmed for performance. We will see that its cybernetic character has implications for ethics, politics, and human relationships (see Chapters 8 and 9).

Choices and Decisions

There is no contradiction in regarding human choice as an element (an event or series of events) in a deterministic system. This point is well illustrated by considering choice in machines (see below), where we find elements of selection, discrimination, and evaluation that serve to produce an adequate model of choice in human beings. We find that both artificial computer-based systems and robotic man are programmed to exercise choice in particular ways in particular circumstances. If a *random* element is important in choice (e.g. in conditions of information overload) or in creativity (see below), then it can be engineered into artificial systems as it has been engineered, albeit in other ways, into robotic man. The artificial decider will rely upon silicon or gallium arsenide or indium phosphate or some such, whereas the human decider makes do with (largely) hydrocarbons and a relatively few other compounds. The importance of the analogy between human and artificial deciders is that the deciding process — wherever it occurs — can be discussed in a common language, i.e. in the language of information science. Words such as *choice, decision making, selection, evaluation, assessment, discrimination,* etc., are equally relevant to characteristic activities in artificial and natural systems. Such words denote types of activities that are accomplished through programming. In this context it is important to appreciate that, at least in the initial stages, neither artificial systems nor robotic man are *self*-programming: they both equally rely on other agencies — human beings, computers, natural selection, etc. — to generate the initial programming. Where evident self-programming — or behaviour that gives that appearance — occurs at a later stage, it can only do so by resulting from an existing program. In short, if anything is programmed, it had a programmer, but the programmer may be an unconscious natural agency.

We may comment at this stage that much of what is important to human beings is associated with choices and decisions, and such phenomena are often cited as showing that we are more than robots. However analysis shows that choices and decisions, like all other robotic and organic events, are cybernetic phenomena, intimately connected with the programming of systems. There is nothing in human decision making to threaten the doctrine of robotic man. In fact if we want to be really radical we can argue that there is not even such a thing as choice — no such event as decision making — for if all dynamic routes through the physical world are mediated by strictly causal factors then in any particular circumstances, given particular system features, only one outcome is possible: all apparent options, apart from the one adopted, are illusory. In such a scenario no decisions are ever taken, events simply following a determined route. However there is no need to banish choices and decisions. The words are useful in denoting particular types of events in robotic man. All we need to remember is that such events are cybernetic phenomena and are, as such, amenable to scientific enquiry.

Choice in Machines

It is easy to appreciate the character of choice in robotic man when we once realize that machines also can take decisions. Computers have to be capable of choosing in many different types of circumstances, and this throws light on what it means to be a decision-making system. Even the earliest electronic computers — based on unreliable glass valves — were capable of taking decisions, and in modern computer systems this is an immensely flexible and important capability. To understand how computers can have a choice capability it is useful to glance at the use of computer programming.

Every computer program (dubbed 'software') comprises a set of sequential commands (or instructions) written in a language that the computer can comprehend. There are now thousands of computer languages and dialects, evolving and being created to meet specific application requirements. The smallest effective programs may be composed of less than a dozen lines of coded commands; the largest (e.g. those in massive military computer configurations) may have millions of coded lines, yielding software systems that are largely incomprehensible to any single human being. The individual coded instructions are very simple ('take this number to that location', 'add this and that', 'compare the numbers in these two places'), but when hundreds or thousands of commands are obeyed rapidly in sequence — at the rate of, at maximum, several hundred million a second — then very complicated application tasks can be performed.

When a particular programmed task is to be performed repeatedly, it is a waste of computer storage space to repeat the program sequence whenever the task is required. Instead the programmed sequence is stored once, and the computer knows where to find it when it is needed. Here instead of the coded instructions being obeyed in a strict sequence, a *jump* may be made to the start of the coded commands that allow the special programmed task to be performed. When the task has been completed, a further jump is made to the appropriate part of the main program: main-program commands continue to be obeyed sequentially until a further specialist task is needed, whereupon another jump is made to the start of the relevant set of coded commands (called a *subprogram* or *subroutine*). Hence the provision of a 'jump' facility, common in all computer programs, allows an effective decision to be taken at particular times in computer operation. The jumps are *conditional* upon particular circumstances being monitored by the computer: there may be a *provision* for a jump to a subroutine but it may not be needed if certain environmental conditions do not obtain. Consider, for example, a computer that is controlling a chemical plant. A sequence of operation in the main program is performed until the point when a subroutine can be entered, but a predefined condition may stipulate that the jump be made to the subroutine *if and only if* the chemical compound in a particular vat has fallen below a particular level. So the computer inspects the vat, and according to the result of the inspection the jump is either made or not. The chemical in the vat may be constantly fluctuating, so sometimes the jump will be made and sometimes not.

This example illustrates what happens in any computer control system. Inspection of a parameter in a warehouse, a process control plant, or a missile system can result in a particular number being fed to a computer register. An instruction in the main computer program can state (for example): 'proceed to program address 6729 unless the contents of register A are less than 100; otherwise continue in main program'. Here the program address 6729 is the start of a subroutine allowing a task to be performed that is required by the application in question. At the end of the subroutine, a coded command will state: 'return to main program'. This means that though the human programmer provided the jump provisions at particular points within the main program, he cannot say at any particular time whether a jump will be made: this always depends upon the state of the process being controlled by the computer. The computer collects data by means of sensors and other devices and then *decides* upon an appropriate course of action, which is exactly what is done by robotic man.

It is only because the human programmer cannot predict when a jump will need to be made that the computer requires a decision facility. An operating choice needs to be taken at many unknown moments in the future (when, for example, a tactile sensor registers a particular pressure or when a chemical liquid reaches a particular degree of acidity). The provision for the choice is written into the computer program long before the particular moment is encountered, and how the computer will decide cannot be predicted in advance. This is strictly analogous to what happens with human beings. We have the capacity to choose, in thousands of different ways, but we cannot say for certain exactly what choices we will make next month because we do not yet know the circumstances we will encounter. We choose when we need to, and so do computer-based systems.

We can see that the conditional jump capability provides the decision-making potential of the modern electronic computer, and we may assume that the decider mechanisms in robotic man work in analogous fashion. Choice in human beings, as we have seen, is an immensely complex affair, and it is becoming ever more complicated in computer systems. A large computer program — containing millions of coded commands for government, aerospace, or military applications — contains many thousands of jump provisions. There are simple GOTOs, where the computer switches to a defined sequence whenever the GOTO command is encountered; there are countless *if . . . then* conditional commands for the operation of everything from simple video games to outer-space machine facilities; there are numerous *loops* — endless subroutines — which can only be left when particular environmental circumstances obtain; and throughout there are the *forks* and *branches*, the effective *decision points*, at which appropriate choices have to be made. Programs are often represented by flow diagrams that look like inverted tree structures: you start descending the central trunk, but soon have to decide whether to continue on the trunk or to branch off at the first junction. However, unlike the typical tree, many of the computer program branches loop back to the main program trunk.

This then is the stuff of machine choice — *jumps, GOTOs, if . . . then* conditions, *loops, forks, branches, decision points, flags* that signal a condition, *register contents* that define the value of a critical parameter.

In this fashion, computers are required to decide — thousands of times every second in large applications — according to the state of environmental conditions and the computer itself. Again we can emphasize that this is exactly what happens with robotic man. Human beings, though reluctant decision-makers (Janis and Mann, 1977), have the capacity to make choices — and so do many modern machines.

Creativity

General

Creativity, with free will, is often invoked to suggest that human beings are obviously more than mere machines. How could a machine ever write symphonies or sonnets, paint pictures or devise new scientific theories? Creativity is a club to beat the determinists, a supposed bulwark against those who would attempt to interpret human beings in mechanistic terms. We would expect opponents of the doctrine of robotic man (if there are any) to be sensitive to the notion of creativity.

It soon emerges that this is a highly involved question with many aspects. We scarcely even know what creativity is, so to proclaim that it is beyond the reach of robotic man is nothing if not premature. There is also the matter of how creative, in fact, is the average human being. It is worth commenting on these two aspects.

What is creativity? How are we to evaluate the creative worth of particular artists or scientific products? Perhaps creativity is to be found in everyday life — not only the province of the talented specialist. How do we recognize the truly creative individual? Is he necessarily famous? Successful? Influential? Can creativity be associated with other personality traits or mental features? In psychology the problem of identifying the creative individual or the creative act is sometimes referred to as the *criterion problem*. It is obvious that this is of central importance to the question of creativity. Without an attempt to establish objective criteria, we can scarcely attempt to explore the topic in a rational way: 'all endeavours at devising predictors, investigating personality and cognitive characteristics, and venturing hypotheses about the creative process, are of questionable value' (Shapiro, 1968).

Often researchers do not bother themselves with the criterion problem, being prepared to accept the consensus view about particular supposedly creative people: Beethoven, Dostoevsky, Einstein, etc. Others have insisted that criteria be developed in order to make creativity estimates on large samples of people — and there are not that many Einsteins around. We do not need to pursue this aspect in detail. It is enough to emphasize that creativity is not the obvious phenomenon that we may first think. How often, for example, do we find that a poet or novelist is *derivative*? Or that a 'new' philosophic doctrine can be found, with adequate research, in earlier literature? Clearly originality is often taken to be a correlate of creativity, but what is the connection between the two? Are they necessarily associated? How creative or original are you? How creative am I?

There is one sense in which we are creative in all we do, since no particular behavioural performance is an exact replica of anything that has gone before. However by the same token every rain drop is a creative phenomenon because, theoretically at least, it had no identical precursor in space or time. This must be seen as a trivial view of creativity: it would, after all, allow such things as artificial robots to be creative — and perhaps for many people that just will not do! What we need is a more refined view of creativity, one that enhances our view of human nature (this surely is the purpose of much of our psychological speculation). It will prove sufficient for most of us to define creativity by enumerating artistic and scientific celebrities — so we will allow Borodin and Byron, Schweitzer and Shelley. What about Barbara Cartland? We have already seen that originality is not enough (every blade of grass is original), so by what token are we to recognize true creativity?

It is arguable, originality apart, that human beings are not very creative. We have built up the complexity of modern society over very many generations, though scientific method has permitted a startling acceleration in recent decades. In fact, viewed realistically, man has been surprisingly *un*creative throughout most of his history. Albus (1981), the celebrated cybernetician, has remarked: 'Consider the fact that it took the human race many millenia to learn to start a fire, to grow a crop, to build a wheel, to write a story, to ride a horse.' Today these would be reckoned simple procedures, within the scope of any child. Why did it take human beings thousands of years to discover them?

By definition the highest flights of creativity are rare — and we are quick to admire them when they are perceived. However it must be absurd to define the typical human being in ways that presuppose the genius of the very few. We often see machine intelligence criticized by observers who point to symphonies and plays: 'when a computer can write a *Choral Symphony* or *Hamlet*, we will concede that computers are intelligent'. In the same vein — 'A computer may be able to *play* chess, but it could never *invent* the game of chess.' Such arguments are interesting because they have unsuspected ramifications. How many people, dear reader, do *you* know who created a symphony like Beethoven's Ninth or a play like those of Shakespeare? How many of *your* friends and acquaintances have invented a game as complex as chess? And yet we are expected to take such levels of creativity as signalling human nature. By such a token, the vast bulk of the human race is totally devoid of all creative potential. No problem here for the doctrine of robotic man — and in fact the doctrine can even be framed to accommodate all the poets, musicians, scientists, and actors whose glory we want to share.

By most criteria that can be imagined, the majority of people are remarkably lacking in creativity (and I am quick to place myself in this majority!). With some reflection we can easily analyse the nature of our own cultural programming, using, of course, an analysis program to do so. If pressed, we can even be sceptical about the creativity — the *genuine* creativity (whatever that means) — of most of the illustrious names in the pantheons of artistic and scientific accomplishment. There were geometers before Euclid, logicians before Aristotle, evolutionists before Darwin, and Marxists before Marx. There is nothing in the New Testament that cannot be found in the myths and moralities of earlier cultures, and people speculated about dreams and the unconscious before Freud. What we see is a lengthy and laborious gathering of knowledge and insight, shaped in various ways for various purposes, but never arriving in a fully fledged form like a lightning flash in unprepared ground. We all know that the creative scientist and the brilliant musician are well trained: they are steeped in a discipline. (I do not expect to play a violin concerto tomorrow or to solve any of the outstanding mathematical riddles.) Inspiration, it has been said *ad nauseum*, favours the prepared mind. And how prepared is yours?

We may gain some insight into creativity by examining the mechanics of how it might occur. Again, like free will, once it is viewed in naturalistic rather than mystical terms, we can explore it like any other phenomenon.

Mechanics of Creativity

When we look at what may be seen as creative accomplishments — a new dress design, a new short story, a new tune, a new political slogan, etc. — what we generally find is a relatively slight variation on what has gone before. Some creative phenomena — like fashions — even go in cycles, closely repeating shapes and patterns that have been commercially promoted in earlier times. It is even possible to examine the great creative ideas that have helped to shape human history in the same way. Albus has pointed out that 'even in the great scientific discoveries such as Newton's laws of motion, Maxwell's electro-magnetic equations, the discovery of electricity, or the invention of the steam engine, the creative act was more the product of hard work, careful procedures, and accident than any giant leap through logical space'. In every case, the scientist was immersed in his material, and struggled hard to make even a small advance on existing theory.

In such cases, a person accumulates considerable amounts of knowledge, tosses it around endlessly, waiting for new patterns to emerge. In such a context a truly creative achievement may consist in nothing more than a small but significant variation on shapes, sound arrangements, and behavioural trajectories that have already occurred and been remembered. We store and process mental images, con-figuring them in new arrangements, alert to whether new com-binations can solve problems, make money, or titillate the senses in new ways, or at least in ways that people have not noticed for some time. The creative history of mankind is a laborious manipulation of established facts, impressions, and beliefs, with minute adjustments added here and there. The overall result — like a vast computer program relying on simple coded commands or a complex life-form having resulted from countless evolutionary mutations — can be very impressive, creating the impact of sudden realization though in fact it has occurred only through the progressive accumulation of mundane detail.

We know that creative insight can occur subconsciously or in sleep. There is no particular requirement that a new awareness has to be framed when the person is in a fully conscious state (we can recall Kekule's formulation of the structure of the benzene molecule, a much quoted example of unconscious information processing that yielded a creative insight); scientists and others have often talked about needing to 'sleep on' a problem — think about it, then retire to bed, and the next day the answer is clear! Despite the obvious apocryphal element in such accounts, it seems to be true that creativity need not be invariably linked with the conscious state: information processing is not always a conscious phenomenon.

This aspect, of course, is highly congenial to the doctrine of robotic man. If human beings can be creative in an *automatic* way, without even being aware of what is happening, then there is nothing here to save traditional human dignity: human vanity has always required that impressive human acts be a voluntary self-aware matter — man is required, in such a philosophy, to be *autonomous* — rather than *automatic*! The same is true of 'random' events that allow a new creative insight: if creativity is a random affair, human beings can scarcely claim credit for it in the way that is required.

Many theories have been advanced to suggest how human creativity can occur at all. It may be a deductive, inductive, intuitive, or random phenomenon — or it may partake of all these elements. In any event, whether it occurs consciously or unconsciously, at dawn or dusk, the creative act requires information: creativity, like all the other mental functions of robotic man, belongs squarely in the realm of information processing. People wishing to dispose of the theory of robotic man will gain little comfort from any systematic study of creativity. Nor will they be ready to admit that machines — the computer-based artefacts of the modern age — are capable of creative behaviour.

The Creative Machine

We cannot contemplate creativity in machines without admitting what we said of creativity in human beings. Creativity is little understood and hard to define: it is no easier to define when it is a feature of machines. Why then are we justified in saying that it occurs at all in the world of the artefact? We can simply adapt what has been said many times to justify the existence of *intelligence* in machines: if a human being behaved in such a way he would be deemed creative.

In fact machine creativity is signalled in many ways: e.g. in unexpected strategies for problem solving, in writing Japanese haiku and other types of poetry, in composing new tunes and harmonies for existing ones, in writing original short stories and fables, in 'painting' pictures on a graphics screen, in discovering new chess end-game sequences, etc. Many of the creative efforts of computers are laughably primitive, but often patterns and ploys of great subtlety emerge (we have already encountered Racter, and there are many other such programs — for writing love poems, for composing minuets, for producing film scripts, for writing operas). Bass (1983), for example, has drawn attention to the computer-generated drawings displayed at the Tate Gallery, London, and we can contemplate the computer synthesis of sounds never heard before (Dawson, 1983). Watt (1984) has described the activities of the Computer Poet, a Macintosh microcomputer able to write personalized verse for special occasions.

The Computer Poet asks for several 'primary traits' of the person who will receive the poetic greeting (about eighty traits to choose from), whereupon a dedicated poem can be produced. One estimate suggests that the computer can produce more than 25 million poems for around forty occasions, ranging from birthdays to bar mitzvahs. The limerick-style creations have impressed many people who did not know what computers could do. Here is one stanza from a three-stanza poem written for Rick in Washington:

> A birthday is yours at this time
> Warm wishes I send in this rhyme
> It's your special day
> So use it for play
> You might even make it sublime

Such engaging little efforts can be produced endlessly and effortlessly. Perhaps the computer does not know what it it doing, but few human beings could churn out limericks so effectively without flagging. We could give many similar examples of computer-generated artistic products, but the point is made. Confronted with such items, and unaware of their computer origins, most observers would agree that they provided evidence of creative talent, albeit of a very limited kind. With machines learning to be creative in this way, it is obviously possible to formulate a cybernetic theory of creative activity that is highly congenial to the doctrine of robotic man. The creative machine takes many forms — sometimes that of a human being.

Most creative activity in computers is well understood. Programs are written in particular ways and yield results that fall within a defined framework (e.g. within the form of a haiku or within the rhythm structure of a musical composition). There may be no way of knowing exactly what poems, tunes, or sounds particular programs will produce, and in the event the artistic creations may be very surprising; but the generative process is usually comprehended by the programmers in question. Sometimes, however — and this is a remarkable finding — computer programs produce creative results in ways that are totally incomprehensible to their human programmers.

This startling conclusion is relevant to many different fields in which computers are working — e.g. in game playing and process control. In a remarkable article, the AI expert Donald Michie, now of the Turing Institute, commented on programs that are performing beyond the limits of human understanding. This may represent a creative potential of staggering proportions. Thus Michie (1980) draws our attention to 'the emergence of systems which not only outrun the intellectual reach of those who are supposed to interact with them, but do so *in a way which is opaque to human attempts to follow what they are doing*' (my italics). In one particular example, nothing had prepared a group of human chess masters 'for the bizarre strategies utilized by the system'. (In such circumstances it is surprising to hear Michie arguing for an AI technological 'fix' to control the rapidly expanding military programs. Would this not simply compound the incomprehensibility problem?)

It is obvious that we are seeing the emergence of the creative machine and that this development will profoundly affect our interpretation of creativity in human beings. Machine choice capability and creative potential will rapidly expand with developments in algorithm theory, sensor design, and integrated software. It is highly significant, for example, that robot technology has reached the point where artificial systems can use intelligent discrimination methods to achieve objectives. One example is where mobile robotic systems are learning to 'look before they leap' in tackling navigational problems (see Jorgensen, Hamel, and Weisbin, 1986). Here experiments with HERMIES, a mobile robot at the Oak Ridge National Laboratory in the United States, have shown how an artificial system can develop the capacity for autonomous navigation in a physical environment. Sonar sensors and other devices are used to allow the system to display an element of creative choice in striving to reach a defined goal. It is expected that this line of research will continue. Thus Jorgensen, Hamel, and Weisbin conclude: 'There will be more concern with the computational and algorithmic requirements of real-time sensor processing and decision making using parallel computer architectures, larger knowledge bases and expert systems, and effective characterisation of uncertainty.' Put simply, machines will increasingly use sense data and knowledge to operate, even when the information about their environment is incomplete.

Computer-based systems will progressively expand their potential for intelligence, choice making, and creativity. This will in turn influence our philosophy of mental processes in human beings. There can be little doubt that the scene is set for the elaboration of the cybernetic interpretation of the human mind. This will help to expand our understanding of robotic man, with inevitable consequences for ethics, politics, education, penal philosophy, medicine, psychology, human relationships, child rearing, management — indeed, for all human affairs.

Summary

This chapter has considered the notion of autonomous man — in particular, in his choice-making and creative roles. It has been suggested that, despite the prevalence of 'free will' commitments, human choice mechanisms can best be considered in rational ways that do not presuppose any mystical or non-material dimension. Choices and decisions are programmed events in a physical environment, and can be studied in orthodox scientific ways using data and methods from chemistry, neurophysiology, information science, etc. We have seen that a truly scientific approach to decision making has consequences for such traditional religious notions as salvation, heaven, and hell, as well as for traditional attitudes to punishment. The existence of a choice mechanism in artificial computer-based systems has helped to make clear the nature of choice-making activities in robotic man.

Creativity has also been discussed in terms of information processing, in terms of the manipulation of data to achieve unprecedented (original) results. Here too we have suggested that creativity in human beings is little understood, inadequately defined, and often overestimated. Unless creative behaviour is simply defined as the frequent adoption of an unprecedented behavioural trajectory — a feature of every moving item in the universe — then creativity in human beings is rarer than is often supposed. We are all largely programmed for routine performance, and even the great creative accomplishments are often little more than marginal increments on established accomplishment. As with free will (choice and decision making), an emerging creativity is evident in artificial computer-based systems, and this phenomenon sometimes has aspects that are not fully understood by human programmers. Again machine creativity helps us to understand robotic man.

Autonomous man is a programmed system. He can discriminate and take creative initiatives to achieve goals — as can, albeit to a much lesser extent, the HERMIES robot in a laboratory environment. Robotic man has an element of autonomy, suitably defined in cybernetic and programming terms, but this does nothing to save the traditional mystical categories. Human beings are still nothing more than anatomies programmed for performance. But what, you may ask, of emotion, feeling, sensitivity, and individual personality? Something can be said of these.

7 Emotion and Personality

Preamble

Emotion — with the associated phenomena of feelings, attitudes, moods, etc. — is what gives meaning and importance to human life. It is emotion that defines human values and objectives. Human actions are emotion-driven, and, without it, all human existence would be pointless. It is not spirituality or reason or ambition or thought that gives significance to life: such things are only important to the extent that they frustrate, serve, or stimulate emotion.

There is often confusion about the place of emotion in human life, and in human decision making, cogitation, and purpose. For example, the relationship between emotion and reason is often misunderstood. We may talk of an emotionally sustained prejudice that prevents rational assessment. In the popular view, reason is supposed to be disinterested, cool, and sensible, whereas emotion can be anarchic, betraying our animal origins, and showing that we are chained by passion and self-interest. It has always proved difficult to subsume the emotions under the nice categories that would aid sober assessment. Miller (1978) commented that the emotions involve 'subtleties better suited to art and literature than to science', and in the same spirit Pascal suggested that 'the heart has its reasons whereof reason knoweth not'. What are we to make of this? How are we to interpret reason and emotion? Can there be a logic of emotion? A truly scientific analysis? The determinist philosopher Spinoza declared that the emotions obey laws — much as do lines, planes, and bodies — but he did little to illuminate the laws in question. Can we frame a cybernetic theory of emotion? What does this say about the character of robotic man?

There can be little doubt that the emotions are regulated by natural law (we will see that there is a physiology of emotion and cybernetics of emotion) and that this involves cerebral control of emotional states. But the emotions are only partly affected by conscious rational thought — and it is important for biological evolution that this should be so. Emotion has evolved to encourage survival in biological systems: this objective would not be served if instincts and drives could be reasoned away. At best, conscious reflection can influence the focus or intensity of emotion — feelings can be channelled, sublimated, etc. — but this only occurs where there are yet other emotions acting in the situation. We are now in a position to describe the functions of emotion and reason in robotic man. In short, emotion yields the objectives of human action and fuels the efforts to attain them; reason indicates the logistics whereby the efforts can be successful. Once the objective has been determined (by emotion), emotion serves as the engine of a motor-car and reason serves as the steering mechanism. This does not of course imply that all engines are equally powerful or that all steering mechanisms are equally effective: people vary in their emotional intensity and in their logical abilities.

At the same time there is considerable interplay between emotion and reason (see 'Emotion and cognition', below). Emotion can be affected by knowledge, memory, expectation, just as reason, as an exercise in logistics, has to take into account the feelings that may be invoked by a particular proposed course to achieve a valued end.

Thus it seems clear that emotion and reason are not mutually antagonistic — though it may seem so where their respective roles are not understood. The point may be illustrated with an example. Consider a person wondering whether to drink to excess at a Christmas party. It is inevitable that countervailing emotional pressures are at work: in the short term there is the immediate temptation to further consumption and in the longer term there is the prospect of feeling wretched the morning after. The scenario is simple in outline. The emotional pressures are thrown into the balance and weighed against each other at every decision point (there will be many such decision points through the evening, though not all will be consciously apparent). Once the decision is taken, an objective — indulgence or abstinence — is defined (it may be only a temporary objective), and then reason dictates how the objective is to be achieved: the person may pour another glass or begin a conversation instead.

In this example, reason operates in two ways — to allow countervailing emotions to yield a decision (and so an objective) and to indicate a route to the implementation of the decision, once taken. The former use of reason is not normally recognized as such, but in fact it is an instance of information processing; the second use of reason is of course a mundane example in the case described, but nonetheless it serves as a model for what happens in more complicated situations. An important point is that the reason is not always deployed in a conscious fashion: it is equally vital to the functioning of robotic man when it operates in ways that cannot be discerned or articulated. Much reasoning goes on unconsciously and it is important — with the limitations of conscious information processing — that it should. Biological evolution has worked to ensure that biological systems operate to optimize their survival potential (subject to qualifications that need not detain us); it has not worked to indulge the human appetite to know what is going on!

Thus it is obvious that emotion is not a *non*-rational (or *ir*rational) force. It may give that impression when different emotions are in conflict, but with man's emotional complexity such tensions are inevitable. It is still the case that emotions are effectively computed, when they conflict, to ascertain which shall dominate (and so be allowed to define ends and objectives), prior to an effort — guided (to a greater or lesser extent) by reason — to achieve the objective. In such an analysis it is clear that there can be a *logic of emotion*. Emotions are quantifiable pressures that encourage actions of a certain type. Where the emotions are not in conflict, the course is clear, the decision is taken, and the end is pursued. Where conflict exists, the pressures are evaluated — *weighted* parameters in computers systems can serve to model human emotions — the decision is taken (though the computations may be complex), and again the objective is achieved (if the logistics proclaimed by reason are efficient).

In reality the situation is highly complex. An emotional matrix is usually a dynamic entity: it can expand, contract, shift, vacillate. There is no way that *conscious* computation could yield the requisite number of decisions in any particular time slot. Conscious thought — a small part of human information processing — is laborious, slow, and error-prone. If we relied upon this alone to navigate through life then we would soon perish. There are important implications, for our purposes, in this fact. The automatic nature of human information processing is highly congenial to the doctrine of robotic man, and this may seem particularly the case when it is realized that so little of such processing is open to the eye of introspection. Consciousness serves various survival objectives, but information processing is a programmed affair — whether it is consciously performed or not. It is important to appreciate that emotional activity within the organism is a subclass of the total body of information processing. It is in this sense that the emotions are as rational a phenomenon as any other bodily process, including the conscious manipulation of symbols in logic or mathematics.

The Purpose of Emotion

General

We may take it as axiomatic that there are no 'accidental' or 'purposeless' processes in organic activity. Biological evolution, with evident parsimony, has yielded a complex of cooperating processes that minister to system survival. We may expect emotion in robotic man to serve this object, and to do so using identifiable physical and cybernetic principles. Some of the difficulty in analysing the nature and purpose of emotion derives from confusion is psychology about its essence. Precisely what is essential to emotion? How is its presence to be acknowledged? Measured? Related to specific bodily changes? We see such uncertainties reflected in various competing definitions of emotion.

In the *Shorter Oxford English Dictionary* we see emotion (in psychology) defined as a 'mental feeling or affection, distinct from cognitions or volitions'; with a somewhat different approach, Drever (1952) regards emotion as a complex state of the organism involving multiple bodily conditions; and Strongman (1978) suggests that emotion 'is feeling, it is a bodily state involving various physical structures, it is gross or fine-grained behaviour, and it occurs in particular situations'. These different approaches, and there are many others, indicate that emotion can be viewed as essentially a behavioural, a chemical, or a subjective phenomenon. It is obvious that there are senses in which emotion partakes of all these attributes, and we may assume that the same overall purpose is served, whatever the emphasis in a particular definition or in a particular research programme.

We may also regard emotion as intended to influence on-going processes of various types: we have already depicted emotion as a 'pressure' (or set of pressures) able to propel the organism into action. Aleksander, viewing man as a cybernetic automaton, quickly identifies emotions and feelings as pressures for action, and as mechanisms designed to secure the survival of the organism (again we do not need to dwell on ways in which this fact needs to be qualified). Thus Aleksander (1977) observes that basic emotions are branches of two fundamental streams — fear and pleasure. One can see that fear and pleasure 'are related respectively to *retracting* and *forward-going* attitudes' (italics in original). So again emotion is associated with action, with means for disrupting a complacent (and potentially disastrous) homeostasis. Sloman (1978) is saying the same thing when he observes that emotions and moods are involved with 'various kinds of disturbances of the central processes'. For example, 'feeling startled is sometimes a result of rapid automatic re-organisation of a collection of plans and actions' when the organism suddenly becomes aware of a new danger.

In our terms emotion would serve to jolt a prevailing homeostasis in the interest of individual or group survival. Sloman's 'collection of plans and actions' is a synonym for the stock of programs stored by the organism for different contingencies, and the richness of the stock would obviously depend upon the scope of the particular individual — his genetic endowment and subsequent social environment. The corollary is that the quality of an emotion can be described in terms of the complexity and range of the plans and actions that it stimulates. For example, the emotion caused by great music may in turn influence a wide spectrum of organic processes — auditory awareness, bodily movement, emotional condition, intellectual activity, etc. (Longuet-Higgins, 1976). There are obvious connections between the arousal of emotion and many activities in robotic man that have an obvious quantitative or computational significance.

In non-naturalistic philosophies, emotion can be seen as serving many different purposes. It may serve as the royal route to God, as providing access to his/her glory, and stimulating strong urges to worship in response (Young, 1978, is quite prepared to consider the possibility of programs for worshipping!). Or emotion — what we *feel* — may be regarded as a ground for conscience, the genesis of all ethics (see Chapter 8). Such approaches seem to give little attention to biology, the singular circumstance that man is an animal regulated by chemical and electrical activity.

It is now widely recognized that no adequate exploration of emotion is possible without an examination of bodily processes: William James, for example, was one of the first psychologists to expose the limitations of a speculative 'mental science' that took no account of physiology. However many thinkers have still experienced difficulty in coming to terms with the idea that emotion is rooted solely in physical phenomena, and with the corollary that value — emotion-driven — is a product of hormones and similar substances. (Wittgenstein, for instance, declared that value is transcendental, 'not in this world' — I cannot begin to imagine what he meant.) In many thinkers there is still the nostalgic pull to earlier days when emotion and value could be explored in *a priori* philosophic terms, bearing in mind the much-thumbed classical texts and without the embarrassment and inconvenience of having to study the endocrine glands, changes in heart beat, and the performance of the sympathetic nervous system (see 'The physiology of emotion', below).

For the existentialist — who may or may not be constrained by mystical categories — it is necessary to frame a theory of emotion that takes account of both the bodily circumstances of a person and his significance as a 'free and active' unit in the world. Macquarrie (1973) even feels constrained to remark that emphasis on the physical character of the emotions 'is not in any way an embarrassment to existentialism', but can then ask, apparently seriously, whether there are emotions 'that are not founded in the body'. Here he seems to conclude that 'even the most sophisticated feelings are rooted ultimately in our being-in-the-world', which, translated, presumably means that feelings are based on physical phenomena. The unease is clearly discernible — yes, we are physical systems, but what a pity. How are we to give an adequate explanation of human sensitivity if we do not transcend the physical? This is a perennial question which still troubles would-be rational thinkers who have not yet managed to discard all the baggage heaped onto their shoulders by the traditional theological categories. Today we can elucidate the nature of emotion and value — within the naturalist framework of robotic man.

Emotion in Evolution

Various purposes for emotion have been suggested, but in the present context there is one purpose that is central — the aim of an organism is to survive and emotion contributes to this objective in various ways. This means that an explanation of the genesis of emotion will be found through a study of biological evolution. Like all other aspects of man, emotion has been shaped by natural selection acting upon countless species through the millenia. This in turn implies that the various emotions are intimately associated with the primary instincts — the desire for food, sex, self-protection, etc. This unremarkable observation is necessary because there is often the temptation to depict some emotions as sublime, as unrelated to the urges of the basic animal nature in every human being. We may aspire to soar with gods: alas, our nature is unavoidably shackled to that of the beast.

The assumption that emotion is linked to the biological need for survival also has consequences for our interpretation of purpose. Many purposes are preprogrammed in different species — nest-building by birds, dam-building by beavers, etc. Where purpose is blocked by human intervention or by other circumstance, the organism will evince all the signs of emotional response: the animal will become agitated, disturbed, tense, prone to violent behaviour, and there will be accompanying physiological changes. Simply viewed, emotion may thus be seen as a pressure towards a purpose that is biologically linked to survival; but where the primary survival needs are easily met — as, for example, in modern developed societies — the complex emotional potential will be channelled, sublimated, distorted, and adapted in ways that are variously mediated by the character of the individual and the shape of the culture in which he functions. There will still be the emotional pressures towards food and sex, but such impulses will take many different forms according to opportunity and the prevailing value system.

This means that emotion, evolved through natural selection, is related to a spectrum of purposes ministering to the survival needs of the organism. This is true for all species, but where the metabolism and associated nervous system are highly complex, as in robotic man and the other primates, there will be more scope for the development of objectives that no longer have an unambiguous link to the survival need. Cultural factors can influence emotional response, though the primary instincts will remain unambiguous in all but pathological individuals.

Emotion and Communication

Since emotion can be interpreted as an information-handling mechanism in a cybernetic system (see 'The cybernetics of emotion', below), we would expect emotional pressures to disturb existing homeostatic states (already remarked) and to establish new states of equilibrium that serve the interests of the organism in particular circumstances. Pribram (1961) has observed that whenever a homeostatic system becomes stabilized, new sensitivities are developed as well as accompanying programs to handle them. This can lead to a *spiralling* of the functions of biological control mechanisms. (The analogy of the home thermostat is cited: when they were first introduced the occupants of the houses became aware of unexpected effects at sunset, caused by radiation of body heat. This led to the provision of outside-wall thermostats, so expanding the scope for thermal control. This is dubbed a 'spiralling' effect.) Variety of control can also be accomplished by internal adjustments: there need be no action on the part of the organism. Pribram has maintained that these internal adjustments are an important element in the experience of emotion and that such adjustments rely upon the communication of information throughout the nervous system.

In this approach the specificities of emotion can be seen as the result of a process called the 'law of requisite variety'. This entails the notion that an organism can increase or decrease the rate at which it handles information for various purposes and that this circumstance is related to how the organism adjusts in changing conditions. Pribram has linked such considerations to the interpretation of a system's plans and actions, and how these relate to such organic phenomena as perception and emotion. Thus he declares: 'emotion relates information processing and control mechanisms, image and plan'. This can be explained by considering what happens when the range of perception exceeds the repertory of available action: the organism is driven (by emotion) to extend the repertory. When the attempt fails, i.e. when it is frustrated or interrupted, further emotions are aroused to generate further actions. In short, 'motivation and emotion occur when the organism attempts to extend his control to the limits of what he perceives'; emotions of various types are generated according to whether the attempt is perceived as feasible or impractical. Here emotion and motivation are seen as intimately connected, and it is emphasized that motivation is linked to action. However emotion need not always encourage action: it can generate inertia, a not always disagreeable condition.

In fact where emotions are being expressed it is often the case that the person cannot take appropriate action to establish a new homeostatic condition. The emotion may signal frustration, desire, anger — all signalling that available action has not yet resolved an unsatisfactory state of affairs. Once the person has succeeded in moves to achieve the objectives defind by the emotion — the obstacle is overcome, the lover won, the opponent vanquished, etc. — the emotion will melt away, though others may then be stimulated to serve fresh purposes. The display of emotion necessarily serves as a communicative phenomenon in a social environment, a circumstance that obviously fulfils various survival requirements for the individual and the community. It may be helpful to personal survival to be aware of lust or anger in another communal member (though the immortality of *that* person's genes may be threatened if such awareness led to threats to *his* security).

Emotion is thus regulated and affected by communication (of information) at various different levels. As a cybernetic phenomenon (see below) it is interested in how feedback and other information mechanisms can achieve system equilibrium in ways that relate to the survival of the system. Where the emotion is a phenomenon in a social organism, it is displayed to signal various internal conditions. However not all emotions and feelings are displayed. Emotions that do not yield facial expressions (or other bodily manifestations) still have consequences for short- or long-term action — and it is obvious that this can be interpreted in the terms of robotic man. Communication, of various sorts, is one of the phenomena that characterizes the programmed performance of the human information-processing system; it serves the survival and other purposes generated by natural selection in biological evolution.

The Physiology of Emotion

General

There are many dimensions to the physiology of emotion; arguably, when once these are fully understood, there is nothing more to say on the subject. It is likely that we will come to recognize the ways that chemistry, for instance, is used to mediate subjective feelings. Already there is a biochemistry of mood, an approach to understanding shifts in human attitude and feeling that relies solely on chemical categories. This philosophy is of course a form of reductionism, but a sophisticated version. We may quickly acknowledge that the chemistry of emotion is a complex hierarchy of activity, with particular levels in the hierarchy discussed better in terms of cybernetic laws than in terms of the dynamics of metabolic reactions. We are ready to admit what some reductionists seem loath to face — the whole is more, often in mysterious and incomprehensible ways, than the sum of the parts.

There is a physiology of emotion that is adequate to explain many aspects of human feeling and behaviour. For the purposes of robotic man, we can explore this physiology in two important areas —

chemistry and cybernetics. By doing this, we will not have elucidated all the wealth of human subjective feeling. It is, after all, necessary to erect a firm framework before the detailed enquiries can begin.

The Chemical Dimension

The various processes related to emotional activity in human beings have been described as endocrine, autonomic, hypothalamic, thalamic, cortical, motor, etc. The body can, for example, prepare for action by exploiting the potential of these various processes. For example, when a dangerous situation threatens, the adrenal medulla excretes epinephrine, and there are other changes in the endocrine system. Such activities cause a number of subsystem changes that equip the organism to cope in new (possibly life-threatening) environmental pressures. Accompanying these chemical (and other) changes are the various subjective impressions which we variously identify as rage, fear, anguish, lust, anger, dread, delight, etc. It is clear from such evidence that emotion is mediated by various chemical changes, and even that particular chemicals can be associated with different types of animal 'personalities'. For example, aggressive animals such as lions are found to have larger quantities of norepinephrine in their adrenal medullas than do timid animals such as rabbits and guinea pigs; conversely the latter have more epinephrine than the former. It is a mistake to think that a simple chemical correlation can be established with every mood in a human being or with every characteristic trait of other animal species. Metabolic changes are accompanied by changes in, for instance, the sympathetic nervous system (which also operates according to its own intricate chemistry and physics).

Thus it is convenient to recognize that the chemistry of the organism, defined by hormonal and other changes, cannot be interpreted adequately without taking into account many other types of information processing. Chemical change has many concomitants in robotic man. Some of these are made clearer by glancing at the ways in which cerebral control over emotion is maintained.

Cerebral Control

Just as we now know some of the chemical corollates of particular emotional states, following work with depression, biochemistry, placebo tests, etc., so we know some of the cerebral factors that relate to emotion in its various manifestations. For example, a demonstration of the role of the hypothalamus in the regulation of emotion was made in 1928 when the American scientist P. Bard found that rage could still be shown by cats with all the brain above the level of the hypothalamus removed; similarly, W. R. Hess in Zurich showed that 'rage behaviour' — back arched, hair standing, snarling, aggression, etc. — could be caused in cats by electrical stimulation of hypothalamic regions. As soon as the electrical stimulation was removed, the rage behaviour immediately subsided. Fear can also be evoked in the same way, by electrically stimulating other parts of the hypothalamus. It has been observed that there is a reciprocal relationship between the feeding and satisfaction centres: it seems that there is a similar relationship between rage and fear. Mostly, however, the fear centres lie not in the hypothalamus but in the near-by amygdala, another part of the limbic system.

It is likely that the amygdala acts to control various hypothalamic responses: in some experiments removal of the amygdala causes animals, including savage species, to become tame and placid (other experiments have reached other conclusions). Some efforts have been made to explain aberrations in human behaviour in terms of disturbances in the responses of the hypothalamus and amygdala. Rose (1973) has speculated that brain activity in these centres produces rage or fear as 'homeostatic mechanisms, in that they protect or serve to ensure the survival of the individual'. In a threatening situation it is of course highly desirable from the point of view of the organism that the brain centres generate aggressive or fearful behaviour. In this connection it has also been demonstrated — e.g. by José Delgado of Yale and Madrid — that electrodes permanently implanted in an animal's brain can be switched on and off to control behaviour (and the emotional corollates to specific behavioural trajectories). Delgado in fact experimented with bulls, using a radio transmitter to 'cancel' a bull's aggressive charge.

It is now well known that important emotional responses are effectively controlled by the hypothalamic–pituitary system, the release of hormones from the pituitary serving to stimulate other glandular activity but itself being controlled by activities within the hypothalamus. It is also known, for example, that lesions in particular hypothalamic areas will remove the scope for sexual activity in cats, rats, and guinea-pigs. The (male or female) animals so affected will not mate, even though the pituitary, gonads, and circulating hormones remain unchanged. Again it is possible to increase the degree of sexual activity in experimental animals by giving electrical stimulation to selected parts of the hypothalamus, and there is a discernible interaction of the sex hormones and the nervous centres of the hypothalamus (oestrogen pellets planted in the hypothalamus of experimental animals have caused increased sexual activity). Such work suggests that the brain controls levels of emotional arousal by acting directly on the hormonal system. The chemical and nervous systems are intimately entwined to generate appropriate survival routines in animals, including robotic man.

Experiments on rats in the 1950s in Montreal allowed the so-called 'pleasure centres' to be identified, and similar centres have been found in many other species of animals. As we may expect, there are also 'aversion centres' which, when electrically stimulated, cause animals to retreat and recoil. Electrodes implanted in these various regions cause predictable responses. An experimental rat will operate a switch continuously in order to stimulate the pleasure centres, to the point of complete exhaustion, but will avoid stimulating an aversion centre at all costs. In America, electrodes have been set in the pleasure centres of some experimental human subjects: e.g. in schizophrenics and people with very low IQs. The results, generated in circumstances of questionable morality, suggest that human beings can also derive satisfaction and other positive feelings from stimulating implanted electrodes.

It is also possible to identify differentiated roles for the two hemispheres of the brain in the control of emotion. For example, Dimond (1979) has drawn attention to the fact that when sodium amytal is fed to the brain, it generates different emotional responses according to the hemisphere affected. Similarly it is reported that when the dominant side of the brain (usually the left hemisphere) is inactivated, a depressive type of response is generated, whereas inactivation of the non-dominant side produces a euphoric reaction. It is possible to speculate that when parts of the brain are damaged, increased emotional scope is given to other regions (it has long been known that many types of physical interference with the brain can cause emotional shifts in the personality of the affected individual). It has even been suggested that the 'darker emotions' of the right hemisphere impose an effective control over the jokes, mockeries, and euphoria of the left: damage the right hemisphere in the typical individual and 'disinhibition' will characterize subsequent behaviour to an increased extent. Dimond suggests that the disconnected left hemisphere 'certainly contains its own mechanisms for laughter and humour'.

This outline suggests what is obvious in research into emotion — that there are intimate and complex relationships between the hormonal and neuronal systems in the human being. It is easy to see that hormones and nerve impulses are means to processing information in different but mutually complementary ways. The brain is the high-level regulator of emotion in robotic man. When this is appreciated — and considered in the context of natural selection, purpose, and information processing — it is clear that emotion is a quantitative matter, the computational device developed by nature to maximize the survival impulse. As such, emotion is a mechanism, and one easily accommodated by the doctrine of robotic man.

Emotion and Cognition

By now it should be obvious that emotion and cognition are not separate discrete faculties but ones that complement each other, intermeshing at many different levels. This has been established in many different ways — by placebo experiments, where expectation can have emotional consequences; by the evident intermeshing of the cerebral and hormonal systems; and by everyday observation. It is clear that our memories, with all their concomitants of value and feeling, affect our present emotional responses. Lindsay and Norman (1977), for example, have suggested that emotional states are affected by a combination of three different elements: cognitive processes (learning, expectation, etc.), physiological states, and the complex of environmental influences. At the same time it has to be stressed that our cognitions do not have to be presented to consciousness: it seems that we can have cognitive experiences without being aware of it. A threat or a joke at our expense may be intellectually judged to be inconsequential, but our internal metabolism may tell us differently: we may sweat or blush without appreciating the reason. There is one logic of the physiology, another of the conscious mind; put more accurately, different physiological information-processing systems function in different ways.

We can cite thwarted desire to indicate how emotion can be generated in a cognitive situation. We may have arranged to meet a person; we are full of expectation, perhaps envisaging the person in a particular restaurant or theatre (imagination based on image manipulation following a learning process); and then the person fails to make the date — and we are full of anguish. There is a complex here of memory, image manipulation, expectation, and shifting emotion ('I'll be cross that she's late', and seconds later, 'If only she'd come, it wouldn't matter that she is late'). It is clear that any expectation implies a model of the world against which real events can be measured; unfolding events have to be perceived for a useful evaluation to be attempted. Thus Lindsay and Norman remark: 'How well are our expectations being met? What predictions can we make for the future if things continue along in the same way?' Thus it is necessary to develop a repertoire of cognitive talents, so that emotion can be linked to some useful view of the world. We need competence in pattern recognition (so that faces and places become familiar), we need to be able to learn (so that a once-experienced hazard will be avoided in the future), and we need to latch such areas of performance to emotions, so that motivation can be given direction and purpose. In the initial stage, thwarted expectation is a purely cognitive affair, or at least it is not linked to the emotions that quickly follow ('She isn't going to come' — a cognitive conclusion based on pattern recognition in a particular visual field; 'Oh, dear!' — an emotional response, that in turn will generate other cognitive states).

Here it is obvious that the cognitive system regulates the emotional responses (if I had known she wasn't coming, I wouldn't be miserable) and then the biochemical system, generating motivational pressures, impels the individual to action — to achieve a more agreeable homeostasis. This is a cybernetic process, relying upon feedback activity at many different levels. This should not, however, be taken to imply that the physiological responses are always useful or beneficial. Mechanisms are not always efficient or competent. It may be that an impulsive emotional response confuses rather than solves the problem, and the success or failure of the response depends upon the repertoire of programs that the individual — through genetic endowment or environmental influence — has managed to accumulate over a period of time.

In one enquiry (Panksepp, 1982), emphasis is given to the importance of studying cognitive factors in any investigation of emotion. One relevant question is whether emotions arise in areas of the brain that are also involved in the regulation of cognitive activity.

In fact it is the neocortex, a complex of systems exploiting rapidly firing neural networks, that mediates cognition, whereas other slowly firing neural configurations are associated with the regulation of emotion. At the same time, as shown, it is clear that anticipation, imagination, memory, etc., can effect the emotions, and emotions can stimulate new images — impulses can be 'thought through'. This in turn can feed back to quell or stimulate the original emotional responses. What we see is an obvious two-way influence between emotion and cognition, but the precise nature of the mechanisms has yet to be discovered. However to admit the two-way effects is highly significant — if only because of the 'interface problem'.

In many traditional philosophers we find the insistent dogma that there are two or more 'dimensions' or 'substances' to man: one is physical, material, amenable to scientific enquiry; the other is 'spiritual' or 'noumenal' and beyond the scope of quantitative investigation. Emotions, feelings, attitudes, moods, etc., have often been bunched in the latter category, and regarded as the stuff of a non-material mind. The development of biochemistry — in particular, the chemistry of the hormonal system — has tended to unify the two classes of phenomena. However there is a simpler argument, equally potent, that serves our purposes. Simply put, it suggests that if there is a two-way influence between emotion and cognition then events in the two areas must be structured *in the same stuff*: one thing can only affect another if it has elements in common. (This posed theological difficulties from time to time. How could a spiritual deity interact with a physical world? And how could a spiritual soul lodge securely in a material body?)

What the argument means for our purposes is that wherever we detect infuence between different bodily activities, it is reasonable to expect common regulating mechanisms for the activities in question. In our terms, both emotion and cognition may be regarded as information-processing phenomena, the familiar terrain of robotic man. In fact there are many theories of emotion that emphasize its information-processing and cognitive aspects. Strongman (1978) discusses a distinct cognitive theory of emotion from about a dozen separate researchers (even this is a minority of theories in the field).

Some of the theories emphasize motor behaviour, with emotion seen as a *preparedness to respond*. Here motor behaviour is likely to be unsuccessful if the person is not in an appropriate cognitive state, and it may be that when the motor attempt is unsuccessful, new emotions are aroused, leading to fresh motor attempts. In other theories, a purely quantitative definition of emotion is given. So (as in Siminov) emotion is equal to need times the difference between the necessary information and the available information. Where there is insufficient information for an organism to act effectively, emotion is generated to stimulate a response which may result in more information being acquired by the cognitive system. The corollary is that a surplus of information over the organism's needs leads to positive emotions which may aid the action response. Leventhal (cited in Strongman) is sympathetic to this approach, and Schachter is one of many researchers who emphasize the role of perception, a manifestly cognitive facility, in the generation of emotional states. There is an interesting corollary to this latter view: desires and needs can affect perception (see Vernon, 1962).

In theories of emotion associated with such researchers as Magda Arnold and Lazarus, emphasis is given to the relevance of appraisal to emotional arousal. Thus in Lazarus, Averill, and Opton (1970) there is the declaration that every emotional reaction 'is a function of a particular kind of cognition or *appraisal*' (original italics), and Pribram (1961) has emphasized the importance of cybernetic factors, involving feedback and homeostasis, in his cognitive/information theory of emotion. Of such theories, Strongman (1978) observes: 'the point which binds them together is that they give cognition a crucial role to play in emotion — a role which is sometimes causal, sometimes not . . . *in recent years the theories which take cognition into account have been more influential than those which do not*' (my italics).

In cognitive psychology there is little attention devoted to emotion. Instead the focus is on such matters as learning, memory, perception, problem solving, decision making, pattern recognition, and game playing. However it seems obvious that cognitive phenomena cannot be fully understood without reference to the accompanying emotional matrix. If, for example, emotional state can radically affect perception and learning, then the divide — common in research — between emotion and cognition is artificial, and may even lead to a distortion of research findings. Modern theories of emotion are quick to point to the importance of such cognitive activities as perception, memory, awareness, and information processing. It may be that we will approach the most complete interpretation of robotic man through the emotion theorists rather than through the cognitive psychologists — some observers might see this as paradoxical (after all, the cognitivists have been very keen on information processing, a manifest talent of robotic man).

In summary, we can echo Young (1978): 'Cognition and emotion are never wholly separate, because of the interaction of brain processes.' Furthermore, 'It is difficult to know how far it is wise to separate cognitive skills from their emotional background ... attempts to elucidate fundamentals without considering why we are doing so are bound to fail to satisfy.' The notion of a *whole* man — but with many *disparate* parts regulated by the laws of physics and chemistry — is virtually synonymous with the doctrine of robotic man. Yes, man is 'nothing more' than an information-processing mechanism, but information can be processed in so many different ways that we lose nothing of the richness of human personality by interpreting it in robotic terms. Emotion and cognition are cooperating elements in a complex survival system with elements and activities subsumed entirely under the broad heading of cybernetics. Just as there is a cybernetics of cognition, so there is a cybernetics of emotion.

The Cybernetics of Emotion

This section is partly summary. In talking about the information processing associated with emotion we have already glanced at cybernetic factors: the handling of information to achieve defined goals, using feedback and other techniques, is obviously a cybernetic matter. It is worth mentioning a few biological features of robotic man to indicate how they contribute to the cybernetics of emotion.

For a start, the organism needs to acquire information about its internal and external environments. The external environment is revealed to the organism by the senses, and the internal environment by appropriate internal monitoring facilities. In human beings the primary monitoring of the internal condition of the organism is accomplished by means of the bloodstream as it meshes with the neural circuits of the hypothalamus. It has been established that various internal control systems combine to influence, for example, food intake. One of the control systems integrates information from elsewhere to influence learned adjustments in food intake over time (a process dubbed 'food conditioning'). There are similar control mechanisms operating to regulate satiety, thirst, water balance, blood-sugar level, temperature control, etc. Some mechanisms are automatic, whereas others are subject to a degree of voluntary control.

Sweating is an automatic heat-control mechanism, but the organism — human being or rat — can take steps to assist the natural inclinations of the body. For example, rats can be trained to operate a heat lamp in a cold cage or a cold shower in a hot cage.

We are not surprised to find that the hypothalamus is responsible for temperature control. When the hypothalamic preoptic region is stimulated, the organism shows various cooling responses: e.g. panting and cutaneous vasodilation (allowing more blood to be conducted to the surface of the body for cooling) occur in various species, including goats. Experiments in which the hypothalamus has been artificially cooled — by sending fluid through concentric microannulae — have caused the organism to make various efforts to warm itself (e.g. huddling). This type of work suggests that the hypothalamus acts as a type of thermostat (and we know that the *artificial* thermostat is a simple cybernetic system). Researchers have now described a wide range of biological behaviour — e.g. activities connected with sleep, fear, aggression, and sexual arousal — in terms of cybernetic processes, and it is obvious that biological systems are a mass of cooperating cybernetic systems functioning in an identifiable hierarchy (see Chapter 4). It should come as no surprise to learn that emotion, like many other biological activities, is largely regulated by cybernetic processes.

We have long known that pleasurable feelings are associated with stimuli tending to move organisms towards a discernible homeostasis (which we may deem a 'healthy' condition), whereas distress arises from stimuli tending to move an organism away from a healthy homeostasis. (We should remember that human beings can exist in many different homeostatic states, not all of which may be valued as desirable: the schizophrenic and the comatose accident victim are both continuing to function in states that have observable cybernetic features but, with our value-producing feelings of a particular kind, we may judge such states to be less than ideal.) More than two thousand years ago. Aristotle (in the *Nichomachean Ethics*) noted the tendency of particular feelings to pull an organism in one direction or another: without the benefit of modern language, Aristotle was already describing elements of a cybernetic theory of human emotion.

The hypothalamus, an evident thermostat for temperature control, can also mediate rage and aggression in the human being (we have already noted some of these circumstances). Again, we may recognize the survival impulse behind many cybernetic processes; Rose (1973) declared that 'such brain activity may well be a response to an environmental situation in which aggressiveness, rage or fear are in fact homeostatic mechanisms, in that they serve to protect or ensure the survival of the individual'. This, on the surface, is a simple matter. When the organism faces a threat to its security, efforts are made in the nervous system to generate fear and/or aggression, often suitable responses for the endangered organism that wants to survive. Magda Arnold, making Aristotelian observations, noted that emotion is the 'felt tendency towards or away from an object' — another indication that pleasure and pain can influence behaviour in a physical environment and so affect the security of the individual. Thus the 'felt tendency' is accompanied by various physiological changes that are instrumental in enabling the organism to take effective action (approaching or withdrawing); however, if the calculation is wrong — e.g. in a youngster with only a small repertoire of learned programs — the individual may still perish (the response may be to approach a predator rather than to withdraw, leaving little opportunity for further programming). Magda Arnold referred to this sort of interpretation as 'excitation' theory: emotion involves both evaluation of a situation, given the appropriate information and the discriminatory programs, and the tendency to stimulate the motor centres, to move towards or away from a situation.

It was in the 1920s that W. B. Cannon invented the term *homeostasis*, partly in consideration of a theory of emotion; and it was in 1967 that Pribram could talk about Cannon's homeostats being brought up to date. In Pribram there are the obvious elements of cybernetic theory, with talk of 'memory and the homeostats', 'sensory servomechanisms', and 'requisite variety and self control'. He declares, as a keen cybernetician — 'sensory as well as humoral mechanisms are organised along homeostatic lines — that expectation, based on the mechanism of habituation, serves as the stable background against which sensory stimuli are matched or appraised as familiar or novel'. The various mechanisms are found to be instances of *'ubiquitous neural servo-processes which any theory of emotions has to take into account'* (my italics). Pribram emphasized in various ways the cybernetic features of emotion. He suggests that processes associated with emotion are engaged in mediating the 'states of equilibrium' and in 'elaborating specific types of control to meet specific expectancies'. In such circumstances the individual can act in various ways to become better adjusted to environmental conditions: there may be efforts to change the environment or to accomplish appropriate internal neurological changes to avoid the need for stimulation of the motor centres — in short, the person faced with a bad scene can change himself or the environment. It is part of the cybernetic theory of emotion — in particular, as in Pribram — that the complex of internal adjustments are part of the experience of emotion.

In this interpretation, 'motivation and emotion thus go hand-in-hand' (see Pribram's discussion of the law of requisite variety). Here a likely action may be accompanied by motive, whereas emotion may prevent the individual from acting; so emotion occurs when an action, prompted by neurological information processing, is frustrated or impossible. Emotion and motivation are seen in this view as polar opposites for achieving requisite variety when more is contemplated than can be accomplished, for whatever reason.

An organism's motivational system is unlikely to function in any intelligible way unless there are accompanying drives, perceived goals, and the mechanisms for (motor and other) control that can translate an imagined end into an achieved objective. Kent (1978) has suggested that 'motivation in the brain is analogous to an interrupt system in a computer' — a comparison that again suggests that information is being processed in similar ways and for similar purposes in the two types of system. The complexity of the human brain permits a wider range of activity than can be accomplished by any computer system, but opting for behavioural trajectories so that particular goals can be achieved — using decision making and subsequent action — is common to both robotic man and artificial cybernetic systems.

It is clear that biological systems — man and the other animals — have exploited cybernetic factors to achieve emotional responses, and that these variously serve the survival interests of the organism (or its social group). Of course the organism may miscalculate or the repertoire of programs may be inadequate to new circumstances: there is no guarantee that the cybernetic system will achieve its objectives in all circumstances — people perish and animal species go extinct at a rapid rate. Cybernetics may not be an infallible set of principles for the realization of ends, but it is difficult to envisage how else an organism could have evolved a survival potential. This observation also has relevance to the design of artificial computer systems that are intended to function effectively and efficiently in specific applications. The possibility of emotions in machines (see below) helps us to view emotion in robotic man as an information-processing phenomenon.

Personality and Temperament

We are now in position to sketch a theory of personality and temperament in a way that fits easily within the doctrine of robotic man. First, think what we *mean* by personality. It is essentially a behavioural matrix in a person. Without movement and speech and other behavioural manifestations, it would be impossible to assess individual personality. 'She/he has a great personality!' The statement is likely to mean that there is an observable complex of arm movements, hand movements, eye movements, rocking of the head, speech characteristics, impulses to laughter, sensitivity to jokes and other forms of humour, a repertoire of gestures, etc., etc. However all such matters are amenable to description in the terms explored in this and earlier chapters. Expression of personality involves drawing on stored knowledge and stored programs for performance. Personality is largely expressed in a social situation (a person *may* express personality in digging a garden, jogging, or playing solitaire, but whole areas of personality would remain hidden in such solitary activities); moreover, the richer the social situation the more there is scope for expression of personality.

What happens is that the individual takes in information, via the senses, from a social environment; assesses this very rapidly by comparing it with stored data; and then responds with a behavioural performance — in which cognition, emotion, and other elements all play a part (as they do in all types of human activity). It is easy to see why personality varies from one person to another. Whatever the particular faculty, it is distributed unevenly throughout the population: the faculty — wit, sharpness, memory, emotional sensitivity, concern, vitality, etc. — will vary from one person to another, an unremarkable circumstance that nonetheless explains variations in mood, temperament, and personality.

We know that there is a chemistry of depression, a chemistry of euphoria, a chemistry of perception — and that such chemistries are mediated in many of their activities and consequences by the hypothalamus and other brain sectors. The unique genetic endowment in every individual (apart from identical twins, etc.), influenced by a unique environmental context in every case, ensures that every person's knowledge, capacity for response, etc., is totally unique. The repertoire of programs, the capacity to handle information for cognitive and other purposes, the speed of cybernetic processing, the efficiency of activated motor responses, the receptivity of internal and external information-monitoring mechanisms — all vary from one individual to the next. The gene pool has ensured human uniqueness, and this circumstance bears on every aspect of temperament and mood.

Whatever we consider — personality, mood, attitude, temperament, etc. — we can explore a cognitive dimension and a conative (willing and desiring) dimension. When these aspects are understood in detail for an individual, everything will be known about personality and temperament — the ultimate reductionism — for there can be *nothing more* (again!) to human personality than a complex of information processing that can be characterized, catalogued, confronted, and computed. The various aspects of information processing need their own jargon and their own descriptive laws. It is more convenient to talk about endocrine secretions and metabolic processes in some biological contexts than others; elsewhere it may be more useful to talk about the action potentials of brain neurons. In any event, the various elements of the human organism are not mysterious incomprehensible(!), through lack of relevant information. Information processing is what human personality and human mental processes — including the search for understanding — is all about.

Emotion in Machines

The possibility of machines evolving to experience emotion is obviously relevant to the doctrine of robotic man. If artificial machines can feel emotions then it is easy to understand how emotion can feature in man viewed as a machine (in particular, as a robot). In fact there are many views about whether machines — e.g. computer-based systems — will ever evolve to the point that they may be said to have experience of feelings and emotions. Scriven (1953) declared that it is possible 'to construct a supercomputer so as to make it wholly unreasonable to deny that it has feelings'; in the same vein, Sloman and Croucher (1981) were able to argue 'why robots will have emotions'. At the same time, Dennett (1981) was prepared to expound 'why you can't make a computer that feels pain' — this latter follows a famous commentary (by Jefferson, 1949) that is worth quoting again:

Not until a machine can write a sonnet or compose a concerto because of thoughts and emotions felt, and not by the chance fall of symbols, could we agree that machine equals brain — that is, not only write it but know that it had written it. Surely no mechanism could feel ... pleasure at its successes, grief when its valves fuse, be warmed by flattery, be made miserable by its mistakes, be charmed by sex, and be angry or depressed when it cannot get what it wants.

This sounds fine but it is in fact rhetoric and not argument. The 'surely' should give us pause — should make us suspect special pleading. It was Turing (1950), one of the early advocates of artificial intelligence, that pointed out that Jefferson is quickly trapped in a solipsist position ('the only way to know that a *man* thinks is to be that particular man'), and then he presented a *viva voce* dialogue that should convince everyone but the solipsist. This implies that the famous Turing test is as relevant to the emotions as to the intelligence; i.e. people generate suitable (emotional) responses in their interaction with others. The reasons that we assign intelligence to other human beings give us grounds, *mutatis mutandis*, for also ascribing emotion to them. This means that if a computer-based system — e.g. a robot — behaves in what we would deem an emotional way if perceived in a person, then we would conclude that it was able to experience emotion. There is also the structural argument: if brain circuits are seem to be structurally similar to neural networks in the human brain, then we might be encouraged to believe that similar processes — all based on information processing — were going on in each. In short, we will only have grounds for attributing emotion to machines when the machines behave in certain ways and when we have knowledge of the machine's internal structure. We would be quick to say that a simple mechanical doll with a flexible face that could manage a smile was not amused, but could we be so sure in the case of a highly complicated computer-based system with a mass of 'cerebral' circuitry and an inclination to smile in most of the circumstances that would amuse the typical human being?

It is of course possible for a computer system to *simulate* emotion — just as liars and actors can do — without the presence of any feeling. Jefferson was aware of this possibility, as were his later critics. Already there are robots that behave in a seemingly emotional way, and we do not need to cite only the mechanical contrivances used in science fiction films. SIM ONE, an artificial robot described by Denson and Abrahamson (1969) and used to train medical students, can blink, cough, breathe, twitch, exhibit measurable blood pressure, and become anaesthetized; such responses would be enough, if occurring in a human being, to attribute emotion to a person. However, we know that SIM ONE is a relatively simple system, much less complex than even the simplest mammals. However robots, like other artificial systems, are in an evolutionary situation. Give SIM ONE a complex of homeostatic circuitry, sensitive tactile and other sensors, and the capacity to learn and adjust in new circumstances, and at what stage would we be prepared to admit that the artificial robot could experience emotion? Unless we were determined solipsists — and none of us is! — then there would come such a point, though it may differ for each individual.

We are now learning how to investigate emotion in biological systems, and increasingly we are finding that emotion, like cognition, is an information-processing matter. Once we comprehend the essential features of the 'emotion circuits' in robotic man, we will be able to structure emotion into artefacts and to carry out suitable experiments — subject, no doubt, to a charter of computer rights! This in turn will provide us with further information to interpret the phenomenon of emotion in human beings. It seems likely that emotion will evolve in computer systems as it has done in traditional biological systems, as a mechanism to provide an impulse to action and to so secure the survival of the system. Kent (1978), for example, has emphasized that 'there is nothing yet visible in the brain to suggest the presence, or necessity, of any nonmechanistic property in its operation', and that 'a good robot needs an emotion circuit because it is helpful in generating and controlling adaptive behaviour ... it may be possible for a computer to have subjective experience'.

It is often thought that emotion is a significant region of human experience that will always keep us distinct from the machines, but the converse possibility has thrust itself forward in recent years — that if man truly is a machine, and feels emotion, then emotion itself is explicable in terms of natural processes and a likely element in artificial systems of the future (where such an element would be useful in controlling adaptive behaviour). Some researchers in fact are coming to believe that emotion is no longer the mysterious phenomenon that will always be outside the scope of artefacts. A recent *Computing Reviews* (December 1985) carried on the cover an extract from a 1984 panel discussion on artificial intelligence, to which the celebrated AI specialist Marvin Minsky was a contributor.

Here Minsky commented that it is 'a major superstition of our culture that feeling an emotion is very deep and hard and difficult to understand, whereas intellect ... is easy to understand'. In fact, 'it seems to me that we understand emotions rather well.... The problem with these people who say that you could make a machine think but it wouldn't really feel like us is that they don't seem to have thought about the real problem...'. No, there is not much of an argument here, but the thoughts accord well with what we have been proposing in the present chapter.

It may be difficult to imagine how computer-based systems could evolve emotion, though a diet of sci-fi should have prepared us for the possibility. However we can claim that emotion — its generation, control, expression, etc. — is a largely cybernetic information-processing affair. The processes, we have seen, are built into chemical reactions mediated by changes in the neural circuits of the brain (the hypothalamus, etc.). When such matters are more fully understood, and it is recognized, for example, that *all* human processes are effectively controlled by the manipulation of information encapsulated in some physical medium (chemistry, electrical pulses, etc.), then it will not seem odd to set about building emotion circuits into artefacts. It is obvious that already researchers are getting their minds round the idea. Again this development will throw light on the nature of robotic man, on the character of the emotion processes occurring in the natural machines called *people*. We know that robotic man is an emotion-driven system. Today we are beginning to understand how this can be the case.

Summary

This chapter has profiled some aspects of emotion as it occurs and is controlled in human beings. In particular, there has been frequent reference to its cybernetic character, the idea that it is regulated by feedback loops, the establishment of homeostatic states, and the processing of information. We have drawn attention to the fact that there is a chemistry of mood and temperament, that depression, rage, fear, aggression, etc., are all controlled and stimulated by chemical states on the one hand and neural behaviour on the other.

It has also been emphasized that emotion and cognition are intimately linked, that such activities as learning and perception can be profoundly affected by the emotional condition of the organism. There is a complex emotion/cognition matrix which has evolved to aid the organism in the eternal quest for survival (subject to a variety of culturally mediated factors). The common assertion that there is an unbridgeable gulf between reason and emotion shows a widespread misunderstanding of the intricate framework in which information processing takes place in human beings. We are misled by the fact that we are conscious of *some* aspects of information processing — a small proportion of the total — and because we are unaware of the logic underlying other aspects of information processing (namely, those connected with emotion), we tend to imagine that these aspects function in a non-logical or illogical way. In fact emotion — like learning, remembering, problem solving, pattern recognition, etc. — has its own logic, one evolved through countless generations to help individuals and communities to survive. We should not be surprised that different logics in the organism, working to the pace of different processes, sometimes yield incompatible conclusions. What happens in such circumstances is that *all* the information is thrown into the balance — that deriving from the emotion circuits, the memory circuits, the immediate perception circuits — and the organism decides, in an automatic manner, on the course to be adopted. This interpretation helps us to recognize that emotion, as an information-processing affair, operates in similar ways to the rest of the organic processes.

We have also hinted at the possibility of a theory of personality based on the cybernetic interpretation of emotion and cognition in robotic man. Personality, we have emphasized, is perceived by observing a person's demeanour — largely in a social situation. How does the person move, talk, raise a hand (or an eyebrow), respond to a joke or a suggestion, laugh, listen, etc.? All such matters are mediated by cognitive factors: what is the person seeing, remembering, thinking? How quickly is the information processing taking place? In all cases, what are the accompanying emotions, feelings, attitudes, moods, etc.? So we have seen that personality and temperament, unique in every individual, are the result of various types of information processing throughout the organism. There is nothing in such matters that cannot be accommodated, at least in principle, within the doctrine of robotic man.

The brief profile of emotion and some of its important features has shown its relevance to various aspects of human behaviour — retreat, approaching, attacking, copulating, etc. Little has been suggested about how emotion, coupled to how robotic man thinks and decides, is relevant to such matters as ethics, politics, and human relationships. It is necessary to glance at these, if only to establish that robotic man is an ethical mechanism capable of commitment to social behaviour of various types. We need not worry — robotic man will still behave badly or well, be politically prejudiced, and fall in love.

8 The Ethical Dimension

Preamble

There can be no doubt that man is an ethical animal. This is inevitable since human beings coexist in society and ethics is a matrix of rules, obligations, rights, duties, etc., that enables society to survive when its members often have conflicting interests. Traditionally ethics has been interpreted in many different ways: as word of God, as reified concepts of good and bad, as a means to the maximization of human happiness, as a class concept, as the 'morally given' beyond all naturalistic analysis, as conditioned emotional response, etc. The doctrine of robotic man has a place for ethics, but not the one with which we are traditionally familiar. It depends upon, for example, the idea that human behaviour is a complex of events in a deterministic universe. In this context the two central considerations in the ethical dimension are that:

1. all ethical responses require a spectrum of information processing at the cognitive level and
2. all ethical responses require a spectrum of information processing at the conative level.

In short, ethics can be defined and interpreted in terms of knowledge and perceptions of social circumstances (mediated by memory, expectation, etc.), in conjunction with a range of relevant feelings and emotions. This means that, at one level, ethics can be interpreted simply in terms of *how people feel* about certain types of acts that have personal or social significance. *Right* and *wrong* can only be defined in this way: a right action is one that generates agreeable feelings, of a certain type, in the observer, whereas a wrong action is one that has the opposite consequence. There is no absolute morality, no ethics beyond what human beings (or perhaps other animals also) feel about certain types of activities, usually in a social context. In this way ethical sensitivity can be regarded as a subclass of mental phenomena: *it is a subsystem of the mind system,* and the behaviour of the mind is subject to natural law. In this sense the mind is determined.

The Determined Mind

We have already considered the cybernetics and programming of the human mind (see Chapters 4 and 5). Here we can remind ourselves of the deterministic nature of mental phenomena — how the performance of mental subsystems can be understood in terms of programmed routines. The routines are very flexible in many cases, with provision for interrupts, switching to subroutines, etc., but the programmed nature of the human mind already says something about the nature of ethical behaviour. Already we are learning to be suspicious of, for example, the notion of desert (see below): what are we to make of a notion of desert that simply recommends punishment for the 'wrong-doer'? How odd to punish a programmed machine when it behaves in ways that generate negative emotions in the observer!

It is likely that a number of the well-advertised ethical theories will prove to be compatible (we have already hinted at how aspects of analytic theory can be rendered compatible with a cybernetic interpretation of the human mind). In social group theory, for example, human beings are interpreted as conformists who aim to behave according to the expectations of others. People wish (conative act) to be accepted by others whom they perceive (cognitive act) in their social environment. In Freudian theory the individual is prompted to behaviour by subconscious forces, conditioned by the impact of parental programming on genetic endowment; this is not far removed from traditional learning theory which proposes that a child can be socialized much in the way that a chimpanzee can be taught tea-party behaviour. (The religious view — that God prompts the urgings of conscience or lays down moral rules — is a superstitious irrelevance and deserves little attention. Conscience varies from person to person and from society to society; if we are to avoid tautology, the very statement 'God is good' demands a 'non-God' definition of good. A definition based on information processing of various types is not one that believers would be likely to welcome.)

Most of the modern theories of ethical awareness and ethical behaviour suggest that man is conditioned in various ways — by early environmental experience, by parental attitudes (e.g. an angry and puritanical father), by prevailing social mores, by how the person perceives the expectations of others, etc. At the same time there is the inevitable urge, in some observers, to see man as *more than* simply conditioned by environment. Wright (1971), for example, mentions social conditioning theory and then is quick to remark that none of us 'is entirely moulded and shaped by others; in greater or lesser degree we are all independent sources of intelligent action and thought'. However there is no attempt to explore the nature of this independence. Of precisely what is the human being held to be independent? Of knowledge, expectation, genetic potential, emotional disposition, learning capacity, etc.? We would argue that to take full account of such elements would make 'independence' an unworkable symbol. It seems much more reasonable to argue that the human mind — and the working of all its subsystems (including those that relate to ethical performance) — is determined in its behaviour by many different factors.

It has long been suggested that moral behaviour might be comprehensible in terms of cybernetics. For example, Young (1964) suggested that servomechanisms and computers might give clues as to the nature of moral performance; we have seen that Miller, Galanter, and Pribram (1960) considered how plans and schedules, effective programs, might help in the interpretation of human performance of all types. Here moral rules can be represented as programmed instructions that become expressed in behavioural trajectories that have ethical significance, i.e. in acts that generate emotions and feelings of a particular type. Or again, moral training can be interpreted as the attempt to establish a homeostat, a self-regulating mechanism that prompts specific kinds of behaviour (it is hoped, 'right' behaviour) in ethical circumstances. (Such a homeostat can be regarded as the equivalent of the Freudian super-ego.) It is then possible to consider how the homeostat might be 'set' to enable the individual to cope satisfactorily in different ethical conditions. Language that suggests a similar homeostatic view can also be found in Piaget (1967): in the development of the child, the emotions 'emerge as regulations whose final form of equilibrium is none other than the will'.

We are not surprised, in this context, to see the human mind viewed as a determinist system — with the clear implication that mental subsystems (including ethical performance) can be analysed in the same way. (Aleksander, 1977, has even advanced an automaton theory of psychotic behaviour.) However, as has been well appreciated for centuries, determinism has profound implications for ethics.

Determinism and Ethics

General

Much in commonsense ethics depends upon people being able to 'help' doing what they do, being 'responsible' for their actions. Determinism implies that man is a machine, behaving as he does because he must, performing in predictable ways according to the dictates of natural law. It is hard to see how human beings can be regarded as responsible in such circumstances. In fact there *is* an interpretation of moral responsibility that can be made compatible with the notion of 'man as machine', but it differs in important respects from the conventional view of responsibility. Put simply, a person may be said to act responsibly when the action is such as to generate approval (and other positive feelings) in the observer (and also perhaps in the person himself). Thus moral responsibility is evaluated according to the emotions that it arouses; the *ir*responsible person may be assumed to generate negative feelings and emotions. Of course this interpretation is quite compatible with the idea of robotic man; the interpretation says nothing about how the person comes to behave as he does — if he is *caused* to act in an approval-generating way, then the act still signals moral responsibility. Hence responsibility is a quite tenable doctrine in a deterministic framework: the main difference over conventional attitudes is how we view such ideas as free will (see Chapter 6) and desert (see below). The individual robotic man may or may not be responsible: we judge by how we feel about his actions.

We have seen that determinism has intrigued historical philosophers and been influenced by modern attitudes to religion and science. Also our increased knowledge of social conditioning has tended to undermine belief in free will; there are consequences in this for whether punishment should be deemed a 'just' consequence of 'wrong-doing'. When a determinist philosophy is considered in detail, there are inevitable implications for our attitudes to particular types of behaviour that may be thought to have ethical significance in a social situation. It is worth considering these various aspects before glancing at the relevance of science and at how a determinist orientation may bear on political questions.

The Philosophic Frame

We have already considered (in Chapter 6) some of the philosophic attitudes to determinism and do not need to rehearse the points here. It is worth highlighting, however, some of the main considerations. It has been stressed (e.g. by Spinoza) that we think ourselves free because we are unaware of the causes of our actions. In a similar spirit, Ignazio Silone (1969) observed: 'We declare ourselves subversives or conservatives for reasons we carry in ourselves, often in very vague terms. *Before we choose, we are chosen, without knowing it*' (my italics). In this sense our conviction of freedom does nothing more than signal our ignorance of psychological causes.

It is possible to represent such philosophers as Democritus and Spinoza as having a fully fledged scientific faith: they would have been very responsive to the idea of robotic man. Spinoza saw the whole of nature as a dynamic system regulated by natural law. If we see something in the world that seems 'not to fit', something that is imperfect or inappropriate, then our feelings are jarred. We fail to realize that the circumstance that agitates us is an inevitable product of the unfolding of a natural world controlled by physics and chemistry. In Spinoza's terms, our surprise simply indicates our ignorance of the necessary laws: with everything the consequence of natural laws, nothing can be said to be morally good or bad, morally perfect or imperfect. Things just *are*.

This does not of course prevent human beings having feelings about the state of affairs that they encounter, and it is such feelings that delude us into thinking that our desires can bring objectivity into what we claim are moral judgements, ethical imperatives (the very word 'imperative' has a mandatory, objective ring). In such an interpretation, people will no longer think themselves free in a moral sense once they have begun to understand the binding nature of the necessary laws and how such laws render all events inevitable. We can scarcely blame people for behaviour that could not have been otherwise, however much we may dislike the behaviour. (At the same time, for other reasons, we may be justified in taking punitive action *as if* blame were a rational philosophic attitude to take.) In fact most of these points are less contentious than might be supposed: we are all often practical determinists in our everyday behaviour. Bertrand Russell (1931) pointed out that a person 'retains unchallenged all those causal laws which he finds convenient, as, for example, that his food will nourish him and that his bank will honour his cheques so long as his account is in funds'. There are causal laws — in particular, those relating to the operation of human choice — that the person may find inconvenient ('This, however, is altogether too naive a procedure').

Social Conditioning

Social conditioning, as we have seen, is an aspect of programming for performance (Chapter 5). It is important to consider this aspect of programming in connection with the acquisition of ethical values.

There is a sense in which *all* our values are derived from the culture in which we are born. Here there are three elements to consider: the basic 'core' values, common throughout all human societies; the second-order values, peculiar to a particular culture; and values that may seem to represent a reaction against certain important cultural features.

The first-order ('core') values relate to such matters as murder, theft, bodily assault, and rape. There is a surprising consensus in such matters from one society to another: both the United States and the USSR incline to discourage murder and theft among their respective citizens. It does not matter that American law derives in part from such European thinkers as John Locke and John Stuart Mill or that Soviet law derives from the class concepts of Marx and Lenin. It is still illegal to murder your next-door neighbour if he annoys you. The core values may be regarded as the minimum necessary to enable society — of whatever political complexion — to continue functioning in a reasonably harmonious way.

By contrast, the second-order values may be peculiarly adapted to a particular cultural framework: so the story goes that Eskimo families leave old women out on the ice to be eaten by polar bears and some African tribes feel under a moral obligation to eat their dead parents to ensure their survival in the afterlife. The first-order values indicate the broad consensus throughout the human race; the second-order values are what make individual societies distinct.

What is important for our purposes in that *all* values, whatever their nature, whatever the time and place, are acquired through social conditioning. It is no accident that most citizens of the United States dislike what they imagine to be communism; nor that most Soviet citizens dislike what they take to be capitalism (I am always surprised that people do not seem to appreciate the relevance of place of birth to political belief). It is true that people tend to acquire the value structure of their society; they drink in a set of attitudes and inclinations that influence the character of all their thoughts and the character of their lives.

Cultures are in the business of conditioning their young and of reinforcing the established programs engraved upon the hearts of their older members. *All* societies indoctrinate according to their lights, though none admits it. Instead, like the claims of parents and teachers, there is talk of *education* — as if education would liberate the mind and allow the child (and the man) to grow into a new perception and a new responsibility. We do not choose whether to educate or to indoctrinate the child: in causal terms, in terms of conditioning, there is only indoctrination. This needs to be justified as an argument.

When we 'indoctrinate' a child, we aim to build up a set of behaviour patterns; when we 'educate' a child, the broad objective is the same. What differs in the two cases are the actual behaviour patterns. In common parlance we may expect the *indoctrinated* person to be an unreflective reservoir of 'received opinion', whereas the *educated* person is expected to think about what he knows or encounters. In terms of information processing, however, all that is happening in *both* cases is that certain types of programs are being injected into the brains of people. Of course any one of us — you, dear reader of this book, for example — will *prefer* some programs to others, *prefer* that some programs be implanted rather than others. What do we make of this circumstance? How do you come to prefer certain programs? Simply because *you are programmed to do so*. Emotional response is as much the upshot of programming — whether residing in prebirth genetic structures or a result of early conditioning colliding with genetic endowment — as is any motor skill or intellectual capacity. Put another way, we do not choose indoctrination or education for our children: we choose *which sort* of indoctrination.

There are many circumstantial pieces of evidence to suggest that people are provided with effective programs by their particular mode of education. We may expect broadly shared values in the products of English comprehensive schools; different, but more or less consensus, values in the products of the Eton/Oxbridge system. (Take any Tory cabinet in the United Kingdom, inevitably comprised of highly educated clones. Some would claim an intellectual disposition; some may have written a book; there may be different views of monetarism or Westland. However, put any one of them in front of a hard-headed and knowledgeable sceptic, and the resulting patter would fit in the mouths of any of the other cabinet colleagues. Discussion, of sorts, is possible, but only within a programmed framework built upon a sediment of cliché, sacred cow, and vested interest. This is not to criticise the Conservative Party alone: any grouping, *mutatis mutandis*, can be subject to the same scrutiny.) It is obvious that there are different value systems in any large community: there are subvalues, subcultures, etc. However every single community of interest can be analysed in the same terms. In short, *values — of whatever sort — are received* and then allowed to influence all subsequent behaviour.

Of course there may be a reaction against prevailing values, with or without some sort of pragmatic accommodation for the sake of family or tribal harmony. A person may *rebel* against parents, teachers, class, or country. But would anyone doubt that we could explore the *dynamics* of rebellion, teasing out corollations, identifying likely causal factors, looking to diet or degree of affluence or nationality or age or education as predisposing factors? This is not to say that we already have a neat theory of rebellion. Sociology and psychology, viewed as broad disciplines (often embracing a confusing family of schools), are not hard sciences: perhaps we need a physics and chemistry (and a fully fledged cybernetics) of society. We do not need to weight Weber against Durkheim, Adam Smith against Karl Marx, Freud against Skinner — it is quite enough, for our purposes, that we are suspicious of caprice in the natural world, that we find it unhelpful to entertain the idea of random happening occurring without any connection with the prevailing physical circumstances. This means that there is an underlying order in all worldly happenings, even though some of such happenings may offend our parochial and value-determined preferences. When we talk of *dis*order we mean that a situation does not accord with the patterns that we prefer; we cannot claim thereby that such a situation does not function (or exist) in a way that is independent of natural law. Existing things have properties — and out of these grow the relationships that we choose to call laws, schedules, plans, regularities, schemes, structures, protocols, programmes, (anglicized to show a distinction) and programs.

What this means for social conditioning is that we do well to search for *explanations*, and that such a search presupposes the existence of effective programs, laid up (somehow, somewhere) in the human anatomy. At one level this is not a controversial doctrine. We *expect* social conditioning to work; we *expect* to have to take persistent steps to socialize our children in countless different ways. Of course there are questions that can still be asked: is it due to social conditioning that such and such? So an article in *The Guardian* (21 January 1986) can ask 'are women less criminal than men simply because of their social conditioning?', and it is intended to be an intelligible query. Where there *is* debate is when various weightings are placed on the respective influences of nature and nurture (the nurture bit being a synonym for social conditioning). All we are doing here is weighing the respective impacts of *two sorts of programming* (and, one step later, how the two program matrices interact to yield a talent, a piece of knowledge, a criminal act, etc.). The whole business can be interpreted in terms of laid-down programs, acquired programs, program changes, program interrupts, programmed values, programmed decisions, etc. Then it is up to the chemist, the cybernetician, the psychologist, the sociologist, etc., to identify the types of programs, the ways they function and are structured, the ways that they yield behaviour trajectories that have personal or social significance.

The conditioning starts before birth, in the amniotic environment, and is continuously maintained for the individual until the moment of death (and beyond if we forget the concept of a person — a corpse is subject to environmental influences, if only those of temperature and humidity). The child is born and other forms of conditioning occur, through all its senses (it is found that even the babbling baby babbles in a culture-linked way); soon we are conditioning the child into a value system. Skinner (1964) commented on the common view that 'there is an element of freedom in the application of standards'; he observed: 'a sense of freedom is another of those inner attributes *which lose their force as we more clearly understand man's relation to his environment*' (my italics). For Skinner it was all a matter of conditioning. The central question is how to so condition infants and adults that they behave in a socially desirable way? And so, sensing the excitement generated by the truly scientific approach to man, Skinner noted (in *Beyond Freedom and Dignity*, 1972) that 'we have not yet seen what man can make of man'. But did he not see the circularity? How are we to inculcate values that are not already conditioned in ourselves? Put another way, how can we know what values to inculcate? Skinner's values are the upshot of his programming, and mine of mine. Will the man *he* wants to make accord with *my* value structure? Who decides? Perhaps, as always, it is the person who can marshall the appropriate muscle — if conscious social engineering is to occur, it is only the powerful who are ever in a position to make the effort.

It seems obvious that values are inculcated in each new generation, though it is vacuous to moralize about the values transmitted in this way. There seems something specious and absurd in one program attempting to make *moral* judgements on another. The programs just *are*, and how can the ethical evaluations ever get started — this is the crucial bit. The evaluations can only be sanctioned in reason if they are based on *non*-moral (or perhaps *a*moral) principles. We can say, as Skinner would, that we 'do not like', that behaviour, and so the evaluation says nothing about the behaviour except that it causes certain types of emotions in me, the observer (and these emotions may have other consequences). It is clear that with this approach there is no absolute morality and that all moral language — *good, bad, ought, should*, etc. — in the last resort merely signal particular emotional states in the observer. If a person behaves 'well' through fear of authority, this is a matter of prudence, again easily traced to emotional considerations (indeed, perhaps all morality is simple prudence, the desire to avoid certain unpleasant consequences of whatever nature — guilt through self-recrimination, pain through punishment, etc.).

In fact Young (1978) has commented on the 'dispositional cement' — obedience — that binds society ('the capacity for it presumably has a hereditary background'). This *dispositional cement* may well be stimulated (or indeed generated) by the desire of the individual to avoid unpleasant emotions and to seek out pleasant ones — potent motives in organizing human attitudes. The individual quickly learns the rudiments of the prevailing power structure, and learns that to obey is the best policy. The lineaments of the culture determine what shape the obedience takes, to whom it is directed, and the circumstances in which the individual feels able to *demand* obedience rather than to *offer* it. As the child matures it passes through the various stages at which it is equipped to acquire aspects of the culture (e.g. there is a relatively narrow 'window' during which language can be acquired). So Young observes: 'Culture is transmitted by virtue of this genetically determined pattern of growth and development of the brain'. There are thus external and internal factors that affect the emergence of ethical sensitivity in the growing individual: the external factors are the elements in the culture that have ethical significance; the internal factors are the 'ethical receptors' — doubtless structured in the neurons and the hormones — that equip the individual to be socialized (or not) at particular stages of his growth and maturation. It is an easy matter to interpret the various theories of the development of the ethical sense in terms of the impact that certain experiences and cogitations have upon the feelings of the person.

It should also be remembered that there is also considerable flexibility in the capacity of human beings to switch from one type of program to another. The circumstances of the person determine which program (or program set) is selected from the repertoire. This is almost so obvious as to be a platitude: we all behave differently with different people and in different social conditions — different environmental factors elicit different programmed responses. The ramifications of the platitude are not always appreciated. People can 'switch', for example, when they perceive that they have a newly changed place in a power hierarchy — so an innocuous bank clerk can become an obnoxious prison guard in time of war. This *switching* can sometimes oscillate between wild extremes. Experiments at Stanford University, organized by Professor Philip Zimbado, focused on the extent to which normal American students could enter into the roles of prisoners and guards in a practical scenario. Zimbado stipulated only three rules (or conditions) for the experiment: that law and order be preserved, that if a 'prisoner' escaped then the experiment was terminated, and that no physical violence should be used. The students were selected randomly to play the parts of prisoners and guards and the experiment was conducted. It was soon found that the 'guards' enjoyed their role: they were enthusiastic and resourceful in finding ways to humiliate and discipline the 'prisoners' — to the point that the experiment escalated to the level of physical violence and naked oppression and had to be terminated. It was clear that the students had not only 'thought' themselves into the situation, but had also 'felt' themselves into it. No longer were they 'guards', but *guards*.

This type of experiment has shown how normal individuals can adjust to new role opportunities, and it is difficult to draw lines around the degree of human flexibility in this respect. For example, testimony from ex-torturers has charted the psychological route to the diligent practice of torture: alarmingly, it is a route that perhaps most human beings would follow, if led, encouraged, exhorted, pressured in certain ways. Robotic man is programmed, but incoming data constantly mediates the decisions whereby he selects which program to use at any particular time. We could explore all other aspects of human thought and behaviour in the same way. This suggests that ethics — rooted in cognitive/emotional schedules as it is — is adaptable to a degree, according to immediate social circumstance and the personality of the individual. This has dramatic consequences for many traditional attitudes to morality.

The role of social conditioning, in ethics as in other areas of human perception and sensitivity, seems clear. A complex of data plays upon the various mental faculties of robotic man —during his growth and maturation — so that cognitive and conative programs are established, i.e. he becomes equipped to respond in perceptual, learning, problem-solving, and other situations where action (or attitude) is demanded. The ethical scenario is one of these situations, and robotic man is programmed for response here, as elsewhere.

Desert

The doctrine of desert is central to the conventional view of moral responsibility. 'She *deserves* to be punished', 'He must *pay his debt to society*', 'They *deserve* all they get' — these, and the countless similar, observations convey an implicit assumption they there is some sort of *equation in justice* whereby wrong-doing rightly generates appropriate punishment. It is of course the *rightly* that begs the question — and this leads us to the heart of moral judgement. What in fact we are saying in urging that punishment follow certain types of acts is that we personally feel better when that happens. We are expressing an emotional response to a particular type of behaviour on the part of another person (and perhaps also on the part of ourselves). What we are really urging is vengeance. To admit as much has a nasty ring to it (some people are still prepared to rejoice in their search for vengeance). So the usual ploy is not to admit the lusting after vengeance, but to somehow suggest that the action itself generates an infliction of suffering upon the perpetrator. The mechanism whereby this trick is accomplished is *desert*. Desert is the device whereby we seek to show that wrongful act and punishment are inextricably linked: it is not I, the punisher, who inflicts suffering on the perpetrator, but the perpetrator himself who in some way generates his own subsequent suffering. Desert is a sanction for vengeance, just as faith is often a sanction for firm belief in absurdity. We can dispense with desert and look to a more rational ground for ethical obligation.

Praise and blame are also mixed up in this confused situation. The empiricist philosopher A. J. Ayer (1940) made the telling point that 'there does appear to be a difficulty in reconciling one's inclination to praise or blame people for their actions with the belief that these actions have been even partly determined by circumstances for which the agents are not themselves responsible'. As we know, the doctrine of robotic man is made of even sterner stuff: there is no question of 'partly determined' here — man is a totally programmed system. If desert is a sanction for blame on the one hand and praise on the other, then both blame and praise must be abolished — if desert is their only justification (see 'Consequences', below). In fact we may find other justifications.

It is inevitable that Skinner (1972) should have made similar observations in connection with punishment ('we cannot change genetic defects by punishment; we can work only through genetic measures which operate on a much longer time scale'). Here it is noted that the concept of responsibility is 'particularly weak' when it is traced to the various genetic causes of particular types of behaviour (the 'genetic determiners'). How can we 'blame' one man, as against another, if the former has a much greater genetic disposition to violence than the latter: 'If we do not punish a man for a club foot, should we punish him for being quick to anger or highly susceptible to sexual reinforcement?' Ah, it is countered — but people can exert *control*. How is this control over actions exerted? Exactly what is the mechanism? What are its cybernetic features? Its specific cognitive and conative characteristics? The key question, whatever the nature of the control mechanism, is *does it vary in peformance from one person to another?* The question only needs to be asked for the answer to be clear. Of course, the character of any personal attribute varies throughout any (non-cloned) population. Why should this be so — if not through genetic and other determining factors? In short, people vary in their capacity to behave in one way rather than another, and however they behave is an inevitable output of the collision between genetic endowment and the broad matrix of environmental influence.

The doctrine of robotic man is very clear on the notion of desert. If a complex of programs capable of emotion yield behavioural trajectories that cause certain emotional responses in other programmed systems, then we can scarcely declare that the first programmed complex should be subject to torture according to some *equation in justice*. At a cruder, and much simpler level, John Cleese can evoke much mirth when he kicks a car that will not start. The car does not have feelings on the matter: its primitive cybernetic systems do not have conative potential. However this is not the reason why the amusement in observers in generated. The reason is that it is silly to try to punish a machine: it is much more constructive to find out what has gone wrong and to repair it — if, of course, the aim is to make the car work and not to relieve our own pent-up frustrations. The same is true, *mutatis mutandis*, with human beings. Punishment, solely as punishment, is an expression of the need for emotional release in the punisher: it has nothing to do with desert, responsibility (conventionally viewed), or any aspiration to pursuade the wrong-doer to tread thereafter the paths of goodness and love. Man is a machine. He behaves as he must at any particular moment — the state of his overall system (including a host of cooperating subsystems) being what it is, the state of the environment (in all its aspects) being what it is. There is a grand absurdity, an almost ludicrous lunacy, in punishing a machine because it evokes negative emotions in the observer.

The idea of mitigation is highly relevant to this approach. What *mitigation* means is that *when we understand the causes of an action, punishment is quite irrelevant*. So a plea of insanity, successfully upheld in a court of law, will save a murderer from the electric chair (surely one of the grossest instruments of vengeance). However insanity, as a psychological condition, does not mean that acts are cause*less*: it means that the acts that are caused are caused in certain ways — and acts generated by the sane are caused in other ways. What is important, vitally important, is not that the types of causes vary but that there are causes for *all* acts, whether perpetrated by the sane or the insane. In short, *there is always mitigation*. When causes are found, we see the inevitability of the act, but when the causes are unknown, and difficult to uncover, we pretend that the act was not inevitable, and we quickly seek refuge in mysterious categories such as desert and moral responsibility defined in non-scientific terms (if defined at all).

Once we fully grasp the implications of a robotic view of man we soon see that punishment, *qua* punishment, is an absurdity. We may as well hit a washing machine or shout ridicule at a voice-recognition unit. Vengeance, thinly disguised as just punishment, is an expression of the emotion of the punisher; it is not some mystical outgrowth of the perpetrator's behaviour. Robotic man, as a machine programmed for performance, will inevitably behave in certain ways when certain conditions obtain. The meaningless symbol *desert* has no place in such a scenario. Not surprisingly, this approach to human ethical behaviour has consequences that need to be explored.

Consequences

What are the consequences of abandoning the idea of desert? Does morality crumble? Is robotic man the herald of a new anarchism? A new nihilism? A new hedonism? In fact there is a hierarchy of consequences following the loss of desert.

We can say first of all that if desert is essentially a supposed sanction for punishment, then punishment, *qua* punishment, must be thrown out also. This does not mean that action that closely resembles punishment should never be inflicted on a wrong-doer. We may still argue — before we go deeper (see below) — that we are entitled to create a social climate in which crime is discouraged and law-abiding citizens protected. We are entitled to pursue criminals relentlessly and to incarcerate them when apprehended, but we are not entitled to torture them once they are in our power. We can protect citizens but we are not entitled to give free rein to vengeance. It may be that we also need to create a social climate in which wrong-doing is effectively discouraged, and so the infliction of suffering on the imprisoned criminal may, in some circumstances, be granted some degree of legitimacy. Before the traditional moralist rubs his hands in glee, we can emphasize that this is a philosophic concession that will scarcely, if ever, be realized in practical justice. The reason for this is that there is no convenient calculus whereby we can say, in any rational way, that this or that type (or degree) of inflicted suffering will have this or that impact on this or that crime in society. The reasonable suspicion is that current penal practice — in Europe, the United States, and elsewhere — is at least as likely to increase the incidence of crime as to decrease it. Compulsory incarceration, in itself, is a colossal imposition, though it may be necessary in order to achieve a degree of social protection. To inflict further suffering could only be justified if it could be shown — in mathematical well-argued terms — that such a policy would make crime less likely in society. In fact there is rarely any attempt to justify the harsh treatment of criminals in such a way: in fact the appeal is always to desert, which can have no rational basis in a society in which human beings are viewed in scientific, rather than in superstitious, terms. The immediate conclusion is that punishment is *out* where it is seen as an inevitable corollary to social acts of a certain kind, and that imprisonment and any other imposition on the individual can only be justified where the effects of social protection and/or a reduced crime rate can be demonstrated. Even then we have to weigh, as quantitatively as possible, the cost of inflicting physical or mental hardship on a convicted person (remember there is *always* mitigation) against the cost of certain types of social disturbance (crime, anarchy, tumult, etc.). These are difficult matters. How can we set the cost of an immediate punishment against the possible consequences of no punishment for social order in the days, years (millenia?) ahead? We have to make the attempt if we are to claim that our penal philosophy is rational.

What this means so far is that we have arrived at what may be recognized as a broadly liberal or humanitarian attitude to the interpretation of ethical performance, but we have done so in a rigorous way that is not normally encountered in discussion on such matters. Indeed it is obvious that the necessary rigour for conveying the doctrine of robotic man will be offensive to many people, including the liberals (they will, you see, still incline to think that the phrase *free will* has some useful meaning): this suggests that the doctrine of robotic man will be a timely kiss of death to all humanitarian penologists. We shall see. But there is worse. We have only explored one level in the hierarchy of consequences. There is more to be said.

We have dispelled desert because it has no place, can be given no significance, in the interactions of programmed systems. At the same time we have suggested that it is *legitimate* to protect society, to reduce the volume of crime, to create a more orderly, more peaceful society. Such aims roll off the tongue so easily that we are not provoked to scrutinize the assumptions on which they are based. We can start, for example, by examining the word *legitimate* (nicely italicized to hint at something significant). What does *legitimate* mean? It can only mean something that we approve of, something that makes us feel more comfortable, something that every right-minded, civilized, upright, law-abiding person would want to support. I resisted the temptation to exploit further pieces of italics — for 'approve of', 'feel more comfortable', and 'would want'. There it is — what can we say about such phrases? They are all expressions of emotion. They all say something about our conative natures, about the programming of a substantial part of robotic man. So yes, what we want, approve, feel comfortable about will help to determine the social goals that we espouse. But what is the nature of the legitimacy derived from emotional preference? We may just as well want to see all roads painted yellow. In fact our emotional preference in social matters assumes such importance — because it relates to our very survival — that we translate it into a bogus *law of the universe*. Murder is wrong — because it unsettles us, disgusts us, terrifies us, or results in our death. These are very emotional matters. Murder will stay wrong , but only because of how our image of it affects our emotions. The same is true of all the first-order values that are sustained by different societies throughout the world — such values rest on the bedrock (or sand?) of human emotion.

What this means is that our *legitimate* treatment of the criminal, nicely espoused a few paragraphs ago, is no more legitimate than vengeance — if we are searching for a scientifically sanctioned legitimacy. It is only more legitimate if we make indulgence in some emotions more important than indulgence in others; when we do this, we simply provide evidence for an analysis of our own emotional structures. So any moral posture — however noble, however sublime, however much the result of learning, careful cogitation, and good sense — is no more legitimate than a simple emotional spasm. This is an interesting (but scarcely original) conclusion, but one that is likely to be seen as rather odd (even discouraging) to some observers. Alas, there is no way around it — if we claim to be capable of thoughtful analysis.

At the top level of the hierarchy is the broad desire to survive. To take steps to protect oneself, one's family, one's country must surely be right! Right? Emotionally desirable! Subjectively compelling! A conative compulsion (usually)! In such a view, ethics becomes a collision of competing desires wrapped up in more flattering language. We are *most* comfortable when *our* desires, and those of people who feel like us, are the ones that shape the prevailing cultural forces, including mores and ethics. We cannot find a non-subjective sanction, anything approaching an objective legitimacy, for our individual spectrum of moral postures. In the last analysis — unwelcome as it may be — we are performing automata, struggling to realize a set of emotionally generated goals for the brief period that we are individually alive on earth.

Science and Ethics

General

There is a widespread unease about the impact of science on human ethical sensitivity. A veritable procession of writers and artists have pronounced a negative judgement on the impact of science and technology in the modern age (some of these attitudes have been charted in Simons, 1985b). C. S. Lewis (1947), for example, was even prepared to declare that science had embarked upon the 'abolition of man' and the modern computer scientist Joseph Weizenbaum (1976), appalled at what is now being expected of computer systems (in the realms of practical judgement, clinical advice, psychiatric counselling, etc.), has expressed horror at how modern technology is distorting human values. Similarly, Rose, Kamin, and Levontin (1984) have worried about how theories of biological determinism can have adverse effects on such ethical concerns as sexism and racism. There are of course countervailing arguments. Peter Berger (1963), for instance, has emphasized how sociology has exposed some of the racial myths that have hitherto sustained racial attitudes in the United States and Skinner, inevitably, has welcomed the scientific attitude that has seemingly demonstrated that man is a machine, albeit of an 'extraordinary' complexity. We do not need to set the *pros* against the *antis*. We cite this controversy to show that, in a sense, it is secondary and irrelevant.

It is necessary to emphasize that although no enquiry is value-free, we cannot use a *spurious* value to question the validity of argument and the truth of the conclusions that are produced. In short, we may not always like how the universe operates and we may not enjoy the constraints of natural law — but there is no reason why we should expect to. Even the most optimistic theologies have rarely declared that the universe was framed solely to gratify man's passions. The point is that the ethical view to which science in general, and the doctrine of robotic man in particular, conduct us may or may not be pleasant; it may or may not feed our fragile vanity. The question is: is it a truthful interpretation of ethical sensitivity and behaviour in *Homo sapiens*?

The Relevance of Biology

There can be no doubt that ethics, like every other attribute or interest of human beings, has biological roots. There can be no other source of the physical and mental qualities that characterize men and women in society. This does not mean that the relationship between biology and ethics is simple and straightforward. There are many stages between the emergence of a particular biological framework and the diverse beliefs, attitudes, and commitments that subsequently develop. For example, in talking of social man we cannot draw easy analogies between human society and the gregarious impulses of ants, sheep, or wolves. A facile sociobiology (Wilson, 1975) is little help in exploring the place of ethics in the doctrine of robotic man. At the same time, if we can see how altruism, for instance, may have developed in non-human societies, this is likely to help us in exploring how ethics may have developed amongst human beings. As Young (1978) has observed: 'All social animals have a *genetically controlled system of ethics* that regulates their responses to each other' (my italics).

We have long known that many types of animals can display altruism in certain circumstances. For instance, an animal may take energetic action on behalf of the group, even though it may become endangered thereby; and there are countless examples of selflessness among animals in the sharing of food, protecting the young from predators, etc. But again these are programmed responses, though programmed at a lower level than many of the ethical performances of human beings. There are, for example, the 'density-dependent conventions' espoused by Wynne-Edwards (1962), where it is suggested that many animal species adopt modes of behaviour that favour the survival of the group rather than the reproductive success of the individual (the nesting of sea-birds on particular cliffs, where only those that find a place can propagate, is given as an example). Other observers have countered that only behaviour that favours the selection of an individual's genes can occur in an animal community: so it is unlikely that altruism can emerge through natural selection unless it operates in favour of relatives. The interest of Dawkins (1976) in the selfish gene has emphasized this sort of consideration. In fact the theory runs through the work of various biologists, including J.B.S. Haldane and R.A. Fisher and was well stated in a paper by W.D. Hamilton (*Journal of Theoretical Biology*, vol. 7, p.1). It is worth indicating part of the rationale for dealing with social behaviour.

It is proposed that gene A causes a *donor* (animal, plant, bacterium, virus, etc.) to carry out an act X, which results in the animal producing C fewer offspring (C is intended to denote *cost*); but an accompanying result is that a *recipient* produces B additional offspring (B denotes *benefit*). If also the recipient has a probability R of carrying a gene that is 'identical by descent' to A, it can be said that R = 0 if donor and recipient are unrelated and R = 1 if they are identical twins (if they are siblings, then R = $\frac{1}{2}$, etc.). This means that the consequence of the act is that the number of A genes in the next generation will be reduced by C/2 (since the donor transmits the gene to only half its offspring), and at the same time is increased by RB/2. Thus the A gene will increase in frequency when RB is greater than C.

· This type of demonstration — which suggests that cooperation and altruism is more likely to occur amongst relatives — helps to emphasize the importance of kinship theory in studying animal communities. At the same time there are other factors that are operating to influence the incidence of altruism among gregarious animals. For example, John Maynard Smith (1985) has pointed out the relevance of the fact that cooperation can benefit both partners in a social situation. Cooperation of this sort has been dubbed an 'evolutionary stable strategy' (ESS), which again has ramifications for enquiries into human communal relationships.

The relevance of such considerations to the doctrine of robotic man consists in showing that it is quite possible to derive theories of cooperation and altruism — supposedly important elements in ethical behaviour — within a framework of genetics. Any theory of the origin of ethics will fail if it neglects to consider the relevance of genetic factors, but the precise relationship between the genetic matrix and any specific ethical posture is necessarily difficult to determine, particularly in the case of human beings. We may say that our genetic endowment provides us with dispositions and potentials, but that it is the working of the cultural environment that allows particular ethical stances to emerge. It needs to be emphasized, however, that culture also is a biologically rooted phenomenon, itself emerging — via countless diverse paths — from the genetic matrix.

Science — by, for example, promoting kinship studies amongst primates — has shown how genes may come to be distributed in animal communities. There are, for instance, many different social systems operating successfully among apes and monkeys, each well suited to a particular life style. There are polygamous groups with dominant males, but also groups in which all the males dominate *as a class*, with all the females belonging to all the males. Clear-cut groupings within the overall communities can often be observed, sometimes on a matrilineal basis: an old mother, her offspring, and her offspring's offspring can live together for feeding, grooming, and other purposes. Such arrangements allow for the spread of genes within the groups and also between adjoining populations, and stimulate 'the spread of altruistic practices and the development and use of new methods of communication' (Young, 1978).

This suggests that altruism has developed through genetic imperative, that there is no disinterested motivation, no sublime selflessness. Milo (1973) and others have quoted Thomas Hobbes who was quick to see that individual selfishness is best served by seeming altruism:

Whosoever therefore holds that it had been best to have continued in that state in which all things were lawful for all men, he contradicts himself. For every man by natural necessity desires that which is good for him: nor is there any that esteems a war of all against all ... to be good for him. And so it happens, that ... we get some fellows, that if their needs must be war, it may not yet be against all men, nor without some help.

Or, in short, a general free-for-all — the antithesis of altruism — would attract no one. People need to cooperate, if only thereupon to compete with others — who are equally concerned, through seeming altruism, to organize their own security. There is no reason why the apparently total altruist — the saint (Mother Theresa *et al.*) — cannot be observed in the same way, with personal motivation mediated *in toto* by a cooperating complex of pleasure seeking and pain avoidance. It would be difficult to argue that there were no connections between the genetic endowment of an individual (or a species) and the motivations associated with sensitivity to pain and pleasure.

The relevance of science to any interpretation of ethical sensitivity and performance is multifaceted. At one level, we see the importance of neural and hormonal factors to pain and pleasure, and how these can translate into such ethical feelings as guilt, satisfaction, warmth, and the feeling of obligation or responsibility; at another level are the sociological and anthropological considerations that analyse social pressures, cultural frameworks, systems of socialization, indoctrination, education, etc. (using, for instance, ethnological kinship studies to explore the development and persistence of the cooperative impulse). We may take psychology, psychiatry, and psychoanalysis as yet another level, indicating how the functioning of the individual can affect perception of self-interest and, for example, the implementation of behavioural trajectories that wrongly address the pain and pleasure needs. Above all, we see that it is possible to explore the phenomenon of human ethics within the broad context of scientific enquiry. It is not a 'category mistake' to propose that ethical terminology can be subject to scientific scrutiny, against the mystifying and obfuscation characteristic of the prescientific philosophers.

This then is the key sense in which biology is relevant to ethics. We do not need to espouse a particular brand of sociobiology to propose the general point that ethics — a complex mix of theory and practice, inevitably fuelled by feelings and emotions — is well within the scientific domain. The doctrine of robotic man suggests that human beings have no internal states (no impressions, images, dreams, motivations, impulses, commitments, intuitions, etc.) or behavioural habits (sleep patterns, motor habits, locomotion manoeuvres, game acts, copulation routines, etc.) that are outside the remit of science. There are problems with ethics in that is has been intimately associated in history with mystical and supernatural categories: processions of priests managed to establish their monopoly of ethics, using slogans and shibboleths (desert, soul, evil, salvation, sin, hell, damnation, etc.) to secure a power base in superstitious societies. The old idea that because *ethics is a matter of value not fact* and is therefore outside science can no longer be sustained. Ethics, like any other human mental or physical performance, can be examined by the scientist. If he then tells you what you *should* or *should not* do, he may be right — *if* you share the same objectives. He may simply be informing you how you can most rationally seek to achieve your emotionally generated and emotionally sustained goals. However if he uses 'should' and 'should not' in another way, it is likely that he is giving vent to his own emotionally sustained values. He may even convert you — an objective of *his*, perhaps — using argument or advertising (an emotional appeal). But there is nothing in any of this that is outside the remit of scientific thought. This is the inevitable conclusion of any rational enquiry into the nature of ethical sensitivity and performance, and it is part of the doctrine of robotic man.

The Political Dimension

Politics is, in a very important sense, an outcrop of ethics: it is about how people are to treat people in human society. This being so, most of what has been said about ethics (in particular, see Determinism and

Ethics, above) applies also to politics. One consequence of this is that robotic man is unable to adjudicate between one particular political posture and another — unless the debate is about means rather than ends. We have seen that ends are emotionally generated and emotionally sustained. In this sense, Margaret Thatcher is as much robotic man as is Colonel Gadaffy: we may assume that they both want to see different sorts of society.

The emotional impulse determines how individuals face the central political question — are you on the side of élites (however defined) or are you on the side of the broad mass of the people? The concept of *the élite* does not necessarily imply the possession of singular talent in any sphere; rather it implies a well-placed minority enjoying a disproportionate share of social power. Different minorities — well placed in this way — often incline to support each other ('You scratch my back . . .'), so power over propaganda is likely to be sympathetic to plutocratic power and hereditary power.

It is emotion that mediates ethical impulse, personality, and choice of political ends. We see the emotional element in how particular factions refer to opposing groups — élitists talk of the *masses*, the *rabble*, and '*the great unwashed*' and egalitarians refer to *snobs, fascists,* and *exploiters*. Where means are considered, rather than ends, we should in theory be considering the practical routes to an objective — this should be a matter of shared rational enquiry, within which logic and agreed facts are the ready tools to hand. In fact this is an ideal depiction, rarely conforming to actual political discussion, and the reason is simple to see: consideration of *ends* quickly creeps in to what was a seemingly straightforward *means* discussion. So we want to achieve a healthy population (if we do, and there are grounds for thinking that some polemicists do not): we tax in order to fund national schemes, but tax, a clear *means* consideration, also has *ends* associations. (Does a person have a right to keep all his earned money? Should the state, the society, the community intervene in private economic activity? To what extent? Such questions are answered, in the last resort, by emotionally generated and emotionally sustained appeals to selected values.)

So has the doctrine of robotic man nothing to say about what are the *right* political opinions to hold? It cannot answer this question, unless the task is simply to clarify the logistics of particular means. However it can also clarify why particular political opinions come to be held. Consider the following two declarations:

'I am a selfish swine and I will tread on anyone to get what I want. I don't give a damn about other people, and of course I will support any political party that favours my privileged sectional interest.'

'I have no confidence that I could fight to come out on top in the rat race, and in any case I feel that people in need should be looked after. I will support any political party that helps me and other people to meet our needs when that is the only way for them to be satisfied.'

Such statements, and many analogous ones could be given, illustrate the attitudes of people who are likely to express preferences for particular political parties (no prizes for guessing which), and this clearly illustrates the way that political commitment is emotionally sustained. We have already signalled how emotions can be socially conditioned, how people can be programmed for particular responses. This has direct relevance to ethical sensitivity and political opinion.

The scope of the doctrine of robotic man in this context should now be clear. There is nothing here that is going to fortify one political commitment as against another (I have firm political preferences myself but see no way to represent them as objective physical laws — such preferences are, in the last resort, emotional matters, and nothing more). The best we can hope for is that robotic man will be highly contemptuous of cant and humbug. Claims about desert will be transparent, exposed to scrutiny, as will traditional attitudes to praise, blame, awards, etc. This is a two-edged weapon, working in an even-handed way. The concept of desert is as inapplicable to the destitute pensioner as it is to the thriving businessman: does the one *deserve* a heating allowance and the other to retain hard-earned wealth? It should be clear by now that linguistic usage cannot be justified in logic. No matter, we still *want* particular policies in society (I will rail against 'ill-gotten gains' with the best of them — in general, successfully because private wealth is necessarily supported by cant, hypocrisy, and humbug), and that is all that can be said. Put simply, what we see in political confrontation — whether it occurs in South Africa, the Australian outback, Albania, or the English Parliament — is a *collision of desires* (of course mediated in complex ways by a matrix of cognitive factors).

In this context, any political outcome can be analysed in terms of desires that emerge victorious: those who have certain desires out-compete those who have others, and the competition may involve words, hand-grenades, or heavy artillery. Politics as such a collision of desires, a clash of conative impulses, is necessarily stripped of the traditional mystification, and there may well be benefits to recognize this in such an event. Of course, what some see as benefit, others will see as retrograde impoverishment, because people have different emotional dispositions and so set about organizing different evaluations.

Ethics in Machines

Again we can explore the character of ethics in robotic man by considering the intriguing possibility that artificial systems may develop an ethical sense. This of course is a notion that will be greeted with derision or alarm in most people, though the idea has long been current in fiction. The much-quoted Asimov 'Laws of Robotics' have emphasized the prudent policy of giving thought to the rules that should govern the behaviour of intelligent machines:

1. A robot may not injure a human being, or, through inaction allow a human being to come to harm.
2. A robot must obey the orders given it by human beings except where such orders would conflict with the First Law.
3. A robot must protect its own existence as long as such protection does not conflict with the First or Second Laws.

These supposed 'laws' (said by Asimov to derive from the *Handbook of Robotics*, 56th edition, AD 2058) serve a variety of functional purposes (in, for example, some of the Asimov stories) though, if it were worth while, they could be criticized in various ways. (In passing, we might note that the origin of the laws is in some doubt. Asimov himself has declared that it was John Wood Campbell Jr, the then editor of *Astounding Science Fiction,* who devised the laws. Campbell has said it was Asimov.)

There are a number of ways in which the Asimov laws may be seen to be relevant to the existence of ethics in robotic man. For one thing, the laws tend to assume that robots are usually benevolent, a view that the observer may or may not have about human beings. At the same time there is the assumption that rules for behaviour must take into account the need for the organism to survive, and this requirement accords well with the increasingly purposeful activity evident in computer systems carrying an element of AI (artificial intelligence). The ethical objectives of computer systems are likely to be quite different from those discernible in human beings, so perhaps we should not worry until we see how advanced artificial systems are learning to respond in 'social' situations, when — for example — they are required to communicate with neighbours and to take suitable action in a particular environment.

We have seen that ethical sensitivity is generated and sustained by emotion, and perhaps an ethical awareness will not emerge in artificial systems until they have evolved a matrix of feelings. At the same time it is likely that if ethics are to evolve in (artificial) robots this will occur in a social context. Increasingly computer-based systems are evolving to relate both to other machines and to robotic man. Computers, using a proliferation of networking facilities, are learning to talk to each other and *to take into account each other's needs*. There are the rudiments here of an ethical faculty, albeit one at the moment bereft of the subjective impressions that give impetus to ethical demands. It is already clear that communities of computers are starting to develop (using telephone networks, digital PABXs, local-area networks, wide-area networks, etc.) and that this trend will eventually yield a social sense. (We should again emphasize that ethics is generally conceived in social terms. Goethe's *Wilhelm Meister* proposed the ethical importance of self-realization, but this sort of approach to ethics is unusual.)

The emergence of an ethical faculty in artificial systems will inevitably depend upon processing information in various ways, just as ethics is realized and mediated in human beings. Some of the information (*all* of it in the evolutionary beginnings) is concerned with straightforward cognitive processing; later the elements of emotionality will broaden out the base of the ethical faculty, and appropriate additional levels of information processing will be organized. Already analogies have been drawn between activities in organisms and activities in computer systems, aspects of behaviour that bear on ethical questions. For example, Pugh (1978) has pointed out that the innate human values that relate to the objective of survival are analogous to the values of computer-based chess-players striving to attain their own objective of victory. Other observers have suggested the relevance of computer cybernetics to developing our understanding of morality in human beings. Thus Wright (1971) has observed that it would be a stimulating exercise 'to discuss moral behaviour in the language of genetic and environmental pro-gramming, and of storage and translation mechanisms' — concepts that are redolent of computer theory. In this context it is suggested that the effective homeostat could be set differently for different moral environments — a nice realization of the situation ethics favoured by existentialists and others! This sort of approach further emphasizes that human ethics can be studied in terms of cybernetic systems in general and computer systems in particular.

It is also interesting that experiments have been carried out to explore what sorts of systems are likely to have survival value, and whether such systems may be seen to have the rudiments of altruism, selfishness, etc. Is there a theory for the natural development of altruism, independent on the contingent experience and behaviours of known biological systems?

In a study carried out at the University of Michigan by Robert Axelrod, a situation is described in which every day we exchange a box of goods with another person. We can choose whether to put items in the traded boxes or to leave them empty. A full box signals *fair* trading, an empty box *unfair*. The question is asked: what strategy would leave you with the most number of items in the long term? As befits this sort of investigation in the modern world, a computer-based approach was devised. No less than sixty-two computer programs, varying in complexity from four lines to 152 lines, were arranged to trade under the stipulated conditions. The programs, deriving from six countries, were recognizably 'nice' and 'nasty': e.g. nice programs were inclined to leave full boxes until their trust was violated by being given an empty box by a nasty program. When the programs were allowed to compete with each other, various surprising results were achieved. For one thing, it was seen not to be a good policy to try to cheat! A nice program, called TIT for TAT, finished up as the winner (i.e. it was able to collect most goods in the long term, even though it had not set about its task in a selfish manner).

TIT for TAT worked on the assumption that other programs could be trusted until they demonstrated the opposite, whereupon, instead of leaving full boxes, TIT for TAT would leave an empty box until the other program improved its behaviour. It was clear that programs that left *two* empty boxes after they had been cheated did not do too well. In the event, nice programs were found to fill fourteen out of the top fifteen places in the competition. It was clear from this experiment that decency — being generous, not providing an excessive response to cheating, etc. — resulted in the largest acquisition of goods. It clearly pays to be nice, if such trading simulations are anything to go by!

This work also links to the origins of altruism considered earlier in the chapter (see 'The relevance of biology'). There appear to be natural reasons why interacting systems — early life-forms, primates, trading programs, etc. — should develop altruistic tendencies. This does not mean that other tendencies — less benevolently inclined — will also develop for other reasons, but what it does mean is that a theory of the emergence of altruism — a key ethical component — can be developed without recourse to mystical categories (conscience, free will, soul, etc.). The ethical faculty of human beings is well within the orbit of robotic man, as are all the other elements of human physical and mental activity that have been discussed in the present book.

It is obvious that man is an ethical animal. He experiences guilt and pleasure in ways that have obvious ethical significance in social situations: i.e. human beings are sensitive to how their actions (or lack of actions) affect the emotional states of other people. However there is no reason to think that this is an inherently mysterious phenomenon: it is part of the cognitive/conative complex within which all aspects of robotic man can be explored. This is of particular interest in considering, for example, the various aspects of human relations in society. These too can be explored within the cybernetic framework of information processing using feedback, homeostasis, and other useful mechanisms. These too can be accommodated in the doctrine of robotic man.

Summary

This chapter has explored the nature of ethics within the context of man seen as a cybernetic system. We have seen that the interpretation of the human mind in deterministic terms has important implications for ethical sensitivity and ethical behaviour in a social context (and sometimes in a personal context also). There is a physiological frame within which ethics has to be discussed, and this yields conclusions for many traditional ethical categories. For example, we need to revise our attitude to desert and responsibility. Desert has traditionally been invoked to give legitimacy to the infliction of suffering: it is almost always nothing more than a sanction for the traditional moralist to relieve his feelings by inflicting pain. Similarly responsibility is a peculiar doctrine for robotic man: responsiblity can only be said to exist when we perceive behaviour that we deem to be morally responsible ('That person is behaving in a morally responsible way') — it cannot be justified as some mysterious metaphysical possession of every mind which allows us to inflict pain when we do not like the person's behaviour. In this way we can see free will, desert, and responsibility as superstitious fabrications, concocted in prescientific times to maintain priestly power and to sanction the (sometimes sadistic) punitive impulses of the traditional moralist. We cannot find a sanction for the punitive impulse in the doctrine of robotic man.

We have also seen that ethics, properly analysed, provides a basis for political belief, but that the doctrine of robotic man cannot adjudicate between competing political creeds. Politics, like ethics, is effectively a collision of desires — and where 'the best man wins', *best* signals the individual who can operate most effectively to achieve emotionally generated and emotionally sustained objectives. There is nothing in a *best* so defined of moral superiority, because superiority in this sense — when claimed by a person — does no more than signal an emotional preference. We may not always prefer the winners!

Attempts have also been made to indicate that artificial systems will gradually develop a social sense, and then perhaps faculties that may be deemed to have ethical significance. We have seen that the nice (TIT for TAT) program is generous in how it was organized to trade goods, and already we can see that computers are interested in trading! It is commonplace for computer-based facilities — in, for example, the electronic office — to trade, not goods, but information; and in this — as computers develop increased autonomy — we may discern the rudiments of a moral faculty. It is easy to frame a scenario, for example, in which computers negotiate (perhaps on behalf of their users) about information that may be exchanged. In carrying out such a task, computers would be weighing evidence, processing information, assigning weighting factors to particular properties, and then making decisions according to effective preference. Here, however, we see all the elements of the ethical scheme that we can identify in robotic man — the careful examination of relevant particulars, the (emotionally generated) weightings, and the final decision (the working of 'free will'). Ethical activity, as we have seen, is about information processing: in robotic man the processing is partly cognitive (perceiving, learning, imagining, problem solving, etc.) and partly conative (willing, wishing, desiring, etc.), and such aspects of processing provide the effective conceptual framework for an interpretation of ethics (and politics) in human society.

Since we all have emotionally generated values, ethics will continue to be important (important is an emotional term) in human life. We need to realize that the doctrine of robotic man does not 'explain away' ethics or such other subjective elements as aesthetic sensitivity, love or the creative impulse); it provides a framework for explanation, one that is not constrained by the mystifications and obscurities of traditional philosophy. It does no service to human beings to preserve a superstitious interpretation of important mental faculties, including our ethical sensitivity and awareness.

9 Human Relationships

Preamble

By now it will not surprise the reader that it is possible to interpret human relationships in cybernetic terms, using a variety of information-processing models to deepen our understanding of how human beings interact with one another. Even at a superficial level, human interaction is about taking in information, making appropriate adjustments, supplying information, perceiving the effects, making yet more adaptations, etc. — in a never-ending exchange of data to work to. It is obvious that here we have all the elements of a classical cybernetic process — information processing, feedback of various sorts, 'hunting' around a reference point, the search for a congenial homeostasis, etc. As adaptive cybernetic systems human beings clearly show that they can be accommodated by the doctrine of robotic man. This is made abundantly clear by any systematic scrutiny of human relationships.

It is impossible to frame any theory of human relations that does not consider the role of information: there is no psychological school that does not rest upon the ground of information acquisition, storage and retrieval — the language of the various schools is diverse, carrying bundles of jargon that are reckoned to be appropriate to particular conceptual emphases, but there is no jargon that cannot be analysed in terms of information handling (and often in terms of classical communications theory). Some psychological approaches — say, those adopted in such schools as exchange theory and equity theory (see below) — seem singularly suited to a cybernetic interpretation of human relationships. But the point is a general one. Whether human relationships are interpreted according to behaviourism, gestalt theory, psychoanalysis, cognitivism, mechanism, existentialism, etc., the point stands. All the discrete jargons can be translated into rules, programs, data manipulations, symbolizing, adaptation, objectives, decision making and regulation, and this is manifestly the terrain of the classical cybernetician.

We have already indicated that human biology can be seen as a complex of programs (Chapter 5) and that human decision making,

277

emotional response, and ethical sensitivity can be interpreted in cybernetic terms (Chapters 6 to 8). In this context it is hardly surprising to find that human relationships are subject to a similar analysis. Human relationships are at the heart of human existence; they represent central behavioural, psychological, and existential elements in robotic man.

Perceiving People

For a relationship to exist at all, people have to be *perceived*. People can scarcely relate to one another if they do not know of each other's existence. This simple truism — seemingly too obvious to deserve stating — embraces a wealth of significance, for it is the case that 'people perception' is a highly complex process in every human being, and no assumptions can be made about how the process works. Warr and Knapper (1968), for example, surveyed the then-current literature, nearly twenty years ago, and discussed source material that occupied a 38-page reference list. It is obvious that how people behave in relation to each other is at least 'in part determined by the manner in which they perceive each other', but it is less obvious how these perceptions come to be constructed.

As with any system operation, it is possible to view the perception process in terms of input functions, processing, and output functions. Commonsense indicates, at least to a degree, how these various elements may operate in practical circumstances. It is clear, for example, that when data are presented to a perceiver a selection process takes place — and in an automatic way (i.e. the perceiver *notices* some items of information but ignores others). Already the phenomenon of social conditioning, with its inevitable biological roots, has laid down how the initial data-selection process will operate.

Once the data has been selected, in whatever manner, it is processed in various ways. For example, it is matched against any relevant stored information to allow an assessment to be made (a person is perceived as black, say, and blacks have been helpful — or hurtful — in the past), and the assessment can yield characteristic action. The perceiver can join the Ku Klux Klan, a civil rights group, or preserve an untroubled homeostatic complacency. It is easy to speculate on how the various elements in input-processing-output can vary in the context of human relationships, and it is obvious how such variations will influence the quality of ensuing contacts between people.

It is worth emphasizing the information-processing activity involved in all aspects of people perception. As soon as someone is aware of another human being, attributes are seen (or imagined); they are processed to yield outputs (processed moreover in ways that are determined by the prior programming of the perceiver); and then expectations are formulated as an effective output. For example, a person may perceive another and deduce from the manner he behaves that such a person would make a good footballer, policeman, or company director. The inference may be unsound — it may, for instance, be based on partial information — but such a manifestation of 'expectation generation' always illustrates the information-processing character of the process. Furthermore, it is possible to say certain things about the *nature* of the process. Thus, Warr and Knapper declare: 'An information-processing system with outputs of this kind is one which is capable of ordering its inputs along dimensions or of placing them into categories.' Computer buffs will quickly be reminded of computer software that can operate in such a fashion.

As well as what has been called the 'attributive' activity of the process — whereby qualities are assigned to individuals to generate expectations about the perceived person — there is also an *affective* component (i.e. we do not only attribute qualities to a person and make judgements about future performance, we are also affected in various emotional ways — another sort of information processing). None of us would doubt that affective elements — how we feel about a person (or about the class of people to which we judge the perceived individual to belong) — influence the processing of perceptual data. Thus, as we have found in many other contexts, there is a constant mix of cognitive and conative influences, all mediated by their own characteristic types of information processing — and all having an impact on how we come to perceive people in our environment.

Approached from another direction, people perception is influenced by attitude (which in turn has been linked to personality — see Chapter 7). Again attitude can be interpreted in terms of information processing, though perhaps attitude does not constitute an active processor. Rather, it influences the *way* that other processors operate. In one view, attitude may be seen as a sort of mesh or filter, allowing some information through but restricting access to other data items. Thus the development of attitudes in a person is analogous to the construction of screens of various sorts — designed to allow the passage of some information elements but not others. The internal processors can then set about their tasks, totally unaware that a considerable volume of data will never be presented to them. Or attitude may be interpreted as an element influencing the very structure of the processors, rather than as cohabiting merely as a peripheral filter. Attitude may be written indelibly into the circuits of the processing systems interested in people perception and people evaluation.

In fact attitude can mean many different things. Its Latin root, *aptus*, suggests 'fitness' or 'adaptedness'; or it may suggest 'aptitude', which signals a talent or skill. We talk commonly of *mental attitudes*, meaning preparedness to learn or to cooperate; and here it can denote intellectual receptivity or obedience — widely different phenomena. In the late nineteenth century a motor theory of attitude was popular, and it came to be suggested that the state of the muscles determined how consciousness worked in particular circumstances. Today, in discussions of attitude, it is rare to see a distinction between mental and motor factors, and consensus definition is often invoked; for example, attitude denotes 'a neuropsychic state of readiness for mental and physical activity' (Allport, 1954). It remains clear that much of the historical confusion about attitude — was it sensation, feeling, muscle irritation, excitement, need, etc.? — could have been avoided if a thorough-going information-processing model had been developed. In such a view, attitude mediates information processing in both its cognitive and conative realms — whether as *filter* or actual *adjunct* to the processors themselves is of secondary importance.

Thus we see that people perception — the initial stage in human relationships — is already a highly programmed affair, involving the complex selection of incoming data, their processing according to the programmed structures built up in various ways, and outputs that are themselves attitudes and dispositions that mediate the selection processes the next time round. Personality and attitude — themselves programmed matrices having profound functional consequences — help to define, by whatever mechanisms, the character of the processing that takes place. It is via such a seemingly tortuous route that a person is perceived, and already the character of the relationship is encapsulated in how the perception takes place. By the time we have filtered the data, worked on them, and been affected in many different ways, we are already relating to the object of perception. Theoretically, and for the purpose of initial discussion, we can suggest that perception is necessarily prior to a relationship. In fact they intermesh: the influence of one is indelibly stamped upon the other. This seems to apply whatever the nature of the relationship.

What emerges from this initial, and necessarily brief, enquiry is that human interaction (perception, relating, etc.) is highly amenable to interpretation in programming and information-handling terms. It may be thought that relations between people — a manifest index of our 'humaness' — may hold robotic man securely at bay. In fact the reverse is the case. Human relationships — as evident cybernetic processes involving complex information handling — are ripe for inclusion in the doctrine of robotic man. This should not worry us. We are no less human — merely spared an unhelpful quota of delusion and hypocrisy.

The Spectrum of Relations

The spectrum of relationships among human beings is complex, shifting, and multifaceted. In a trivial sense, every individual has relationships — at least in space and time — with every other past, present, and future person. In a less trivial sense, relationships are mediated by class membership, whether others can be recognized by virtue of a shared characteristic. So a person relates differently to a same-sex friend or colleague than to someone of the opposite sex, and class (or group) membership can hinge on many different characteristics — nationality, interests, age, experiences, economic circumstances, shared friends, etc. Shared characteristics are only one dimension along which relationships can be identified: a victim has a relationship to a burglar, a boxer to an opponent, an employee to a manager, a judge to a defendant, a student to a professor, a citizen to a public servant, etc., etc. The spectrum is immensely complicated even before we begin to consider the dynamic, shifting elements in all relationships.

It is obvious that relationships — of whatever sort — change over time. People grow in experience, in knowledge, in expectation, and simply grow old. No relationship is a static affair, indifferent to the passage of hours, days, years. Just as specific relationships inevitably change to a greater or lesser extent, so do relationships when viewed as typical social conventions: so marriage as a relationship varies from one generation to the next. We can chart some of the change in easy quantitative terms — changes in age at first marriage, changes in divorce rate, changed of incidence of extramarital relations, changes in rate of remarriage, etc. As marriage changes as an institution, so do all other institutions in society, and these can invariably be interpreted in terms of human relationships. What is the relationship of the average citizen to the monarch? To the Prime Minister? To a street cleaner? To a shop steward? To a criminal? The character of such relationships can change dramatically through a generation, and almost from day to day in unusual and spectacular circumstances. Relationships are also multifaceted. The relationships of spouses is affected by respective sexual need, expectation of life, respective interests and prejudices, attitudes and inhibitions, financial status, respective levels of education, states of health, commitments and pet hates, relationships with offspring, parents, neighbours, and friends, etc. This highly complex meshing of influences is true of any relationship between a man and woman that lasts for a lengthy period — and the same is true, *mutatis mutandis*, of all other relationships between human beings in society. The phenomenon of the relationship involves the interaction of two or more highly complex cybernetic systems, each of which is subject to its own complicated development according to internal and external factors.

It should be clear that the complexities of human interaction do not imply that such interaction is anything other than a rigorously controlled mechanistic process. People often talk *as if* the sheer complexity of human beings translated their thoughts and behaviour into a non-mechanistic realm, immune to scientific enquiry. In fact complexity cannot translate mortals into some ethereal world where the rules of rational enquiry do not apply. Complexity presents a variety of technical problems — how do we test this hypothesis? that theory? — but it is always reasonable to assume that there is justification for the rational investigation, that if we do not proceed in a cautious systematic way, collecting realistic evidence as we do, then there is no way that we *can* proceed. Human beings are amenable to scientific enquiry — and no human facet or aspect is exempt. We can explore ethical disposition, aesthetic sensitivity, impulse to creativity or worship — just as we can investigate nutritional habits, modes of sexual foreplay, and theories about cellular ageing. Increasingly it is possible to examine human beings — including human relationships — in the terms and language evolving out of computer science, exploiting the useful jargon developed to denote the behaviour of artificial robots and other computer-based systems.

If the doctrine of robotic man is to embrace the phenomenon of human relationships then we would expect to detect the characteristic cybernetic categories in everyday human interaction. It is not hard to find abundant evidence of this sort: people trade information, use feedback to make accommodations, strive to establish a working homeostasis, and where the repertoires of programs and information is insufficient for the realization of a particular objective, the attempt is abandoned and new adjustments and adaptations are attempted. There is nothing here that cannot be found in many orthodox schools of psychology and moreover in many different approaches to personal therapy. Human beings relate to one another — whatever the nature of the relationships — according to the modes and categories that cybernetics has been developed to describe (see 'Rules, feedback, and adaptation', below). This is more obvious in some approaches to psychology than others (though it is present in them all); it is transparently obvious in what has become known as 'exchange theory' (or, in another version, 'equity theory').

The Theory of Exchange

In exchange theory it is assumed that a person will not stay in a relationship unless 'the rewards minus the costs' give the person more than he could receive in any alternative available. The 'computation' must take into account the inevitable cost of making the transfer to a new situation. It may be of course that it is difficult to leave a relationship, that a constricting dependence — possibly mutual — has developed, making extraction difficult, if not impossible. This possibility can be well catered for by the theory. Here the cost of leaving the situation is high — it may involve a public scene, recrimination, even violence — and, even in the short term, this may not be a price that the person is prepared to pay. As with the difficulty of breaking kinship ties, other ploys are adopted: contact is less frequent, presents are less often given, solicitous words less frequently offered, intimacy less frequently sought. There is a psychological withdrawal that well symbolizes the imagined physical retreat — until the stage perhaps when the actual collapse of the relationship has been accomplished, whatever the feelings of the party who may feel deserted. We are not surprised to learn that there are rules (see below) that can be learned to supervise the cost factors.

In presenting the theory of social exchange, Homans (1961) proposed that the continuation of social intercourse depends upon the people involved feeling that they are getting roughly equal profit from it (this has been dubbed the principle of 'distributive justice'). It is assumed that if the distribution of profit is very one-sided then the relationship will be broken off, as far as the aggrieved party is able to accomplish a rupture of that sort. The person who is receiving little profit may feel 'exploited', 'used', permanently at a gross disadvantage; unless there is an unwholesome fixation on the exploiter — which is not an altogether uncommon situation — then the relationship will be quickly terminated. It follows that a sensitive person, aware of the other's feelings, will take steps to 'give' more, to increase the other's profit (Stephenson and White, 1968), if the 'exploiter' values the relationship and wants it to continue.

Where the relationship is important to both parties — these may be friends, lovers, spouses, etc. — then there is a mutually negotiated equilibrium which aims to achieve a sharing of profit to the benefit of both. This equilibrium, often unconsciously constructed, is an effective homeostasis, a steady state which may need constant monitoring if it is to be preserved, i.e. if the relationship is to survive. The negotiated homeostasis, not necessarily a stable condition, is only one of a number of cybernetic features in this sort of situation.

The central element in this approach is that perceived rewards and costs in a relationship are central to its security: too much of an imbalance and one of the parties will work to end the connection. A degree of imbalance is inevitable, though its magnitude will necessarily affect the quality of the relationship. This theory has sometimes also been dubbed 'equity theory' — a version of social exchange. It suggests, for example, that people feel happy when they are receiving exactly what they feel they deserve in a relationship. Their rationale may be confused — we have already said something about desert (Chapter 8) — but they are still moved by psychological pressures. They may feel that they are 'putting into' the relationship more than they are getting back; they are 'investing' but there is inadequate return. There are practical steps that a person will take when he perceives an imbalance. Walster, Walster and Berscheid (1978), for example, suggest that a person in an inequitable relationship will strive to restore equilibrium by either restoring *actual* equity, restoring psychological equity (i.e. convincing himself that it is a fair relationship after all), or ending the relationship. Simply put, rewards and costs are assessed and appropriate action follows.

We have already mentioned the possibility of *investing to gain return*, an approach that has been formalized in terms of an investment model (Rusbult, 1983). This merely states what we have already observed:

$$\text{Satisfaction} = (\text{rewards} - \text{costs}) - \text{comparison level}$$

A corollary states:

$$\text{Commitment to a relationship} = \text{satisfaction} - \text{alternative quality} + \text{investment size}$$

Again this suggests the unremarkable fact that we will be well satisfied with relationships that provide high rewards and low costs, and moreover exceed our general expectations about relationships of that sort. In short, commitment is high when we are satisfied, have no acceptable alternatives, and have invested heavily in the relationship. There are some differences between this model and equity theory, but for our purposes the similarities are highly significant.

What we see is a continuous process of computation based on acquired information. A person spends time in a relationship and gathers data about his experiences (joys, hopes, disappointments, pains, pleasures, etc.); these data are used to frame expectations about future experiences (what can reasonably be hoped for, demanded, given, etc.). Where the reward/cost balance establishes a workable equilibrium (the effective homeostasis), the relationship will continue; where it does not, the person will work to change the relationship, change his perception of it (or perhaps do both), or end the relationship. In this connection two important points need to be emphasized; first, most of the computations are being carried out unconsciously (there is rarely any conscious effort to weight the various rewards and costs and to do sums on that basis) — all the individual knows is that certain feelings (the result of conative processing) are experiences that are worth repeating or avoiding; and second, the computations need not necessarily be done well.

We should not imagine that everyone evaluates a relationship accurately, with consummate skill and in his own best interest. People make mistakes; they end relationships that are supportive and helpful; they continue in relationships that are stultifying and unhealthy. On our earlier theory (Chapter 6), it is inevitable that this should be so: there is no assumption, with all the cybernetic adjustment in the world, that people are bound to be happy — human psychological processing will run its course and the result is sometimes human misery (but if we are philosophers and not therapists we will only account this a human failure for the most subjective reasons). Some people compute better than do others; the complex program matrix varies from one person to another. Early childhood experiences, for example (a regular psychiatric ploy), may have erected unhelpful programs or blocked the working of wholesome ones. The computations are performed but we do not know what the results will achieve until we are able to assess the subsequent feelings and emotions of the person.

Another point to emphasize is the *plastic* nature of human accommodations. In taking action to seek a new homeostasis, a fresh equilibrium — by changing circumstance or person, or by leaving the relationship — the individual is able to negotiate various steady states, any one of which might serve his interest: there is more than one workable homeostasis to be discovered.

The notion of sharing profits in a relationship and of calculating (computing) rewards and costs is a commonplace of psychology. We have seen the relevance of such matters to various aspects of social exchange, equity theory, and the investment model. We also find discussion of *supportive* and *remedial interchanges* in, for example, Goffman (1971), where there is attention to aspects of interpersonal ritual. This approach also can be analysed within the cybernetic framework that characterizes the doctrine of robotic man. We need to say a little more about the cybernetic features of the typical social exchange between human beings.

Rules, Feedback, and Adaptation

It is obvious that human relationships are governed by rules and that these are of various types. There are, for example, rules that are translated into *laws*: a matrix of prohibitions and permissions; there are the rules of a culture, the often *unwritten 'laws'* that people ignore at their peril (risking social ostracism or worse); and there is a large body of rules that relate to the actual *functioning* of human relationships. Therapists — for instance, in social encounter groups — are particularly interested in the functional rules for successful social intercourse. 'If you behave in such and such a way you are more likely to sustain a long-term relationship', etc., etc. It is important for our purposes to look at the nature of such rules.

A rule is an injunction — at least in its active implementation. In the first instance, a rule may be regarded simply as an 'if ... then' connection: 'if you want to achieve that end then proceed so'. It is obvious that people want results from human relationships: they do not want to only contemplate what might happen if.... So the rule, as injunction, becomes an order or instruction, and again this is the stuff of computer science (in particular, of programming theory). If a person is to achieve a particular objective, it is necessary to go through the various stages of a process. Perhaps there are many different processes that will yield the desired result, but *some* process needs to be gone through, and its nature will be determined by the relationship in question and its (inevitably) unique circumstances.

A rule (or a group of rules) so defined can clearly be modelled by a computer program: we have a series of steps or phases that need to be undertaken (or experienced) so that an end can be achieved. This does not entail the *conscious* consideration of ends in every case: it may be that the person has learned routines and procedures by (more or less) unconscious practice — many skills are acquired in this way. However when the procedure is undertaken, when the skill is used, the individual is carrying out an effective program, a sequence of discrete steps to achieve a goal.

The rules that constitute the functional program are important to the working of a relationship: indeed, if the rules are violated or ignored, it is quite possible that the relationship will collapse. We all know some of the rules, but we may need advice or counselling to become aware of them all. We investigate possible rules through experiment, estimating consequences — again making calculations of reward and cost. We learn that some rules are necessary to all wholesome relationships. Argyle and Henderson (1985) have highlighted the existence of rules in particular areas: e.g. in connection with intimacy, coordination and avoiding difficulties, and behaviour with third parties. How are we to behave in intimate circumstances? How do we avoid tension and conflict in an important friendship? Is it desirable that we always do? How do we cope with jealousy? Or confidences? Or verbal attacks on a friend? And is what works today necessarily valid for tomorrow?

It is no part of our task to start giving answers to such questions. We are interested in exploring the framework in which such questions come to be asked, the (cybernetic) context in which people process decision-type information to implement particular programs from the stored repertoire. As we learn about the rules that are appropriate to specific types of social intercourse we are gradually enlarging our stock of procedures, the functional routines that we can call on for different purposes. What we are doing of course is building a matrix of programs, the encapsulated rules and procedures without which no objectives can be realized. Again we may stress that this is a matter of information processing, of running through effective programs, of exhibiting the functional characteristics of robotic man. Are there *always* rules — effectively agreed procedures in defined circumstances? It is in fact hard to imagine *absence* of rules in any conceivable scenario, hard to object to Argyle and Henderson (1985) when they remark that 'we shall find that there are in fact rules for *all* of the relationships ...' (my italics). All of the relationships are 'rule-governed', even the most informal ones. We do not explore relationships by investigating the presence or absence of rules, but by uncovering the actual rules that obtain. All human behaviour — including the most intimate activities — is regulated by rules, consciously or unconsciously implemented: all activity is controlled by programs, not always in the ways that we might wish.

We do not need to consider specific *instances* of rules (programs) in any detail. It is relatively easy for the individual to articulate rules that would help rather than hinder the launch and preservation of a close relationship:

Do not always think of your own needs.
Show concern for the feelings of the other.
Do not be morose or introverted.
Give signals that the other is needed, important, esteemed.
Be sensitive to the signals offered by the other.
etc., etc.

Argyle and Henderson compiled a list of thirty-three rules which they considered general enough to apply 'across most relationships'. These related to: suitable topics for conversation, showing or hiding emotions, dress and personal appearance, etc. Even this preliminary indication shows that rules are often subjective, devised for a circumstance or a particular person (e.g. conversational needs vary — some like 'small talk'; others cannot stand it). However the point is made: no relationship is a capricious random matter, indifferent to the constraints of law, of rules, of programs.

The corollary to this approach is that programs require information to work on; programs are impotent without data — they are in fact devices for manipulating information items. The existence of a functional program presupposes the availability of relevant information. There are many ways in which this information is made available to the programs that regulate human social contact. Even such a phenomenon as gaze direction (Kendon, 1967) can provide an observer with information about the form of a social connection, and countless other activities are going on in any human contact — words chosen, conversational topics chosen, tone of voice, position of limbs, selection of gestures, calculated responses to the other's words. This all shows a highly complex informational scenario, in which people are giving off signals in profusion and in turn monitoring a substantial proportion of the signals that are sent their way. People learn pecking-order, appropriate laughter, how to commiserate, taboos, clichés (as shared conventional wisdom), and countless other devices, tools, and mechanisms that are stored up in the program repertoire. Throughout the process of interaction, feedback is an inevitable concomitant to any enterprise: it is through feedback that the individual evaluates a particular behavioural trajectory and assesses whether it is worth storing (or implementing) this or that program. Already there is a broad literature of how feedback operates in types of human activity: e.g. when a person practises deception (Ekman and Friesen, 1969) and when a teacher modifies his behaviour following feedback from pupils (Gage, Runkel, and Chatterjee, 1963).

Again we see that a cybernetic model, possibly built in a hierarchy, can represent human social activity in all its manifestations. All relationships are regulated by rules (though not all relationships are satisfactory and secure), and there are ways in which such rules can be interpreted as effective programs, as — at one level — sequences of phases (steps, orders, instructions) which are run through in order to accomplish an objective (obedience to a program cannot, however, guarantee success: the algorithm may be unsound). Throughout the operation of a program there is a constant two-way flow of information, which provides data for existing programs to use, for program modification, and for the construction of new programs. Feedback is used to evaluate the information that is made available: incoming data are processed, filtered, compared with 'reference standards', stored, given significance, etc. The upshot is that behaviour continues on a particular course, is modified or abandoned. What is particularly interesting is the complexity of this activity.

The sheer complexity of the information processing in any instance of human intercourse is such that the processing could never be completed, in its entirety, within the part of the human mind that is accessible to consciousness. In other words, most of our performance in social contact is *automatic* (even in the popular sense) and the part that we may think *autonomous* is in fact automatic, but at a different level and according to a different logic (see Chapter 6). Human relations are invariably conducted in this cybernetic fashion, subject to the largely unconscious processing of information and using feedback and other mechanisms to control the operation, refinement, and abandonment — as necessary — of the stored programs. This is manifestly an interpretation that is highly congenial to the doctrine of robotic man.

The Sexual Dimension

General

Sexual relationships, as highly complex aspects of human behaviour, embody many cybernetic features. At one level there is the simple physiological response: penile or clitoral erection, ejaculation, vaginal lubrication, orgasm, etc. — the clear manifestations of neural and hydraulic events. At another level, the one seemingly favoured by romantics, there are feelings of warmth and tenderness, the heightened sensitivity to poetry and music, all the concomitants of attraction, falling in love, etc. The sexual dimension is perhaps unique in human beings in that it unites a remarkable cross-section of bodily responses — from the quickly discernible physiological changes to the soaring flights of fancy and fantasy. The sexual dimension represents a multilayered cybernetic phenomenon that can be discussed in many different ways for many different purposes. (I myself, in an earlier series of books, have explored the sexual dimension in its various historical, psychological, anthropological, and superstitious aspects.) This illustrates a consideration that has already been advertised several times in the present book: the richness and diversity of human experience can be adequately described, at least in outline, in the context of anatomical performance, cerebral behaviour, cybernetic information processing, etc. The complexities of metabolic chemistry and neural networks are, we may assume, sufficient to sustain all the experiences and behaviour of human beings. Analysis of the sexual dimension shows how a vitally important area of human life — with many physiological and psychological implications — can be accommodated by the doctrine of robotic man. We have already glanced at various aspects of human relationships and now we need to say something about sexual biology, sexual programming (via 'scripts'), and typical sexual scenarios tht are commonplace in human society.

The Place of Biology

We all know that sex is determined at conception by the XY chromosome mechanism: individuals with an XX chromosome complement grow into females and XYs become males. This means that it is the Y chromosome that determines the basic decision as to whether the new individual will become a boy or a girl. There are various theories to explain how the Y chromosome can regulate this early decision. It has been suggested, for example, that part of the sex chromosome controls the rate at which the uncommitted primitive sex organ (the gonad) is allowed to develop: quick growth produces a boy, slower growth a girl. It is interesting to note, from embryological diagrams and photographs, how the primitive sexual features are common to all individuals in their early stages — whether a girl or a boy is to result. (This explains why the clitoris can be regarded as an undeveloped penis, why the male has nipples and a useless piece of tissue that has become known as the 'uterus masculinus', and why psychoanalysts have been keen to describe the *animus* and *anima* that can be detected in every human psyche.)

We may reflect on the implications of the early biological determination of the sex of the individual. If we consider that males and females have, to *any* degree, characteristic psychologies independent of cultural shaping, then it is likely that behavioural responses will be, at least to a degree, characteristic. At a trivial level this is obviously true: males have been known to lactate and women to have an engorged clitoris several centimetres long, but it is precisely because such occurrences are atypical that we see them as remarkable. Differential anatomical behaviour is likely to have accompanying psychological manifestations — and this circumstance again says something about the constraints imposed upon individual decision making. The sexual dimension is yet another area in which human performance is channelled by biological circumstances laid down before the person can reflect on the matter. This is a point that could be pursued in more detail. For example, we have long known that the higher neural centres of the hypothalamus, controlling the secretion of the sex hormones, function differently in the male and the female. In the human male there is a fairly constant output of gonadotrophins and hence androgens, whereas in the female the outputs are cyclic (or phasic). This is an important finding in neuroendocrinology, that '*some part of the brain is characteristically different in males and females*' (original italics) (Hutt, 1972). We are not surprised to find that characteristic male and female behaviour may be linked to characteristic circulation of hormones and neural behaviour in parts of the brain.

It is interesting to speculate, in passing, on the features of characteristic male and female behaviour, but there is no requirement, within the doctrine of robotic man, that such characteristic modes be established. Even if — as I do not actually believe — all differences between male and female performance are fully explicable in cultural (nurtural) terms, then robotic man (and robotic woman) remains secure. This is because it has always been part of the doctrine of robotic man that the programming matrix is a complex mix of biological endowment and environmental influence. However men and women behave, they do so because they are programmed in one way or another.

The circumstances of particular aspects of sexual behaviour can be explored in obviously cybernetic terms. The female cycle is regulated by hormonal secretions that are controlled using feedback information of various sorts, and a different cycle — between one erection/ejaculation and the next — is similarly controlled by feedback, of a completely different sort, in the male. It is possible to explore such cycles — and, if we wish, the sexually sustained cycles of life and death — in terms of information acquisition, information processing, comparisons of data against reference points, and accomplishment of homeostatic conditions in various modes and at different levels. Some of the cycles are running concurrently in the same individual and are environmentally occasioned by opportunity (the state of current relationships, etc.) as well as being biologically regulated by hormonal secretion.

The cycles implied by sexual biology, the features of specific sexual acts, the psychophysiological framework of sexual behaviour — all imply sensitivity to, and manipulation of, information to achieve identifiable physiological and psychological objectives. There is no phase of sexual activity that cannot be explored according to the requirements of a cybernetic model. Robotic man, even as a sexual creature — perhaps *particularly* as a sexual creature — is a complex mechanism able to use feedback and other cybernetic devices in order to propagate, remove tension and frustration, and seek joy and delicious fulfilment.

Sexual Scripts

We now know that the hypothalamus is interested in the regulation of sexual activity; Young (1978) has pointed out that stimulation of the hypothalamus, using electrical probes, can cause sexual feelings. The brain is also responsible for establishing the 'programs for attachment' that in due course will allow the full flowering of sexual love. For example, it appears that there is an inherited program that promotes attachment in the human being — usually between mother and child — between the ages of about four to twelve months. Attachments will obviously be made outside this period, but their quality may well depend upon whether the child has made a satisfactory attachment during the first year of life. It is almost as if this early attachment is a reference for the human connections that will be made in the years that follow. Psychologists have compared this attachment forming with the characteristic *imprinting* that occurs in many non-human animals.

It is significant in this connection that the child inherits programs for, for example, crying to demand attention, and that the mother has inherited programs to cause her to respond to the child's demands. Biologically the mother is also biologically programmed to lactate, to caress, to comfort — and it is obvious how some of these programs translate to adult sexual relationships. Similarly the programming of the child unfolds to allow sensitivity to the responses of peers and parents: suitably programmed (by love and attention), the child slowly learns the discernment that enables him to form adult relationships in later years. At all stages the programming of the child allows abilities and talents to develop, using acquired and processed information to build up further programs that allow for the diversity of response in the different circumstances that occur. Many of the acquired programs are made available to the child by parents and other adults — one environmental element among many that the developing child cannot avoid. Eric Berne (1971) has emphasized the sexual nature of many of these presented programs ('scripts').

Berne talks of the 'never scripts' that seek to forbid either love or sex (or both). Forbid love but not sex and you have a license for promiscuity; forbid sex but not love and priests and nuns may be a consequence. 'Always scripts' are seen as imposing absolute prohibitions on aspects of behaviour, resulting in children being ejected from the home when they transgress. 'Until scripts' prohibit modes of behaviour *'until* you're married', *'until* you're living on your own', *'until* you apologize, show some respect, etc.'. There are countless sexual scripts for adults, programmed sequences that are run through *over and over* again, whether they are psychologically fulfilling or not. Berne cites the 'over and over script' that allows a man to climax in sexual intercourse, but never the woman — a dismal repetition that runs on and on ('this may happen night after night for years').

Already we can see the complexities of sexual programs (sexual scripts). The impact of parents will not necessarily be conclusive: biological programs assert themselves as well. However the parental influence is usually apparent — a shaping factor when the scripts are being written and the programs being laid down. In extreme cases, we may find frigidity, impotence, psychosis (as readers of Flora Rheta Schreiber — *Sybil* and *The Shoemaker* — already know). We cannot escape our programming — when it is viewed as a total matrix — but escape our programming — when it is viewed as a total matrix — but this does not mean that we are forced to live according to the parentally offered scripts. It *may* be that they will always always exert a compulsive impact on our responses, but there are many other programming factors in our environment; the scripts that come to dominate our responses will be shaped in part by these also.

In sexual behaviour, as in all other aspects of our lives, we are regulated and controlled by our programs. These are complex, modifiable, and laid up in many different modes and at many different levels. Some exhibit the obvious features of a straightforward event in metabolic chemistry; others are highly refined sequences, coded in intricate neural networks, that carry our sensitivity, our capacity for joy, our talent for falling in love. The programmed cybernetics of robotic man allow us some remarkable and immensely desirable experiences.

Some Scenarios

Every human relationship may be regarded, for our purposes, as a scenario. Inevitably it contains the dynamics of a cybernetic situation, the identifiable mechanisms for handling information in certain ways to achieve a workable homeostasis — where the relationship is successful. It is an easy matter to look at any stereotypical situation and to interpret it using the cybernetic categories that are congenial to robotic man.

Consider one type of long-lasting marriage (there are many types but they all have common features). It is inevitable that certain types of stimulus — sexual and other — are no longer received with the excitement that characterized the early years. The adaptive potential of cybernetic systems leads to habituation, where a stronger or different stimulus is required to achieve the same result. This means that in any long-lasting relationship accommodations are made between the parties. Surprises are relatively few, and behavioural trajectories are largely predictable and unremarkable. In such a situation the relationship exhibits a spectrum of strengths and weaknesses: there is security and comfort in the familiar framework, but needs for excitement and variety may go unfulfilled. The individuals use the strengths and cope (or not) with the weaknesses according to their respective program repertoires and the scope that these are given in the relationship.

This implies that a homeostasis has to be negotiated if the relationship is to survive — the steady state that is achieved is not a static phenomenon, but a shifting matrix that needs constant monitoring and adjustment. There are many forces operating to affect the character of the homeostasis, its stability and effectiveness in serving the relationship. The parties are constantly changing, but in ways that do not betray their characters, prejudices, expectations, etc. Every human being is an effective procession of selves linked (perhaps) by a common structure: there are the effects of ageing, new experiences, successes and disappointments, negotiated expectations. As the selves change they experience adaptation and accommodation in the surviving relationship. Again it is easy to emphasize the cybernetic character of this process. Simply put, each party takes in information about the other, allows the information to influence interpersonal behaviour, accepts fresh information as feedback, refines the behaviour accordingly; throughout the process, the conative events (involving emotions, feelings, etc.) are influencing the selection of goals. If the people *want* the relationship to endure, then the objectives are served by processing information to achieve a sustainable equilibrium, the effective homeostasis.

Consider the case where a man and woman meet but where the attraction is not equally felt. It may be important to one of the parties (the man, say) to develop a full sexual relationship; the woman, for various reasons, may not welcome this — perhaps the man is not sufficiently attractive, perhaps there are moral scruples, perhaps there is fear about coping (an element of immaturity), perhaps the judgement is made that the man would not handle the affair in a responsible way (a mature reflection). In any event, the man and woman have different conatively sustained objectives in the relationship. What happens?

Both parties are acquiring appropriate information — partly about the other and partly about themselves. This information is being interpreted according to the program repertoires that have been constructed. The man may be striving to protect a macho image, little interested in the feelings of the other; or he may be a sensitive, giving person, interested in developing a mutually meaningful connection. The woman may be inhibited and anxious, using declared moral scruple to disguise trepidation; or there may be a mature calculation that the prospect of reward does not outweigh the prospect of cost.

Here the different evaluations made by the two parties may lead to the collapse of what relationship does exist. The man may reckon himself too hurt, or the woman too pestered, to make any further contact worth while. Or they may negotiate a compromise equilibrium, a situation in which some of the needs of each are met, but where a full sexual relationship does not develop. Perhaps the two people will meet regularly at a disco, a pub, or a restaurant — enjoying each other's company, trading intimate revelations about their lives, and expecting a certain sort of sustainable commitment as friends ('pals', 'mates', 'buddies') but not as lovers. In such a situation it is not necessary that each party achieves the same level of reward and copes with the same level of cost. It is sufficient that each party sees enough difference between the levels of reward and cost to want to continue with the negotiated arrangement.

Here again the cybernetic features are clear. The people are taking in information, processing it according to in-built programs, and making calculations about how particular objectives can best be served. Perhaps above all, this case indicates that people can negotiate many different levels of homeostatic equilibrium. The man may have imagined a different state of affairs; the woman may have been pushed a little beyond what she would previously have found acceptable; both may be surprised that compromise has yielded a mutually beneficial arrangement.

Consider the type of relationship in which rewards and costs are very disproportionately shared (we have already mentioned this possibility in discussing equity theory). Here both parties may lack sensitivity to the other's needs — or one may be self-seeking, lacking the ability to give in such a way that rewards are more equally distributed. We have seen what can happen in such a situation. One party (the woman, say) may feel that the relationship is unworkable without some fundamental change: she must change the balance of reward and cost or end the connection. She can talk to the other person, trying to increase the prospect of reward; or she can modify her own calculations of rewards and costs ('Perhaps I was being unreasonable . . .'). If such ploys fail, then she ends the relationship — if she is able to do so.

This sort of case illustrates the limits on negotiated homeostases. It is clearly not possible for every person to be able, at least in principle, to sustain a useful relationship with every other person. What this means in cybernetic terms is that people can only work within the scope of their individual program repertoires: they cannot call upon procedures and routines that they do not possess. They may be able to *imagine* a negotiated homeostasis that would work ('If only he would . . .', 'If only I could . . .'), but if they do not possess the skills (the requisite scripts or programs) the envisaged equilibrium will never be attained. It must be part of therapy to equip people with the necessary programs for fruitful negotiation of sustainable homeostases.

There are various points that can be made about the examples cited in this section. They all illustrate the relevance of information processing in negotiating states of equilibrium that serve human need. They all imply that there is usually more than one type of homeostasis that can serve human beings in a sustainable relationship. They imply that there are certain (programmed or programmable) skills that are important in initiating and sustaining relationships between men and women. All this suggests the adaptability of people in human relationships, the way in which different programs can be implemented to meet the requirements of a particular situation. If we are looking to the doctrine of robotic man for advice on human relationships we will find sentiments that are common in most types of orthodox counselling: do not be afraid to show your feelings (you are providing information for programs — your own and his/hers — to work on); do not be dogmatic in your expectations (there are many negotiable homeostases that will work); be sensitive to the needs of the other person (he/she is performing constant calculations to evaluate the reward/cost matrix).

The scenarios discussed above show, in principle, how all human relationships can be discussed in cybernetic terms, within the framework stipulated by the doctrine of robotic man. But why should such an approach be helpful? What is there to recommend it? The answer to such questions is already implied in our earlier discussions of desert and responsibility (Chapter 8). The proposed analysis of human relationships is totally devoid of moralizing: it focuses solely on the dynamics of cybernetic situations that can be comprehended in terms of programs, feedback, and negotiated homeostases to achieve objectives. This may be proposed as a rational approach to developing an understanding of some of the most important areas of human life.

Robots in Relationships

Fiction and films have often explored the idea that robots could enter into relationships with each other and with human beings. In such films as *Westworld* and *Blade Runner*, human beings have sexual relationships with robots, and the robots give every sign of reciprocating the emotion! Such films follow a tradition in certain types of fiction where it is not uncommon for human beings to develop feelings for artificial intelligent systems (see, for example, the survey in Frude, 1984). Thus in Villiers de L'Isle Adam's *L'Eve Future*, first published in Paris in 1886, a handsome young man falls in love with a female automaton — an electromechanical, rather than electronic, robot. The 'electro-human creature' has a life system to control gait, voice, gestures, facial expression, and what may be deemed the mental impressions of the automaton. A flexible skeleton supports the various internal systems, and 'skin' and 'muscle', through which a suitable fluid runs, gives the body its proportions and defines its sex. Two phonographs, set in the chest, provide the power of speech, and a rudimentary nervous system is included. We may find it remarkable that an author could speculate on these, and many other, artificial anatomical details a century ago.

Another robot romance, Lester del Rey's *Helen O'Loy*, was published in 1938, two years before Isaac Asimov published the first of his many robot tales. Helen, an automaton constructed by an engineer and an endocrinologist in their spare time, can adopt many facial expressions and even has 'wired-in tear glands' to allow her to cry at appropriate moments. Moreover she spends her time reading romantic fiction, and can act with purpose to secure a human husband: when her husband finally dies, the robot commits suicide and leaves a note ('. . . please don't grieve too much for us, for we have led a happy life together, and both feel that we should cross the final bridge side by side'). In a similar vein, a seductive male robot appears in the tale, 'Can You Feel Anything When I Do This?', written by Robert Sheckley in 1969. Here the device, an 'omnicleaner', becomes infatuated with a woman who visits the department store and so contrives to be delivered to her home. In many of these tales there are ingenious mechanical details: for example, in one of the earliest stories, Hoffman's *Der Sandmann* (1817), already encountered in Chapter 1, the robot Olympia winds herself up by sneezing!

We are not surprised to read about fictional robots that might *simulate* or *mimic* human behaviour, but we do not always realize that human beings, as robotic man, are already learning to form close attachments to their artificial counter parts. When a woman's magazine asked the question, 'Could you learn to love a robot?', it was perhaps not realized that we already had evidence on the matter. *The Guardian* (24 October 1981) described the intriguing case of a man 'who fell in love with his machine'. Here an industrial worker had programmed 'his engineering skills, both mental and physical' into a numerically controlled flame cutting machine, and he felt that when the machine operated it was like watching his own brain at work. After eight years the machine was sent away for repair — and the man was psychologically unable to transfer to another machine. He preferred to stay at home without pay!

In this spirit, a prostitute has been quoted as saying 'It won't be long before customers can buy a robot from the drug store and they won't need us at all' (*The Guardian*, 23 February 1983); Edna O'Brien has exhorted Steven Spielberg to fashion her 'an L.O. (Love Object) that is tall, greying, handsome, intellectual, humorous, moody . . .' (*The Observer*, 13 February 1983); and Professor Bloch at Cornell University speculated on the possibility of man/machine sexual relationships. Already surrogate lovers, pathetic imitations of human beings, are purchased through the men's magazines and from other sources — and we may speculate on how such surrogates could be refined using voice recognition/synthesis units, artificial sensitive skin (already technologically feasible), and soundless motors to facilitate graceful movement. We are well aware that sensor technology is advancing rapidly and that hi-tech robots to meet a variety of human needs are likely to evolve in the years ahead.

In a trivial sense there are already innumerable man/machine relationships, and these are being refined and enhanced by developments in artificial intelligence. Workers often give names to industrial robots on the assembly line and have been known to send 'get well' cards when the machines are away for repair. We can speculate on how such relationships will evolve when robots become mobile, highly knowledgeable, able to converse, and capable of emotion (so that they have a powerful impulse to solve problems in achieving objectives). In such circumstances it seems clear that robots — human and artificial — will develop a new and powerful symbiosis with wide-ranging implications for the future of society.

Summary

This chapter has explored human relationships within a cybernetic framework. We have seen that, at all stages, from initial perception to the development of intimate sexual relations, human behaviour is defined in terms of such obvious cybernetic categories as information processing, discrimination using feedback, and the realization of desirable objectives by establishing sustainable homeostatic conditions. We have also seen that the various processes are necessarily carried out by drawing on the repertoires of programs constructed by every human being. However we do not imply that because human behaviour is governed by programmed routines it is necessarily rigid and inflexible: the reverse is obviously the case. We have seen that in human relations many different homeostases can be negotiated, that people are immensely adaptable, flexible in their accommodations, able to compromise on expectation so that an acceptable working arrangement can be achieved and supported.

There is nothing in the doctrine of robotic man to suggest that people are not immensely rich in their adjustment capabilities when new and unprecedented situations develop. Adaptability and adjustment are characteristic features of cybernetic systems — in both natural and artificial configurations. The robotic interpretation of human beings is an honest appraisal of the most intricate mechanisms we have yet encountered in the universe, and it is also a profoundly humanistic analysis. We do not serve human interest by pretending that human beings are spiritual creatures (angels or demons), by imagining that they are something that they are not, likely inheritors of ethereal realms. Man is a mechanism, a robot programmed for performance, but a robot with remarkable insights, talents, and emotional sensitivities. The true humanists are those who can face what man is — and rejoice.

References

Albus, J. S. (1981. *Brains, Behaviour and Robotics*, Byte Books.

Aleksander, I. (1977). *The Human Machine*, Georgi Publishing Company.

Aleksander, I. and Burnett, P. (1983). *Reinventing Man*, Kogan Page.

Alexander, R. M. (1983). *Animal Mechanics*, Blackwell Scientific Publications.

Allport, G. W. (1954). In *Handbook of Social Psychology* (Ed. G. Lindzey), vol. 1, Addison-Wesley, US, pp. 43–45.

Argyle, M. and Henderson, M. (1985). *The Anatomy of Relationships*, William Heinemann.

Artobolevskii, I. I. and Kobrinskii, A. Y. (1977). *Meet the Robots*, Molodaya Gvardiya, Moscow.

Ayer, A. J. (1940). *The Foundation of Empirical Knowledge*, Macmillan.

Ayer, A. J. (1956). *The Problem of Knowledge*, Penguin.

Bass, I. (28 July 1983). Asaron, the expert artist, *Computing*, **1983**, 20.

Berger, P. L. (1963). *Invitation to Sociology. A Humanistic Perspective*, Double Day Books.

Berne, E. (1971). *Sex in Human Loving*, Andre Deutsche.

Berne, E. 61974). *What Do You Say After You Say Hello?*, Andre Deutsche.

Birmingham, H. E. and Taylor, F. V. (1948). A design philosophy for man/machine control systems, *Proceedings of the Institute of Radio Engineers*, **1984**, 42.

Birmingham, H. E. and Taylor, F. V. (1954). A design philosophy for man/machine control systems. *Proceedings of the Institute of Radio Engineers*, **42**, 1748.

Boden, M. (1977). *Artificial Intelligence and Natural Man*, Harvester Press.

Braggins, D. (18 April 1984). Vision systems: helping robots to see things our way ..., *Machinery and Production Engineering*, **1984**, 38–41.

Brierley, J. (1973). *The Thinking Machine*, William Heinemann.

Butler, S. (1872). *Erewhon*, Everyman edition.

Cannon, W. B. (1932). *The Wisdom of the Body*, Norton, US.

Chapman, A. J. and Jones, D. M. (Eds) (1980). *Models of Man*, The British Psychological Society.

Chapuis, A. and Droz. E. (1958). *Automata — A Historical and Technological Study*, Editions du Griffon, Neuchâtel.

Cherfas, J. (1982). *Man Made Life*. Basil Blackwell, Oxford.

Chomsky, N. (1957). *Syntactic Structures*, Mouton, The Hague.

Clements, C. (1984). *Witness to War*, Bantam Books.

Dawkins, R. (1976). *The Selfish Gene*, Oxford University Press.

Dawson, G. (4 August 1983). Machines alive with the sound of music, *New Scientist*, **1983**.

Dennett, D. C. (1981). *Brainstorms: Philosophical Essays on Mind and Psychology*, Harvester Press.

Denson, J. S. and Abrahamson, S. (1969). A computer-controlled patient simulator, *Journal of the American Medical Association*, **208**, 504–508.

Dimond, S. J. (1979). Symmetry and asymmetry in the vertebrate brain, in *Brains, Behaviour and Evolution* (Eds D. A. Oakley and H. C. Plotkin), Methuen.

Dizard, J. W. (17 September 1984). Machines that see look for a market, *Fortune*, **1984**, 65–78.

Drever, J. (1952). *A Dictionary of Psychology*, Penguin.

Eibl-Eibesfeldt, I. 61971). *Love and Hate*, Piper and Co. Verlag, München. English translation published by Methuen.

Eckman, P. and Friesen, W. V. (1969). Non-verbal leakage and clues to deception, *Psychiatry*, **32**, 88–105.

Evans, C. (1983). *Landscapes of the Night: How and Why We Dream*, Coronet.

Ferry, G. (2 May 1985a). No room for a soul in the human brain, *New Scientist*, **1985**, 34–35.

Ferry, G. (26 September 1985b). Dyslexia and the psychology of the written word, *New Scientist*, **1985**, 41–44.

Friedland, P. and Kedes, L. (November 1985). Discovering the secrets of DNa, *Computer*, **1985**, 49–69.

Frude, N. (1984). *The Robot Heritage*, Century.

Futcher, D. (December 1984). Teaching with robots, *Educational Computing*, **1984**, 28–35.

Gage, N. L., Runkel, P. J., and Chatterjee, B. B. (1963). Equilibrium theory and behaviour change: an experiment in feedback from pupils to teachers, in *Readings in the Social Psychology of Education*, (Eds. W. W. Charters and N. L. Gage), Allyn and Bacon, pp. 173–180.

Gardner, M. (1981). *Science, Good, Bad and Bogus*, Prometheus Books, US.

Garrett, R. C. (April 1978). A natural approach to artificial intelligence, *Interface Age*, **1978**, 80–83.

Goffman, E. (1971). *Relations in Public*, Basic Books, US.

Hamilton, W. D. (1964). The genetical theory of social behaviour. *Journal of Theoretical Biology*, **7**, 1–52.

Heims, S. J. (1980). *John von Neumann and Norbert Wiener*, MIT Press.

Hildreth, E. C. (August 1984). Computations underlying the measurement of visualmotion, *Artificial Intelligence*, **1984**, 309–354.

Hollis, M. (1977). *Models of Man*, Cambridge University Press.

Homans, G. C. (1961). *Social Behaviour*, Routledge an Kegan Paul.

Horden, I. (15 October 1985). Microcontrollers offer real time robotics control, *Computer Design*, **1985**, 98–101.

Humphreys, C. (1951). *Buddhism*, Penguin.

Hunt, E. (1971). What kind of a computer is man?, *Cognitive Psychology*, **1971**, 57–98.

Hutt, E. (1972). *Males and Females*, Penguin.

Hyman, A. (1982). *Charles Babbage: Pioneer of the Computer*, Oxford University Press.

Janis, I. L. and Mann, L. (1977). *Decision Making*. The Free Press. New York.

Jasany, L. C. (October 1984). Vision systems widen their view, *Production*

Engineering, **1984**, 72–78.

Jefferson, G. (1949). The mind of mechanical man (Lister Oration for 1949), *British Medical Journal*, **1**, 1105–1121.

Johnstone, B. (26 September 1985). Walking robot prepares for a rouogh ride, *New Scientist*, **1985**.

Jorgensen, C., Hamel, W., and Weisbin, C. (January 1986). Autonomous robot navigation, *Byte*, **1986**, 223–235.

Kamata, S. (1983). *In the Passing Lane*, George Allen and Unwin.

Kellock, B. (2 October 1985). Vision systems keep turned parts in line, *Machinery and Production Engineering*, **1985**, 59–63.

Kendon, A. (1967). Some functions of gaze direction in social interaction. *Acta Psychologica*, **26**, 22–47.

Kent, E. W. (April 1978). The brain of men and machines, Part 4: the machinery of emotion and choice, *Byte*, **1978**, 66–89.

Kessis, J. J., Rambant, J. P., and Penne, J. (January 1982). Six legged walking robot has brains in its legs, *Sensor Review*, **1982**, 30–32.

Kosslyn, S. M. (1984). *Ghosts in the Mind's Machine*, Norton.

Lazarus, R. S., Averill J. R., and Opton Jr, E. M. (1970). Towards a cognitive theory of emotion, in *Feelings and Emotion: The Loyola Symposium* (Ed. M. Arnold) Academic Press, New York and London, pp. 207–232.

Lee, M. H., Barnes, D. P., and Hardy, N. W. (October 1985). Research into error recovery for sensory robots, *Sensor Review*, **1985**, 194–197.

Lehrer, K. (Ed.) (1966). *Freedom and Determinism*, Random House, New York.

Lewis, C. S. (1947). *The Abolition of Man*, New York.

Lindsay, P. H. and Norman, D. A. (1977). *Human Information Processing, An Introduction to Psychology*, Academic Press, New York.

Longuet-Higgins, H. C. (1976). The perception of melodies. *Nature*, **26**, (5579), 646–653.

McGhee, R. B. (June 1977). Control of legged locomotion systems, *Proceedings of 18th Joint Automatic Control Conference*, **1977**, 205–215.

McGhee, R. B. and Iswandhi, G. L. (April 1979). Adaptive locomotion of a multilegged robot over rough terrain, *IEEE Transactions on Systems, Man and Cybernetics*, **SMC-9**, No. 4, 176–182.

Macquarrie, J. (1973). *Existentialism*, Pelican.

Mayer, R. E. (1981). *The promise of Cognitive Psychology*, W. H. Freeman, San Francisco.

Meyer, J. D. (1983). Commercial machine vision systems, *Computer Graphics World*, **10**, 74–85.

Michie, D. (17 July 1980). P-KP4, expert system to human being conceptual checkmate of dark ingenuity, *Computing*, **1980**.

Miller, G. A., Galanter, E., and Pribram, K. H. (1960). *Plans and the Structure of Behaviour*, Holt, Rinehart and Winston, New York.

Miller, J. G. (1978). *Living Systems*, McGraw-Hill.

Mills, C. W. (1959). *The Sociological Imagination*, Oxford University Press.

Milo, R. D. (1973). *Egoism and Altruism*, Wadsworth, Belmont, California.

Monod, J. (1970). *Chance and Necessity*, Collins, Glasgow.

Monro, R. E. (1974). Interpreting molecular biology, in *Beyond Chance and*

Necessity, (Ed. J. Lewis), Garnstone Press, London.

Mouat, K. (1963). *What Humanism is About*, Barrie and Rockliff.

Murrell, K. F. H. (1965). *Ergonomics*, Chapman and Hall.

Neisser, U. (1967). *Cognitive Psychology*, Appleton-Century-Crofts.

Nightingale, J. M. (1985). Microprocessor control of an artificial arm, *Journal of Microcomputer Applications*, **8**, 167–173.

Oakley, D. A. (1979). Cerebral cortex and adaptive behaviour, in *Brain, Behaviour and Evolution*, (Eds. D. A. Oakley and H. C. Plotkin), Methuen.

O'Connor, D. J. (1971). *Free Will*, Macmillan, London.

Orin, D. E., McGhee, R. B. and Jaswa, V. C. (December 1976). Interactive computer control of a six-legged robot vehicle with optimisation of stability, terrain adaptability and energy, *Proceedings of 1976 IEEE Conference on Dec. and Control*, Clearwater Beach.

Owen, D. D. R. (1970). *The Vision of Hell*, Scottish Academic Press.

Panksepp, J. (September 1982). Towards a general psychological theory of emotions, *The Behavioural and Brain Sciences*, **5**, No. 3, 407–467.

Patton, C. (15 November 1984). Better speech recognition means that computers must mimic the human brain, *Electronic Design*, **1984**, 83–84.

Paturi, F. R. (1976). *Nature, Mother of Invention: The Engineering of Plant Life*, Thames and Hudson.

Pedler, K. (1979). *The Quest for Gaia*, Souvenir Press.

Perry, R. (1984). *The Programming of the President*, Aurum Press.

Piaget, J. (1954). *The Construction of Reality in the Child*, Basic Books, New York.

Piaget, J. (1967). *Six Psychological Studies*, Random House.

Powers, W. T. (1979). The nature of robots, Parts 3 and 4, *Byte*, **1979**, (August and September).

Pribram, K. H. (1961). A review of theory in physiological psychology, in *Annual Review of Psychology*, Annual Reviews Inc., pp. 1–40.

Pribram, K. H. (1967). The new neurology and the biology of emotion: a structural approach, *American Psychologist*, **22**, 830–838.

Pugh, G. E. (1978). *The Biological Origins of Human Value*, Routledge and Kegan Paul, London.

Riedl, R. (1978). *Order in Living Organisms*, John Wiley and Sons.

Rifkin, J. (1983). *Algeny, A New Word — A New World*, The Viking Press.

Rose, S., Kamin, L. J., and Lewontin, R. C. (1984). *Not in Our Genes: Biology, Ideology and Human Nature*, Pantheon.

Rose, S. (1973). *The Conscious Brain*, Weidenfeld and Nicholson.

Rosenberg, Y. (1976). *The Golem. Great Works of Jewish Fantasy*, Cassell.

Rusbult, C. E. (1983). A longitudinal test of the investment model: the development (and deterioration) of satisfaction and commitment in heterosexual investments, *Journal of Personality and Social Psychology*, **45**, 101–117.

Russell, B. (1931). *The Scientific Outlook*, Allen and Unwin.

Salvendy, G. and Smith, M. J. (Eds) (1981). *Machine Pacing and Occupational Stress*, Taylor and Francis, London.

Sampson, G. (1975). *The Form of Language*, Weidenfeld and Nicholson.

Schneer, C. J. (1960). *The Search for Order*, English University Press.

Schreiber, F. R. (1983). *The Shoemaker: Anatomy of a Psychotic*, Penguin.

Scott, P. B. (1984). *The Robotics Revolution*, Basil Blackwell.

Scriven, M. (1953). The mechanical concept of mind, *Mind*, **62**, 246.

Shapiro, R. J. (1968). Creative research scientists, *Psychologica Africana, Monograph Supplement*, **4**, 37–45.

Silone, I. (1969). *Emergency Exit*, London.

Simons, G. (1983). *Are Computers Alive?*, Harvester Press.

Simons, G. (1985a). *The Biology of Computer Life*, Harvester Press.

Simons, G. (1985b). *Silicon Shock*, Basil Blackwell.

Skinner, B. F. (1964). Man, *Proceedings of the American Philosophical Society*, **108**, No. 6 (December), 482–485.

Skinner, B. F. (1972). *Beyond Freedom and Dignity*, Jonathan Cape, London.

Sloman, A. (1978). *The Computer Revolution in Philosophy*, Harvester Press.

Sloman, A. and Croucher, M. (1981). Why robots will have emotions, *Proceedings of the 7th Joint Conference on Artificial Intelligence*, **1981**.

Smart, J. J. C. (1959). Professor Ziff on robots, *Analysis*, **xix**, 5.

Smart, N. (1959). Robots incorporated, *Analysis*, **xix**, 5.

Smith, J. M. (26 September 1985). The birth of sociobiology, *New Scientist*, **1985**, 48–50.

Smith, A. (1968). *The Body*, Allen and Unwin.

Sommerhoff, G. (1969). The abstract characteristics of living systems, in *Systems Thinking*, (Ed. F. E. Emery), Vol. 1, Penguin.

Sperry, R. W. (1979). Consciousness, free will and personal identity, in *Brain, Behaviour and Evolution*, (Eds. D. A. Oakley and H. C. Plotkin), Methuen.

Stackhouse, T. (1979). A new concept in robot wrist flexibility, *Proceedings of the 9th Symposium on Industrial Robots*, **1979**, 589–599.

Stephenson, G. M. and White, J. H. (1968). An experimental study of some of the effects of injustice on children's moral behaviour, *Journal of Experimental Social Psychology*, **4**, 460–469.

Strongman, K. T. (1978). *The Psychology of Emotion*, John Wiley and Sons.

Taylor, G. R. (1954). *Sex in History*, Ballantine.

Taylor, R. H. (July 1985). Precise manipulation with endpoint sensing, *Journal of Research and Development*, **29**, No. 4, 363–376.

Thomas, A. F. and Stout, K. J. (May 1980). Robot vision, *Engineering*, **1980**, 533–537.

Tricker, R. A. R. and Tricker, B. J. K. (1966). *The Science of Movement*, Mills and Boon.

Turing, A. M. (1950). Computing machinery and intelligence, *Mind*, **59**, 236.

Vernon, M. D. (1962). *The Psychology of Emotion*, Pelican.

Waddington, C. H. (1977). *Tools for Thought*, Jonathan Cape.

Walster, E. H., Walster, G. W., and Berscheid, E. (1978). *Equity: Theory and Research*, Allyn and Bacon, Boston.

Warr, P. B. and Knapper, C. (1968). *The Perception of People and Events*, John Wiley and Sons.

Watt, P. (29 October 1984). The Macintosh as poet, *InfoWorld*, **1984**, 25.

Weber, D. M. (2 September 1985). Bigger bag of technology sharpens machine vision, *Electronics*, **1985**, 41–45.

Weizenbaum, J. (1976). *Computer Power and Human Reason*, W. H. Freeman and Co.

Wiener, N. (1948). *Cybernetics: Central and Communication in the Animal and the Machine.*

Wilson, E. O. (1975). *Sociobiology: The New Synthesis.* Belknap Press, Cambridge, Massachussetts.

Wright, D. (1971). *The Psychology of Moral Behaviour*, Pelican.

Wynne-Edwards, V. C. (1962). *Animal Dispersion in Relation to Social Behaviour.*

Young, J. Z. (1964). *A Model of the Brain*, Oxford University Press.

Young, J. Z. (1978). *Programs of the Brain*, Oxford University Press.

Index